D0225527

SEXUALITY AND THE DEVIL

SEXUALITY AND THE DEVIL

Symbols of love, power and fear in male psychology

EDWARD J. TEJIRIAN

ROUTLEDGE NEW YORK & LONDON

First published in 1990 by
Routledge, an imprint of
Routledge, Chapman and Hall, Inc.
29 West 35 Street
New York, NY 10001

Published in Great Britain by
Routledge
11 New Fetter Lane
London EC4P 4EE

Printed in the United States of America.

Library of Congress Cataloging in Publication Data

Tejirian, Edward J., 1935-
Sexuality and the devil : symbols of love, power, and fear in male psychology / Edward J. Tejirian.
p. cm.
Includes bibliographical references.
ISBN 0-415-90205-3
1. Psychotherapy—Case studies. 2. Demoniac possession—Case studies. 3. Cultural psychiatry—Case studies. I. Title.
RC465.T45 1990
616.89'17—dc20 89-28929

British Library cataloguing in publication data also available

To Elli, Chris and Jeremy
and "Frank"

Each person's life is
in some manner repeated
in that of his fellows,
and every human soul is
a mirror in which other
souls, as well as future
and former events, reflect
their image.
—Alexander Wilder (1870)

If we want to discover what man amounts to, we can only find it in what men are: and what men are, above all other things, is various.

Clifford Geertz (1973)

Contents

Acknowledgments

I would like to offer my thanks to Professor Helen Bacon. It was in a conversation with her that the main ideas for this book began to germinate. I was exceptionally fortunate in being able to draw on her lifetime of study of Greek civilization to help me in addressing issues of Greek myth and sexuality. Any errors in understanding of those issues are attributable to myself.

I would also like to thank Professor Richard Kuhns. Not only was his psychoanalytic theory of art the right theory at the right time, converging with and encouraging me to consolidate my own ideas with respect to symbolism, but his generous personal support for my efforts to integrate an analytic understanding of sexuality with theories of art and symbolism bolstered my confidence that I was not entirely on the wrong track.

I would like to thank Dr. Charles Silverstein for his willingness to read the manuscript in its earliest, incomplete, and rough form. I am also grateful to Professor James Saslow and Professor Regina Krummel for reading a later draft of the book. Their thoughtful comments about and perspectives on the issues raised in this book were particularly helpful.

Finally, I would like to acknowledge my deep gratitude to "Frank," the protagonist of the first part of this book and the inspiration for the second, for his generosity of spirit in allowing me to tell his story in the hope that it might prove useful to others.

Introduction

The first part of this book is the story of the analysis of one man, whom I have called Frank. His story was unusual in that it involved one of the most ancient symbols of our civilization, the Devil—by whom Frank feared that he could be possessed. At the same time that he dismissed this as an impossibility, the obsessive idea had the emotional force of reality. Nonetheless, his incredulity not only meant that the idea did not have the engulfing effect of a full-blown delusion, it also permitted him to enter into analytic therapy in a determined effort to rid himself of the obsession. The idea of demonic possession has a tradition almost as ancient as the symbol itself, but I know of no other instance in which the individual with this idea has been in a position to enter into analytic therapy. At some point in the course of our analytic work, however, I became aware of a paper by Freud (1923) which I had not taken note of previously: his retrospective analysis of a "neurosis of demoniacal possession" in a seventeenth-century painter. I found it intensely interesting that Freud's interpretation of the painter Haitzmann's "neurosis" was matched by ideas I had begun to formulate about the meaning of this obsession in a young twentieth-century professional.

In our time, the symbol of the Devil has tended to serve as a figure of romance, comic opera, teenage satanic pretensions, or trivializing preoccupation by extremist religious groups. However, as I began to question why Frank had chosen the Devil to symbolize his fears, I began to appreciate this symbol more seriously as the dark nexus from which lines of connectedness radiated outwards to a number of disparate points. The first was the problem of ultimate existential evil, with which, ironically, the Devil is now rarely overtly associated. Another point, quite different but historically significant, is represented by the partially buried civilizations of the pre-Christian world; the lines of connectedness also trail backward to the fires of the Inquisition, and to the fear and suspicion surrounding certain forms of sexuality in our own time; finally, they intertwine with the psychoanalytic concept of the complex to which the legend of Oedipus gave its name.

All these issues appeared with varying degrees of implicitness and explicitness in the complex of feelings that the Devil symbol bound together and represented for this young twentieth-century man. It became clear, however, that another factor that had to be considered in approaching these issues was culture. In retrospect, the cultural factor was implicit but significant for the conduct and outcome of the analysis as well. Culture, then, is an important focus in the second part of this book.

The need for awareness of cultural factors in analytic therapy was demonstrated some years ago by Devereux (1969), in his work with a Plains Indian man. I would say that the cultural awareness that Devereux brought to his work with his "Wolf" Indian patient is equally necessary when patient and therapist share the same culture. In fact, it is in this latter situation that the therapist is most likely to introduce into the analytic situatuion unanalyzed distortions from his own cultural background. These distortions are just as harmful to the impartial outcome of the analysis as they would be when patient and therapist are from differrent backgrounds, a situation where unexamined assumptions cannot so easily masquerade as truth. The need for cultural awareness in actual therapeutic work is matched by the need for it in the construction of analytic theory. The theoretical portion of this book attempts to make a contribution to such an awareness.

The Devil as a powerful cultural symbol, with its multiplicity of meanings, both conscious and unconscious, emerged into Frank's consciousnes as the vehicle for expressing a complex of deeply troubling wishes and fears. The symbol of the Devil rose up in Frank's consciousness because other symbols which would have otherwise mediated the complex of ideas and feelings whose repudiation was incorporated in the symbol of the Devil were forbidden by his culture. This book, then, also concerns itself with the function of symbols in cultural life and individual consciousness, with particular focus on the symbolism of sexual action and imagery.

Part I
The Three Phases of the Analysis

The analysis actually proceeded in three separate stages. The first phase lasted about six months and preceded the outbreak of the Devil obsession. The second stage dealt with the discovery of the meaning of the Devil obsession and its dissolution. It began thirteen months after the first phase and lasted about four and one-half years. The third phase, which began two and one-half years after the conclusion of the second, lasted about one and one-half years and involved the working through of the major issues that had brought about the Devil obsession, issues that had remained unresolved at the end of the second phase and that had taken on new life in another symptom, jealousy.

1
The First Phase

I met Frank through a colleague at the college where we both taught. Frank, who was now working toward his master's degree while teaching in a junior high school, regarded my colleague as rather a special mentor. I first met Frank at the home of this colleague where Frank and his wife and I and my wife were invited to dinner. Soon after that, Frank enrolled in my graduate course in adolescent psychology. A few weeks into the course, Frank approached me with the request for psychotherapy. We agreed to meet on a once-a-week basis. I think the circumstances of our meeting are relevant because they probably affected how Frank regarded me and, hence, our relationship, at the outset. I was the friend and colleague of a special mentor, as well as a teacher at the college from which he had graduated. These factors reinforced his predisposition to approach the beginning of therapeutic work in a state of generally positive transference. That is, he had some confidence that I would be both willing and able to help him.

In the first session, he disclosed an adolescent trauma from which he had been trying to recover ever since it occurred. At about age fourteen, he had been challenged to a fight, in the course of a football game, by another boy. The "coach," a man in his thirties, told the boys either to make up or to fight. The other boy chose to fight, but Frank backed down from the fight, and later backed down from a challenge by a friend of the first boy. Subsequently, he was faced by many challenges from other boys in the neighborhood, even from boys smaller than himself. Although he met all the challenges after the first two, the sense of humiliation over the initial incident never left him and as a young man of twenty-four, he still had a dread of reexperiencing a similar humiliation as an adult. He actually felt it a problem that he still experienced fear in certain situations, and he was worried that he might again be presented with a challenge to fight and he would not be able to face up to it. In fact, there had been no repetition of anything like that original, traumatic situation. Still, the fear haunted him, and actually restricted him in some ways. Living in one of the outer boroughs of New York City, Frank sometimes went into Manhattan with his wife. He would want to keep the windows rolled up when driving through certain parts of town—for example, the East Village. He worried particularly that someone might say something insulting to his wife and then he would be honor bound to confront the person and might possibly have to fight again. He was afraid, not only of backing down again, but even of feeling fear in this situation. It seemed that just having the feeling of fear was incompatible with the kind of man he wanted to be.

Frank felt it to be a deficiency in himself that he could not be completely fearless. So it was especially ironic that he would wind up going so far as to avoid coming into Manhattan in order to reduce the chance of having a confrontation in which he might feel fear. In traveling with his wife, he had to stay only in "good" hotels in order to feel safe from the possibility of facing a challenging situation. Frank felt unhappy about having to be so careful all the time in his movements, and his wife sometimes did not understand just what he was worried about and was irked by it. In a reflective mood, one day, Frank said that his wife might not be able to understand his feelings in this situation because she had never been subjected to what he had.

What Frank had been subjected to began to emerge in the course of this first phase of our work together. Frank had grown up in what would probably best be described as working-class neighborhoods that shaded off into poverty, with the kind of racial and ethnic mix that has both vitality and a potential for violent confrontation all at the same time. It was an environment where older, stronger boys might threaten and bully the younger and weaker. Thus, an early memory along these lines was selling lemonade at age nine or ten and having bigger boys coming over to bother him. His mother, he recalled, had come to his rescue and he felt ashamed of that. It was ironic that, while he described her as the only person in his life to care for and protect him, often watching over him from her window while he was on the street, he could also not help but be ashamed of this fact sometimes.

Another memory was from age eleven. He had been told that an older boy, a neighborhood bully, was out to get him. It had something to do with this boy's girlfriend. In that environment, even looking at an older boy's girlfriend could lead to physical threats and humiliation. Frank stayed in his house for two weeks. Perhaps it was this environment, in which strength sometimes frankly preyed on weakness, that accounted for the fantasy that Frank would have at age twelve or thirteen when lying in his bed unable to sleep. He would have the fantasy of being in a bunker, with all his favorite foods as well as arms and ammunition, alone, holding off the Japanese. Later, he would have a girl down there with him. But he remarked ruefully, "Not that I did anything with her—I wouldn't know what to do."

It was an environment where status was accorded the tough and the strong and where physical courage was equated with manliness. Perhaps growing up in this milieu made a particular characteristic of his father especially important to Frank. This characteristic was his father's strength and how he used it. His father was a tall man, a sanitation worker who usually worked two jobs. He was commonly known as "big Mike" among his friends. But he seemed to be a man of even temperament and respected in the family. For example, if a fight broke out at a wedding, Frank's father would calmly and soothingly intervene. In fact, his father had a saying that Frank had heard a number of times: "It takes a man to walk away from a fight."

His father had rarely used his physical advantage to intimidate his son. While he could be afraid if his father threatened him, his father rarely did so. Only a couple of incidents of this kind came to his mind. Once, when he was eleven, his father hit him, knocking him out of a chair. And once, when he was thirteen, his father chased him under a bed with a broom. But by and large, his early memories of his father were fond ones. His father had a taste for dressing in expensive suits, and he would dress Frank in them as well. He remembered going to the shoeshine parlor with his father and, even now, could remember the good, tingling feeling in his foot. He would sometimes go to bars with his father also. There were bowling machines there and Frank became very good at playing those machines.

This, then, was the positive side of Frank's father and of his relationship with him. So far, we have seen a textbook case of a good father-son relationship: a strong, admired father who fosters his son's identification with him, encouraging the boy to feel like his father's son. However, this happy, idealized picture of his father was to change dramatically as his father progressively sank into alcoholism. By the time Frank was in his early teens, his father was a confirmed alcoholic, sometimes drinking up the rent money while the family could barely sustain itself with food. Thereafter, his father rarely spoke to him except to say, "Get a haircut." His withdrawal from Frank and the family seemed to account for the fact that he rarely thought to give Frank anything thereafter, even for his birthday. But he seems not to have been ungenerous by nature and he would give Frank money when he asked for it, providing that he had some.

After the loss of this relationship, Frank went about looking, as he put it, for "father figures." The "coach" of the fight incident had been one such, but disillusionment about him set in. One incident which hurt Frank and contributed to this disillusionment occurred when this man told Frank that he had seen his father go into a back room of a bar with a prostitute to whom he paid one dollar for a "blow job." Frank could not believe this at the time and as an adult offered the cynical explanation that his father was too preoccupied with booze to care about sex. Still, one can see how Frank the boy would have been insulted by this slur upon his father, for whom some residues of the old admiration remained. Indeed, Frank had no recollection of being angry with his father back then. In fact, he simply remarked, " I always loved him."

This "coach" also introduced a kind of a sexual element in his relationship with the boys. He would show them pornographic comic books and took some boys, though not Frank, to prostitutes. It was not clear what effect, if any, those actions had on Frank's estimate of this man, but my impression was that they did not enhance his standing in Frank's eyes.

Besides strength, there were other facets of character that Frank valued in his quest for father figures. He recalled one man whose knowledge he respected, where physical prowess was irrelevant. And sometimes he would be astonished when some boys with giving, attentive fathers complained, "My old man is a pain." He knew how much he missed it and how grateful he would have been for the attention they complained about. Still, in a setting where many boys had no fathers at all, Frank, most of the time, still felt lucky to have a father.

In this initial phase of our work, Frank spoke less of his mother. But a picture emerged of a woman who felt downtrodden by life. She never felt accepted by her husband's family and had virtually no family of her own. Ever since Frank could remember, his mother complained of how her husband's family treated her. Because he found her complaints unbearable, Frank did not like to visit her or even to talk to her on the telephone very often. However, in spite of feeling overwhelmed and burdened with her own problems in life, she nonetheless did communicate some sense of a steadily caring presence in Frank's life. He remembered, as a child of five, being afraid when sleeping alone in his bedroom at the end of a long hall and calling to his mother. But, as we have seen, by the time he was nine and ten, he felt ashamed of needing her protection.

Frank had a sister who was three years older and, in a general way, he found her warm and supportive. However, she did not appear to have had a very deep impact upon his development, as siblings sometimes do. He also had a brother fourteen years younger. Without elaboration, Frank simply observed that he had never felt a desire to be a father to his younger brother in spite of his recognition of his own deep need for father figures in his own life.

Frank recalled arguments between his parents when he was younger.

His father would shout and his mother cry. While Frank would feel caught between them, it seemed interesting that he found himself more sympathetic with his father.

It seemed evident to me that, before the trauma of the fight incident, Frank had suffered a much more extensive emotional trauma—the loss of his strong, idealized father. I reasoned, at the time, that Frank's backing down from the challenge of the other boy might have some connection with this earlier traumatic loss. I suggested to Frank that the loss of his strong father with whom he had felt so identified in the past left him feeling weak and vulnerable and less confident about meeting this sort of challenge successfully. I also said that, in this situation, he had, in one sense acted in conformity with his father's dictum, "It takes a man to walk away from a fight." While Frank was not at all convinced that this explained his backing down, it did seem somewhat comforting to him to be reminded that fighting was not something that his father viewed as a sign of masculinity.

It seemed to me that the question of the values of the adolescent subculture was very important in understanding Frank's anxiety, as an adult, about the fight incident. It appeared that he had, like many adolescents, internalized certain norms of the cultural milieu in which he found himself. Included in those norms was one that was opposed to his father's saying. In the adolescent subculture a "real man" did *not* walk away from a fight. This made his feeling of deep shame at the time quite comprehensible. What was rather more puzzling was the fact that this anxiety had hung on for so many years subsequently and in view of what Frank had done and accomplished since. In contrast to most of the boys with whom he grew up, Frank went to college and was now even earning a master's degree. Furthermore, he taught English, was widely read and had a deep and sophisticated appreciation of all forms of literature. It was as if part of himself—the personal values by which he measured himself—remained stuck in the subculture of his early teen years, while he, the only member of his family to go to college, had progressed far beyond the limited horizons of that subculture. We discussed the fact that he continued to measure himself by the crude standards of masculinity of that subculture: physical prowess, readiness to fight, and a show of apparent fearlessness. As we discussed these issues, he began to get some perspective on them and to question the utility of the adolescent value system.

What added to the puzzle in all this was the fact that, in his behavior since, he had no reason to reproach himself. Even right after that incident, he had met all subsequent challenges. He never again backed down. As a teacher in junior high school he had many occasions to deal with difficult youngsters and had no trouble maintaining discipline and keeping control of a class. In appearance, he was tall, somewhat rugged in his looks, and it still surprised him when he realized that people might regard him as something of a tough guy. He related a recent incident in which a mob outside an arena where a rock concert had been held was being rowdy. The car in which he was sitting with some women friends was rocked to and fro. Later, one of the women remarked on how cool he had remained. He, in thinking about it, however, wondered if someone else would have come out swinging.

Although he had met any number of challenging situations in the school competently and appropriately, he sometimes would feel weak in the knees afterwards. Recently, when he had broken up a fight between a "nutty kid" and a teacher, he had experienced just such a feeling of weakness. Sometimes, he felt anxious when directly confronted by a challenge from a student. In another instance, when he was about to confiscate a wineskin from a boy, the latter had warned, "Don't start anything you can't finish." Rather than provoking the boy further, he allowed him to keep it.

I told Frank that his aspiration never to feel fear was beyond most adult men, while his behavior could scarcely be judged "unmanly" even by conventional, rather stereotyped standards.

At the time, I felt that Frank's anxiety about once again failing to meet a challenge was largely a problem of excessively rigid and narrow standards that were relics from the values of the adolescent peer group coupled with the lingering effects of a deep wound to his masculine self-esteem which had not completely healed. It was these factors, I felt, that accounted for the almost paradoxical sense of vulnerability in this apparently strong and competent young man. In retrospect, this sense of vulnerability might also be seen in one of the two types of recurrent dreams that Frank mentioned. In the first type, he was being chased by people and he could not get away. One might also see his sense of vulnerability in a couple of other of Frank's preoccupations. He remarked on how he was always very careful to make sure that the house door was locked and to check the cellar door upon leaving. He also would turn off the lights in his bedroom when he was dressing or undressing and insisted that his wife do the same. He was concerned lest shadows be visible in the lowered and closed blinds. Since blinds are virtually opaque, this precaution seemed redundant; I did not make much of this idiosyncrasy at the time, however, except to relate it to another theme that emerged in this phase—jealousy.

And it was this theme, jealousy, that was evident in the second type of recurrent dream that Frank reported. In this dream, Frank would find that his wife was being unfaithful to him with another man. He would then beat up both her and the man. Jealousy had troubled Frank earlier in their marriage. For Anne, Frank's wife, it was a second marriage. Her relationship to Frank had begun while she was still married to her first husband and had contributed to the breakup of her first marriage. Now Frank began to worry that since Anne had left her first husband for him, she might leave him for someone else that she had become attracted to. They went together to see a counselor about this problem. The counselor told Frank that a woman's being unhappy with one person did not mean that she would not be able to be happy with another. While Frank had found this approach reassuring and the counseling had helped him deal with the problem, the earlier anxiety reflected an ongoing susceptibility to jealous emotion that could still be excited in Frank.

An incident had recently occurred in which this susceptibility was touched. For purposes of birth control Frank was using condoms, and one day it seemed to him that there were some condoms not accounted for by the frequency of their lovemaking. As he questioned his wife somewhat indirectly about this discrepancy, she caught his drift and was upset. He told her that, if he ever found her cheating on him, he would kill her. Hurt and insulted, she replied, "You're crazy." This incident brought into relief a whole set of tensions having to do with their sex life that were troubling to Frank.

At this point, they were having sex with a frequency of about once a week, which was far below what Frank wanted. His own preference was to make love every day, which had been the case at the beginning of their relationship. In the early part of their relationship, Anne had seen Frank, who was about four years younger than she, as exciting, a "bohemian" type, while Frank experienced her as really alluring sexually. It seemed that the sexual part of their relationship had been a good deal more electric than it was now. He said that his wife had initially been more adventurous and free in the variety of sexual techniques that she would permit than she was now. The use of condoms was another sore point. Frank hated them, but complied because Anne was very fearful of getting pregnant just then. Adding insult to injury, she would ask him to check them for any tears after their lovemaking. But he really could not tell her how upset all this made him. Frank said, "I'm not used to talking to women about my feelings."

There were two further sources of tension in the sexual area. One was their sleeping schedules. Frank was tired and ready to go to bed before midnight whereas Anne would often want to stay up until 2 A.M., doing things like sewing. And finally, Anne herself was very concerned, unduly from Frank's point of view, about her own appearance, especially her complexion. When she felt unattractive, she seemed to lose the desire to make love.

But sex was not the only source of tension in their relationship. There had been some disagreements over money. Frank recalled the time when he was going to school and his wife was the sole wage earner. He would hitchhike and skip lunch in order to save money. However, when his wife used some of the money she earned to buy expensive clothes, Frank had remarked, "You're taking the food out of my mouth." They also disagreed about the timing of having a baby. Frank wanted to start trying to have a baby at this time and have Anne work up until just before the baby was born. Anne, on the other hand, felt she would like to stop working now but delay getting pregnant for a while.

Apart from these issues, Frank sometimes found himself getting irritated with his wife over little things that he interpreted as lack of thoughtfulness or concern for him. For example, she would leave clothes hanging on the doorknob, dishes on the counter, and want to talk to him when he got home after a long day at 8 P.M., when he just wanted to eat and watch something on TV. This last item bordered on the insensitive and callous on Frank's part, and seemed atypical for him. Perhaps unfairly, Frank saw himself as doing more than his share at home and his wife as somewhat selfish. This feeling of doing more than his share also came up in his work situation, where his female assistant principal seemed to take it for granted that he would handle certain difficult discipline situations that she then felt free to walk away from.

Although in these and other situations, Frank felt anger, he was aware of having real difficulty expressing it. He felt that "smoldering with resentment" was an apt description of how he actually wound up feeling. It seemed that something would actually put the brakes on his anger sometimes. He found this very frustrating and wished he could get really angry—angry enough to kill! In reality, however, if he got really angry with his wife, the most he might do would be to hurt her a little, for example, by squeezing her wrist. However, she would then cry and he could not stand that—it reminded him of his mother.

What seemed to be emerging in the latter part of this initial phase was anger with his wife, and a sense of deprivation generated by their disagreements with regard to sex and money particularly. This theme seemed separate and apart from the issue of the adolescent trauma and the subsequent anxieties about his masculinity that had preoccupied Frank.

One other issue, also separate from both these anxieties and the problems centering on the relationship with his wife, emerged in this first stage. It had to do with his physical attractiveness. It, too, went back to his adolescence, when he had been teased because of his nose. His nose, while not straight, was well proportioned in relation to his face. He had never experienced any difficulty attracting women; in fact, it had been his male peers, not the girls, who teased him with "parrot beak" when he was an adolescent. That fact certainly suggested that his peers were displacing their age-specific anxieties about their looks onto Frank who functioned, unfortunately for him, rather as a mirror for their own imperfections. As an adult, Frank would probably have been described by the casual onlooker as ruggedly good-looking. And even in late adolescence, he was attractive to girls. Nonetheless, he wished that he could have been extremely good-looking and that he had the kind of looks that would turn heads. He would have liked to be able to do modeling and he imagined, if he were not married, that he would like to dress really well and pick up attractive women at East Side Manhattan bars.

We had started our therapeutic work in March, and in July Frank raised the question of stopping. Our discussions centering on the fight incident and its aftermath in his feelings seemed to have been helpful to him. However, he seemed to regard therapy as something of a luxury, perhaps even wasteful. He said, "If you spend money on a car, you have a car. If you spend money on talk, what do you have?" He was also reluctant to have anyone know he was in therapy, with its possible connotations of being "crazy." I urged him to continue but by the beginning of September, after some breaks for vacations, he nevertheless resolved to stop. I suggested to him that, as we got into areas of conflict about his wife, he might be experiencing some anxiety about getting deeper into those feelings lest his marriage be threatened. I also reflected on the fact that depending on anyone else for help seemed to have been implicitly forbidden in his family. Perhaps in partial confirmation, Frank said that when he complained to his wife about her expenses, she would reply, "What about your therapy?" So, he felt he could not ask her to economize while continuing to spend money on himself in therapy. And he wanted to be able to afford to buy a house soon and needed to save money for that. In any case, Frank seemed resolved and I felt it would not be helpful to press him further on this. Thus we can to an amicable, though premature, termination.

What in fact turned out to be the first phase of lengthy analysis now came to a close.

2
The Second Phase

Thirteen months after the close of the first phase, Frank returned to see me. He seemed exhausted and nervous, and said he was worried that he might be going crazy. Thoughts about the Devil kept occurring to him. He had read about an exorcism performed in France, and it was after reading that newspaper account that the fear of possibly being possessed by the Devil began to occur to him. It seemed impossible, and even absurd, but he could not get this anxiety out of his mind. It emerged that shortly after we had terminated the first phase, he had had a nightmare that he could not recall—he surmised that it might have had to do with the Devil—from which he had awakened very frightened. He had clutched his crucifix and prayed to God not to let "that" be a part of him. His life situation had changed slightly since our last meeting thirteen months earlier. The house he had aspired to own had been bought, but he did not yet feel at home there. On the contrary, when he returned there after he finished his teaching duties, he found himself restlessly going from room to room, awaiting his wife who returned from work at 7 P.M.. It was quiet, felt empty, and none of his friends lived nearby. He thought he would like to have a child, but his salary would not be able to cover their expenses entirely if his wife should quit her work. About his wife, he made an interesting observation. He said he could talk to his wife now. Previously, he had never thought he could talk to a woman. He said he could look to people for help now, including looking to me. This attitude stood in contrast to his reluctance a year before to think of himself as being in therapy any more than absolutely necessary. It had seemed then that being in a relationship where he looked to another for understanding or help was a threat to his self-esteem and something to be kept secret.

From the outset, I could not help thinking that, in the terrifying dream of the previous summer, something within him had broken through the barriers erected by consciousness, giving Frank a glimpse of something about himself that had appalled him. After awakening, it had been repressed again, to be replaced by the symbol of the Devil, the symbol of something "alien" that threatened to possess him.

If there was any foundation to this suspicion the challenge was surely to bring the terrifying ideas into consciousness without precipitating a reaction of flight from therapy or, worse, a catastrophic slide into graver symptomology. On my side was the successful introductory phase that we had enjoyed previously and the trust that Frank brought to his collaboration with me personally. Most important, however, was a readiness to accept the interpretation, given in the first few months of this second phase, that the Devil actually symbolized a set of powerful anxieties about things within himself. While he could not afford more than once-weekly sessions he was a willing and conscientious patient in every respect and was determined to conquer his symptoms with my help. This last point was, of course, critically important. Had Frank fully believed that he was really in danger of being possessed by the Devil, it would mean that his inner anxieties were so great that they had caused his capacity for adequate reality testing to be seriously unhinged. It would have been far more difficult to help him since he would likely have been virtually unable to enter into a genuinely therapeutic alliance with me. By according credence to the possibility of being possessed, he would have signaled that he could not tolerate any attempt to suggest that he was actually afraid of something within himself. Since analytic work investigates and unearths just such inner anxieties, it would be only with the greatest difficulty that he could be persuaded to work at analysis with me. In a word, he would have been suffering from paranoia rather than from an obsessional neurosis. But Frank himself regarded his fear of possession as irrational and was suffering so much from it that he was highly motivated to work with me to obtain relief.

Other cases of fear of possession by the Devil have been reported. To my knowledge, however, these have either been clear cases of paranoia or, less commonly in the present day, cases that occurred in the context of religious belief and that were treated as such by religious authority. In neither case, of course, could there be any question of the individual entering into psychoanalysis. Rather, psychiatric treatment or religious exorcism might follow. The only instance of psychoanalysis of such a fear that I know of is that by Freud (1923) himself, who retrospectively analyzed a seventeenth-century painter who claimed to have entered into a pact with the Devil. At the time that Frank came to me, however, my decision to treat him had nothing to do with any scholarly interests or with the wish to score a "first" by the psychoanalysis of a person with a fear of demoniacal possession.

Within a few weeks, Frank's overall emotional state was considerably improved. He was markedly less tense, and the intense anxiety and dread that had accompanied the idea of demonic possession had receded. Strikingly the *thought* of possession by the Devil had largely supplanted the dread of it. This was still upsetting, of course. He would think something like, "You're okay now, but you're going to be thinking of the Devil pretty soon."

However, the state of anxiety that had accompanied this thought no longer prevailed. The thought of the Devil would sometimes appear without warning in a paradoxical setting. Early on, he related how he was playing football, having a great time, with "everything so beautiful," and then suddenly thought, "You'll be thinking of the Devil later on." He could not understand why the thought occurred just then. The idea, though not so terrifying any more and seemingly impossible, still retained a mysterious power. Almost as an act of defiance, he found himself saying, while driving in his car, "If there is a Devil, let him take me now." But of course, he said wryly, nothing happened.

The First Dreams

Dreams proved to be absolutely indispensable in this analysis, more so than in most others of my experience. The dreams seemed to tap emotions and perceptions that were far removed from Frank's consciousness, and even alien and repugnant to it. However, the first dream he reported in this second phase did not seem particularly profound. He related, "I was in a subway. A black man was there, I was afraid he might try to mug me, so I left." The elements of this dream are suggestive rather than clear. The "subway" crops up in dreams of New Yorkers. It seems to have reference to the depths of the mind, to the unconscious and its dangers that the dreamer is closer to in dreams than in waking life. The image of the mugger is an urban variation of a theme that occurs in the dreams of most men that I have worked with—the confrontation by a dangerous male. Sometimes a fight ensues, sometimes the dreamer retreats. For Frank, this dream brings to mind the traumatic incident of his adolescence where he chose not to fight. It also was related to the situations in his current life where Frank feared that he might be faced with a challenge to which he would respond by backing down again.

The next dream was rather more perplexing: "A woman is having a nervous breakdown. She is pointing a gun at me. I go to the window. Another, younger, woman is there. All three of us jump out the window. The woman who had the gun says, 'If she had given in, she would not have been killed.' " In yet another dream, that same night, "A woman is saying about Mary Hartmann's husband, 'He's a real Devil.' " At the time, the meaning of these dreams was totally obscure to me. Naturally, I was struck by the occurrence of the Devil theme. It was in this session that Frank remarked that, for him, the Devil signified something "really evil." Inserting this meaning into the dream material would result in coming up with the idea that "Mary Hartmann's husband" was really evil. At that time, that rather simple connection did not occur to me. Another connection that eluded me, in the dream of the woman having a nervous breakdown, was that it was Frank himself who had been afraid that he might be going "crazy" when the Devil obsession began to overtake him. Making that connection would have led to the notion that the dream was representing Frank as a woman. The last of these early dreams was less opaque:

"I was in a house in Manhattan. My family was there: my mother, father, brother, sister, grandmother, and aunt (the "godmother"). I needed help. I went to my father, but he was asleep. My mother was preoccupied, worrying. I knew my grandmother and aunt were useless (they had once thrown my brother out of his bed for my father). I went into another room. My wife was there. She came with me into all the empty rooms of the house. We came to the last room—in the attic. I was afraid to go in and woke up."

I was to come to understand that, in a highly condensed form, this group of early dreams incorporated many of the key elements both of the Devil fear and of the context that generated it. However, for the moment, the dream of the house was more accessible and captured many of the crucial background elements in Frank's emotional life as well as reflecting his relation to the analysis. My office was in Manhattan, whereas Frank lived out of town. The house undoubtedly symbolized his self which he was exploring with me. The dream recapitulates the important themes in Frank's family: the father who is turned to for help, but to no avail; the female members of the family who are not even turned to—the mother because, as in life, she is too preoccupied with her own worries; the aunt and grandmother because they are incapable of offering comfort. The sole woman he can depend on is his wife. These elements were close to Frank's conscious experience. However, the final scene in this dream is most striking: the attic room that he was afraid to enter. Would this room not represent some hitherto secret place within himself that, even with his wife's help, he was afraid of coming to know? Yet, he came to Manhattan (where the "house" is) to my office to rid himself of the obsessive fear that had been haunting him, in other words, to enter that room. In that "room" was a complex of frightening feelings that Frank *unconsciously knew* to be there but that were only "known" to his consciousness via the enigmatic symbol of the Devil.

For some time, Frank had been troubled by some of his sexual thoughts. He used to have no compunction about masturbation but of late he was uneasy about it. And now, in school, when some boy brought in a pornographic magazine he felt it was wrong and did not want to look at it. He remembered how, in parochial school—which he had attended through high school—he had been instructed not to "give in to the Devil." Nonetheless, he did have fantasies in which he would be doing just those things that were "wrong," that he would not do with his wife because she would not want them. One of those things was anal intercourse. Some fantasies were based on something he might have read, for example, a scene from a pornographic novel in which two men were having sex with a woman who was shouting "Fuck me!" In spite of the fact that Frank had been exposed to the standard warnings about sex in parochial school, he had never taken very seriously the straight-and-narrow approach to sex taken by the nuns and the religious brethren who had taught him. I took this as my cue to assume that his newfound religious compunctions were based not on theological conviction but rather on quite unrelated inner anxieties. I told him that in just so many words. As I did so, the thought occurred to him that perhaps it was the Devil who was trying to persuade him that these things were "okay." But even as he disclosed the thought he remarked that he wanted to report it to me, that he did trust me.

All this did make it appear that the Devil had some association with sexual thoughts. And in fact, the next week he reported a series of dreams that explicitly paired the Devil with a sexual act. In the first: "There was a 'little Devil.' He was involved in masturbation or something leading to sexual release. Then maybe it was me and I thought: 'That release would be from the Devil.' " In the second, "It was [a well known actress] and she said something about the Devil. She was with an older man and she gave him a sensual kiss." As these sexual images and thoughts swirled around the symbol of the Devil, I began to sense, without being able to pinpoint exactly how, that something sexual was in the room that Frank, in his dream, was afraid to enter, and that the Devil symbolized that sexual "something." It was interesting that his wife was by his side as he hesitated at the threshold, especially in view of the fact that Frank had noticed that the Devil thought occurred more readily and more often if he had gone for three or four days without making love to her.

Mother and Wife

With regard to his mother, the main female caretaker of his early years, it was clear, as the dream indicated, that her capacity to help him with his problems had been limited. He recalled times when he might have upset her by something he had done. He would tell her he was sorry, but she would not accept his apology, even if he was in tears. She would say, "If you're sorry, you wouldn't have done it." This sort of scene occurred into his teen years. In addition, because money in the household was in such short supply, his mother would always "borrow" whatever money he had, even money he would receive as gifts, for example, even for his graduation. When he worked at regular jobs such as a paper route, most of the money earned would be turned over to his mother for household expenses.

It was increasingly clear that, while Frank had initially described his mother as the only person to protect and take care of him, a significant degree of role reversal had taken place in this relationship as she became overwhelmed by her own life situation. His own needs to be taken care of had to go unfulfilled in whole or in part while he tended to hers. For example, he recalled having, as a teenager, recurrent dreams in which he attacked a child or infant, tearing off its limbs. These dreams, in retrospect, could be understood as expressions of intense and angry rivalry with the little brother born when he was fourteen, who inevitably became a recipient of the diminishing supplies of emotional nurturance in the family.

At an earlier time in their marriage, he had accused his wife of "taking the food out of my mouth." This accusation reflected an implied identification of his wife with the image of the mother who took rather than gave. He had also been unable to talk to her about his feelings. After all, it was *he* who had to understand his mother's feeling when she was upset with him. His feelings of remorse and his apologies were not accepted. But now, he was beginning to allow himself to turn to his wife as an important source of comfort and support. It was, therefore, both ironic and unfortunate that his wife revealed to him, about four months after the commencement of this second phase of analysis, that she was not sure that she loved him any longer, nor did she want children. In spite of this shock, he said that he loved her still. However, a few weeks later, he reported the following dream: "I was asking my wife, 'Did you ever love me?' She said 'yes' but I thought, 'You never loved me,' or heard her saying in my head, 'I never loved you.' She seemed to be smiling a 'Devilish' smile. I stabbed her—once in each breast. Some other people were around and there was some suggestion that she'd been with other men."

In discussing this dream, I said to him that, in his initial reaction, he had suppressed the anger her announcement had stirred just as he must have suppressed his anger toward his mother sometimes. It was striking that he replied that he was not aware of feelings of anger toward his mother. A few weeks after this dream, his wife declared that she had not wanted to be with him for four years. Frank now felt that he could absolutely not be alone. While his wife seemed clear in her determination to separate, she did say that she would stay until he felt able to let her leave. He continued to feel that he loved her and wanted her and hated to think of her with anyone else. When his wife said she had been talking to an older man at work, in the capacity of confidant, Frank wondered if she might be planning to take her upcoming vacation with him, saying "I'll kill him." The contrast between Frank's outburst of sexual jealousy as seen in this last remark and the poignancy of his feeling that he absolutely could not be alone was striking. The dream in which he stabbed his wife in each breast provided an important clue to its symbolism. While a woman's breasts are part of her sexual appeal, they also clearly signify the maternal, nurturing, and tender aspect of a woman. It seems to me that Frank was not only attacking her in a fit of sexual jealousy in this dream. It was not so much her giving her sexual favors to another man that provoked him, but it was rather her withdrawal of her tender support and nurturing love that had so enraged him. However, jealous rage at the older man in whom his wife had been confiding brings to mind the dream in which the beautiful actress said something about the Devil as she was about to give an older man "a sensual kiss." In the dream there was no hint of jealousy but rather of the presence of the Devil. It is interesting to recall an offhand comment by Frank that he had always been obsessed with something. At first, it was money. Later it was fear of his wife's infidelity. The Devil, then, was the most recent in this string of obsessions. And it was the Devil thought that occurred in the dream that, on its surface, seemed to refer to his suspicions about his wife's involvement with the older man at work. This was the first hint, unnoticed by me at the time, that the two obsessions—jealousy and the Devil—might somehow be linked.

As for his wife, she affirmed her intention to separate and had moved out of the house before the end of the first year of the second phase.

In the months before she disclosed her feelings about ending their marriage Frank had permitted himself to turn to Anne for emotional support and understanding as he never had before. A few months after she left, he said that he felt no woman could love him because he was weak and needed people. It seems that the lesson he had learned from his mother's weakness and neediness was that, as a man, his role was to take care of protect the woman and that weakness and need were prohibited to him. He had always attempted to suppress his own need to depend on others. But after the outbreak of his symptoms, he did turn overtly to his wife, and her desertion at this point appears to have reinforced the earlier conviction that women did not wish to be depended upon. However, for some months after their separation, Frank continued to see his wife. They would have sex together, and he continued to be powerfully attracted to her sexually. In this, he saw himself as clinging to her, which he deplored. However, almost another year was to pass before he had sex with any other woman. Feelings in his consciousness that seemed to keep him from approaching other women were anxieties about his attractiveness and the belief that women saw him as the "strong, silent type" and that if they knew what he was really like, they would not want him. Secondarily, he was also somewhat concerned about his sexual performance. These concerns actually reflected a set of ongoing and important themes in Frank's feelings. Ever since the traumatic teasing about his looks that he had suffered in his adolescence, he was super-sensitive about them and he had the conviction that a very attractive woman would not want him. This belief, coupled with his anticipation of being rejected *because of his feelings of need,* made him wary of approaching new women. The statement of these concerns early on were early harbingers of a complex of feelings about women that reflected Frank's deep mistrust of them.

With regard to the question of his attractiveness, a major event occurred in the middle of the first year. In the early part of the year, his nose had been broken in a basketball game and he decided to have surgery to correct a deviated septum and, just as important, to effect some cosmetic changes to his nose. He was somewhat embarrassed about this latter motivation. But the operation was nonetheless performed and the results were rather striking when coupled with the shaving of the fairly full beard which he had previously affected. His face had a decidedly more boyish look while still retaining its handsomeness. Although shaved, his beard was dark and contrasted with a good complexion that had a hint of ruddiness. Combined with a tall, slender but broad-shouldered frame and jet-black curly hair, all this meant that Frank would undoubtedly be considered a rather good-looking young man. In fact, two other patients, both male, one gay and one heterosexual, who preceded Frank and saw him emerge from my office commented vehemently upon his striking good looks. My heterosexual patient asked, "What problems could *he* have?" Nevertheless, a conviction that continued to haunt him was that a very attractive woman would not be interested in him because she would demand someone on the same level of attractiveness as herself.

Father, Men, and the Devil

Another major theme, which received equal time with his concerns about his wife and women, were his relationships with men—including, of course, his father. One of the few negative early feelings Frank had about his father involved the memory of his father coming home drunk, with his mother crying, and he and his sister holding on to her between them, and they also crying. At *those* times, he could feel hatred for his father. However, about a year before Frank returned to analysis, his father had stopped drinking. Until he and his wife moved to the new house, Frank was stopping by his father's home every afternoon; often they took walks together. They even talked of his father's driving again. But after the move, this contact was much reduced.

The first dream in which his father appeared was the following: "I was going to a porno theater with my father. Some people (men) were threatening my father. I wanted to protect him. Then, inside, some kids from school were acting up."

Given Frank's need for support and help during this trying period in his life, it is striking that, in this dream, he was taking care of his father rather than the reverse. However, the setting of the porno theater introduces a sexual element into this dream. And while his father's health was in reality declining rapidly the men who were threatening him had nothing to do with the issue of his failing health. The kids who were "acting up" introduced yet another element. They were reminders of how exasperated and angry he sometimes felt toward the students in his classes when they threatened to get out of control; how he felt real hatred for them because they reminded him of the boys of whom he had been afraid when he was younger. But "control" was important to Frank in other ways. He had given up smoking marijuana a few years ago because he was afraid of losing control, and he cited a couple of instances when, under its influence, he had been very "passive": once, when someone else had grabbed away concert tickets he was about to buy, and again, when he allowed himself to be driven home by a cabbie who was cursing. In the dream, the aggressive men were threatening his father but when he had felt out of control and passive, *he* had been unable to deal with aggressive males. The kids "acting up" represented the aggressive males he had feared as a youngster and also his own fears of being out of control.

With regard to the issue of control, there was an interesting sequence of feelings in two consecutive sessions early on in this second phase. In the first of these sessions, he had been feeling optimistic and said that he realized *he* was in control, regardless of how much he might fear the Devil. This session was a rambling one, and we touched on a number of related topics having to do with masculinity. When he returned the following week he related that he had felt fine for several days until, while waiting for the elevator in an office building, he saw a young black man also about to enter the elevator with him; he did not get on and then reproached himself, telling himself he should not have hesitated. He then thought "Maybe there is a Devil after all." In the imagined scenario of possession, of course, it would be the Devil who would be in control, not Frank.

The foregoing were some of the feelings, events, and dreams that paved the way for a very important dream which seemed to have some reference to his father and which was mistakenly interpreted, as will be seen.

The dream was, "There was someone—a man—possessed by the Devil. He was somehow like a vampire. He was in bed. An old stumblebum came in. The first man sat up and kissed the old man on the forehead. Then, a tail and horns were superimposed on the first man." The first man was described as having hair like mine, and a goatee (I had a beard at the time). But, he emphasized, the man did *not* have glasses (which I wore). He had fine features and looked gay. With regard to the kiss, he said it first appeared that he was going to do something hurtful, but he did something nice instead. The first man was about my age, not old. The association he gave to the old "stumblebum" was from the film *Rocky* which he had just seen. In that film, the hero Rocky had befriended an old stumblebum. Frank had found this film quite moving, empathizing strongly with the hero who desperately wanted to make something of himself. Because of this association, I interpreted the old "stumblebum" to be Frank's father and let the suggestions of my identification with the Devil slip by. Three years later, Frank, in recalling it, mentioned "the dream where *that man kissed me* and then turned into the Devil." This was the correct interpretation, and making it would have of necessity focused attention on the man who turned into the Devil—which, of course would have been myself.

The kiss in this dream is reminiscent of the dream mentioned earlier where the actress said something about the Devil and then gave an older man a "sensual kiss." By now, it had begun to be apparent to me that the Devil must be connected with a complex of sexual feelings charged with anxiety. If it was I who turned into the Devil after kissing Frank, then surely it would raise the question of something sexual between us. And yet, in the dream the kiss was tender, as it would be if a parent brushed his child's forehead with his lips to check for a fever. It was as if the two aspects of kissing had been split up, with the sensual potential going into the dream of the woman and the older man and the parental aspect going into the dream between the two men. Yet, the element common to the two dreams was the Devil symbol, hovering in the background in the first dream, but etched with startling clarity in the second. Both dreams, though separated in time, must have been generated by a single interwoven complex of feelings.

I have realized that I was not really prepared to deal with Frank's wanting something sexual from me at that time, and of course, there was absolutely no question of his own readiness for it. I certainly could not have made any such interpretation but I might have insisted that the man in the dream was myself and left the question of why I should be turning into the Devil to be explored. The answer must have been, of course, in my role as a fatherly person, reflecting the deep complex of feelings about his father. In fact, the old stumblebum was probably a dual figure, referring to both Frank and his father as well.

There was a fragmentation in the inner image of the father that resulted from the different ways in which he had experienced him. First, there was the strong father he admired who took Frank places and who bought him nice suits like his own. Then there was the absent father, who rejected his family's need for him, including Frank's, to spend time and the family's money drinking in bars—that father he sometimes hated. Finally, there was the much weakened father of the present, debilitated by long years of alcoholism, that Frank was caring for; this father he pitied. Through his caring he was trying to reconstitute some few elements of the father/son relationship that had been drastically disrupted years before. It was this fragile relationship that was interrupted anew, but now by Frank's moving away from his father's neighborhood to the new house he had bought for himself and his wife.

The week before the dream just discussed, he had awakened at 4 A.M., with the thought of the Devil—accompanied by the same sort of panic he had felt the year before. But this time, he reassured himself. Instead of praying, he reasoned that the problem was within himself. But he also said, "Let him take me now, if he's going to." It is striking how the two systems of thought stood side by side: on the one hand, the reasoned, analytic explanation and on the other hand the dreadful symbolism of the Devil, nonetheless experienced, momentarily, with all the force of reality. While Frank could not resist this unconscious "reality," he retained the presence of mind to hold up his analytic knowledge as a medieval priest might hold up a cross to keep the Fiend at bay.

The circumstances under which this near panic was experienced are worth mentioning. That evening, he had had a party at his house. As he related it to me, he realized that he was very fearful of saying or doing something that would make his friends reject him. In any case, they had all gotten rather drunk and Frank told a story of how he and one of his basketball friends (who was there with his wife) had once been drunk and tried to pick up a couple of girls. Also, he revealed how he and this friend, Robert, had once gotten drunk in the car after the game. He later worried that Robert might "get it" from his wife afterwards, and that he, Frank, would lose his friendship because Robert would be angry with him. After the 4 A.M. awakening and the accompanying thoughts, he asked his wife to hug him, and she did. The sequence of conscious events here seemed interesting: a felt desire for his friend's esteem and fear of losing it, then a state of near panic in which the frightening symbol of the Devil appeared; then, using his analytic knowledge, he tried to fight off the fear, and then finally turned to his wife and her embrace to help ward off the anxiety. (This event occurred in the months when Frank's wife was still living with him.) It seems important that he turned to her at that moment. The relationship with her represented a comforting bulwark against the unconscious feelings—symbolized by the Devil—that had threatened to engulf him that night. Recalling the analytic explanation signified his identification with me in the role of the ally who was trying to help him regain his emotional strength.

In my own mind, I had begun to formulate the hypothesis that the Devil symbolized not only forbidden sexual feelings but also, more specifically, some kinds of sexual feelings between men. However, the occasional gingerly attempts I made to feel out Frank's reactions had drawn a complete blank. He did not express horror or loathing of homosexuality, which might have suggested a strong reaction against repressed, forbidden wishes. He had no trouble acknowledging feeling flattered when he noticed a gay man admiring him, seeing it as a tribute to his masculinity. But he had no interest himself—period. To make an interpretation about wanting something sexual with Robert would surely have been utterly futile.

In talking about the party, Frank said that he had *always* been fearful that letting himself get out of control would cause others to reject him. He had been in an exuberant mood at the party and a female friend remarked, "I've never seen you like this." The Devil idea was associated with a feeling of not being in control. The unconscious subtext of not being "in control," then, was undoubtedly the anxiety that the door to that "room" within himself that he did not dare to enter in his dream might be opened and reveal something that would lead his friends to reject him. As in the dream, his wife was a reassuring presence. The event that had precipitated the Devil thought must have been an unconscious one—the energizing of a complex of feelings, including something sexual, about Robert—himself a man about eight years Frank's senior, a man Frank warmly admired and who seemed to return these warm feelings.

The First Interpretation

As will be seen, the above sequence of events as well as the incident related below suggested to me and enabled me to propose to him an element that appeared to be behind the occurrence of the Devil idea. Several weeks after the incident just discussed, he related that after a Saturday basketball game, he had gone home. His wife was out and he went down to his basement workshop. He found himself wondering if the other men on the basketball team liked him. He also thought of calling up a friend—a man fifty years of age who had a family. While Frank liked him, this man could be really opinionated. Sometimes, after or during an argument with this man, Frank found himself thinking of the Devil as he then found himself doing. After listening to this, I suggested an interpretation to him: that when he questioned his acceptance by other men, when he felt uncertain of their liking for him, the idea of the Devil sometimes came into his head. I recalled how, several weeks ago, he had awakened in a near panic after he had feared alienating his friend Robert at the party. He felt this observation was concrete and helpful and readily agreed to continue to try to specify when the idea occurred. It was in this hour that he assured me that he was not interested in what gay men did, adding that he would tell me if he had any such feelings.

In Frank I had an ally who was highly motivated and intelligent. It was not difficult to persuade him to use his intelligence on his own behalf in our work. Intuitively, I felt that if we could start by discovering connections between elements of experience that were in consciousness, we could gradually expand the area of his awareness to reclaim for him areas of feeling that were not now accessible to his consciousness. Thus the suggestion I made about when the Devil thought seemed to appear did not go beyond what was available to Frank's consciousness. Nonetheless, it made a connection between elements of his experience that had not been there before. At this time, I did not make the suggestion that the fear of the Devil might symbolize some feared *sexual* implication in the liking he desired from other men. The link between the affectionate and the erotic certainly was not in consciousness. For the moment, it seemed to me that we could work productively on the *emotional* issues involved in his relations with men, which *were* in consciousness.

The Masculine Ideal

I must confess that, in spite of the data that were emerging from the dreams and associations, it was not easy for me to give the idea of repressed homosexual feelings credence. Frank had a history that was exclusively heterosexual, both in reality and in conscious fantasy. He was entirely and even stereotypically masculine in his appearance and mannerisms. For these reasons I felt I had to work closely with him every step of the way and to be wary of straying too far from the actual data of his subjective experiences.

On the issue of his masculinity, a month before we had been discussing the fact that, after his move to the new house, he had been missing his friends and that he had lost a source of masculine reassurance that they had provided. He was very struck by that observation and added that, at this point, the only contact with men that he had was with men on the basketball team where he did not yet feel accepted and where he did not think he was playing well. In contrast, he would have loved to be praised by them, to be carried off the playing field or court on their shoulders. He went on to say that (apart from the Devil idea) his main anxiety right now was about his manliness, an anxiety that continued to center on the feeling that he should be willing to fight to prove his courage. When he saw a "hood" type, he said, he could not help feeling apprehensive. (This apprehension was seen in the first dream he reported in this phase.) He deplored this continuing preoccupation. He sometimes wondered, "What would Ed do?" One could see, in this question, Frank's struggle to alter a set of values that had by now become somewhat alien partly through identification with the trusted figure of the therapist. In no way, however, did he connect fears about his masculinity with fears of homosexuality. He was clear about that. With regard to the fear of weakness, he had just the week before described an incident in his school where a former student was causing a disturbance in the school. He started to go to call the police, leaving some assistant principals on the scene, when a girl said to him, "Aren't you going to help them?" He went back but the boy had already run away. Over the weekend he had been concerned that he would be reproached with dereliction of duty on Monday. The incident was not mentioned again, and he realized that he had really not wanted to fight. He also realized that he had been afraid and, in a sort of milestone, could finally admit to such a feeling without thinking that it meant he was a coward.

It seemed to me that an important therapeutic task, as opposed to an analytic one, was to reinforce Frank's feelings of masculine adequacy. If there were a homosexual element in the Devil obsession, it absolutely could not be acknowledged by Frank if his masculine self-esteem remained very fragile. Insofar as possible, I attempted to steer clear of any charismatic statements by myself. I did not try to define to him what "masculinity" was according to my values, but rather to compare his feelings and behavior to those of other men as I had observed them in my professional experience as a therapist and social scientist. I again observed that his ideals of masculinity had been derived from the extremes of the adolescent peer group and were rather different from the realities of what adult men were generally like. He said that he now could see that actual people were not "supermanly" and perfect, yet he could not help but feel that there were such people somewhere.

A dream that seemed to summarize where he was in dealing with these issues and my role in resolving them occurred about this time: "I was in a 'perfect place' with athletic, competent, good-looking people. Someone, a guide, was showing me around. I asked, 'Is everyone like this?' The guide said, 'No, some people can't handle it.' He showed me some 'cave people' dressed in skins and looking crazy. Someone was showing a woman a 'Frankenstein' head and asking her, 'What do you think of this?' I asked, 'Which kind of person could I be?' The other person said he didn't know; it depended on how well I could cope."

The guide, in this dream, he said, was not a strong person, but "together," like me. One could see Frank still struggling with a polarization in his perceptions of what people were like. On the one hand, there were the perfect people, one of whom he very much wanted to be and on the other hand, the primitive, deranged people that he feared being identified with. The guide, while sympathetic, is also somewhat detached and says the outcome for Frank will depend on himself. In a way, it was a rather accurate picture of an analytic relationship.

In this dream, the figure of the woman is also of interest, and it recalled the woman who was having a nervous breakdown in the first group of dreams recounted above. Some sort of unconscious identification with these women on Frank's part seemed to be implied in these dreams. He found himself worrying if *he* could have a nervous breakdown. At the time, I did not know what to make of the possibly implied identification with female figures in a man in whom there was not the slightest trace of effeminacy.

However, about midway in the first year of this second phase a dream occurred that was very frightening. In fact, he said that it was the closest thing to the fear he had felt two years ago when he awoke from the terrifying dream that preceded the onset of the Devil obsession. The dream went as follows: "I was in a house. There were some people waiting for me in a car or cars." The dream seemed perplexingly brief and, in its manifest content, not at all menacing. When he awoke from it, he thought of an older friend and his son together and his feeling of being excluded. And, the idea of the Devil came into his mind. He turned to his wife and hugged her though she remained asleep.

There was a second dream in the same week: "I was with my wife, crossing on an overpass. There were some 'toughs' below. I was trying to shield my wife from them. I kept trying to twist my body around so she would not be seen. I think she was unconcerned. As I was twisting around, I nearly lost my balance and was in danger of toppling over."

Considering the sequence of the first and second dreams, it was not difficult to surmise that they were tapping into a complex of anxieties having to do with men. The intense fear attached to the first dream was, paradoxically, followed by the father-and-son association. The second dream, which also was an anxiety dream, though not so intense, had as a central element the fear of rape by a group of young toughs—rape directed at his wife, of course. Paradoxically she was not afraid in the dream, and it was he who almost tumbled over into their midst. A third dream, reported in this same hour, was as follows: "I was in a movie theater, next to a woman and a man. The woman was smoking pot. Then, the man was coming after me and I was trying to get away." Here, the man is after him quite openly and he is trying to escape. While it was a woman smoking pot, Frank had told me he used to hang around a pot-smoking crowd in high school when he was not hanging out with the "jocks." Once again, there was an implied identification with a woman, while pot smoking had made him fear being passive and not in control.

Putting these three dreams having to do with men together certainly suggested a fear of something having to do with men, including something sexual. In the first dream, the men were waiting for him, in the second, threatening rape, in the third a man was after him and he was trying to escape.

Although, consciously, Frank had no fear of any sexual implication in his relationships with men, he freely acknowledged at this point his need for friendship and affection with men. In this same session, he mentioned the fact that his friend Robert's wife had said to him about her husband, "He needs you." This made him feel very good. And, with evident pleasure, he said about Robert and himself, "We're alike, just alike." It will be recalled that Robert was about eight years older than Frank and the friend whose wife he had feared angering by his indiscreet anecdotes at his party, after which he had awakened thinking of the Devil.

The Second Interpretation

It seemed to me that it might be possible to broach the *fear* of sexuality in the relationships with men. I noted that he had two feelings about men. Men could be competitors, objects of fear in the sense of challenge. On the other hand, a man could be someone that he wanted to be close to and whose affection and friendship he desired, in a friendship that had nothing to do with women. He readily agreed that his friendship with Robert excluded women. I then made the following interpretation: that perhaps the Devil came into his mind when he felt the need to be closer to a man and, because he was an adult and a sexual person, he felt afraid that it might imply homosexuality. He replied, "But you can't love a man. That's wrong. You love a woman." Yes, I said, perhaps that was his dilemma. After all, I added, the prototype of love between men was that between father and son. He said, "Yes, *that's* it," and then added, "I'm feeling nervous." The hour had drawn to a close, and I said we would look more closely at the symbol of the Devil next time. However, in the next session, the theme that emerged was the theme of identification with his father, the wish to be like his father of the old days, the father he had admired and idealized for his strength. This stood in contrast to the possibly homosexual theme of the previous week.

In retrospect, I should have rested content after my first suggestion that the Devil seemed to come into his mind when he felt the need to be closer to a man. By adding that he might have feared that such a desire implied homosexuality, I was simultaneously introducing the idea of homosexuality while discounting it, implying that it was an unwarranted fear. Nevertheless, Frank caught the drift of what I was hinting at. When I tried to mitigate the impact of what I had said by my comment about the prototype for love being that between father and son, I was unwittingly adding fuel to the fire. After all, he had just finished saying that he felt intense anxiety about a seemingly innocent dream in which some men in cars were waiting for him. In this dream, his associations were all important. The dream brought to mind a father-and-son relationship from which he felt excluded and which had to represent the relationship with his own father, from which he had indeed eventually been excluded as his father left him for alcohol.

The second of this batch of dreams was interesting in another way. Since it was he who almost tumbled into their midst, it was evidently he and not his wife who was in danger of being raped by these "toughs." Here there is no question of a loving or tender father-son relationship. These "toughs" were more reminiscent of the rough boys of the neighborhoods in which he had grown up.

The third dream of this series clarifies the meaning of the other two to some degree. Now the man is literally targeting Frank. However, the woman smoking pot must also represent him. But a woman? This would suggest some kind of identification of himself with a woman in relation to a man. Such an identification would also be the farthest thing from Frank's consciousness. The dream of threatened rape, foreshadowed in its imagery, a major theme that had and would profoundly trouble Frank: jealousy. He would later fear that the woman he was attracted to would prefer some brutally sexual male to himself. The dream reflects that jealousy because these "toughs" are targeting his wife, not him. Yet, once again, the dream reflects the unconscious understanding that it is *he* who is in danger of being engulfed by these feelings, because his wife is not afraid and it is he who almost loses his equilibrium. In the dream, then, there exists an inherent contradiction. Even while projecting his fear onto his wife, he knows that it is really he who has the problem. Even had I understood all that at the time—and I did not—there was no way in the world that I could have persuaded Frank to accept it. The woman in the third dream must have stood for the part of himself that had homosexual feelings.

The identification of himself with a woman harked back to the first batch of dreams reported in this second phase of the analysis. There, too, there was a woman having a nervous breakdown who was endangering Frank by pointing a gun at him. I believe this dream was indicating that something within himself that Frank felt to be female was holding him, as it were, hostage. Strangely, the same woman says that another woman who, with Frank, jumped out the window to escape her would not have been killed had she "given in." It was as if Frank were telling himself, in the language of that dream, that salvation lay in accepting that part of himself.

In the week after his wife announced to him that she had not wanted to be with him for four years, a striking incident occurred when he was out fishing with an older friend. They had been fishing together at night and when Frank looked at him in the moonlight, he thought, for a fleeting second, "He's the Devil." He then went off to fish by himself and began to get upset. Then, he began to look around himself and thought, "*That's* reality, not the Devil." Again, when I inquired, his association as to what the Devil might do to him was that he would make him his helpless slave. In the next week, we reexamined this fishing incident. The man he was with was successful, married, and had a child. The whole scene was a bit eerie in the moonlight. He looked at this friend who was of Greek extraction and dark. His sequence of thoughts was: He would like to be close to this man, have him like him; but he then thought, "He doesn't like me, he's only pretending." Then, for a millisecond, he thought his friend was the Devil. He asked, in mock despair, "Does that mean I'm certifiable?"

The Third Interpretation

At this point, I made the following suggestion: That in fearing possession by the Devil, he was fancying himself in a relationship—as slave or servant—in which he is totally submissive and helpless. At this point, he seemed shocked and near tears, and asked me, "Are you telling me I want that?" I had not said that he wanted that—in fact, my meaning was more that he seemed to fear that.

Frank then made a sort of leap into his own interpretation of what I had suggested. He said that, if he felt afraid of being taken over by the Devil when he experienced the emotion of *inferiority* in relation to another man, it would save him from that inferiority feeling. *He could fear the Devil instead of feeling inferior to other men.* This was acceptable to his conscious mind whereas what he *thought* I meant by what I had just said certainly was not. Frank was well acquainted by now with his painful feelings of inferiority to other men and it seemed plausible to him that he would rather fear the Devil than feel these painful inferiority feelings. While I felt that this could not be the whole story, even if it were one element in it, his very strong negative reaction to my interpretation made me feel that it would be unwise to push that any further.

While I was by now fairly certain that fear of the Devil reflected some complex of feelings having to do with homosexuality, I persisted in seeking ways to formulate these feelings in terms that would be acceptable to Frank's conscious mind. But following the imagery of the Devil symbol and of Frank's associations to it led with startling directness to what appeared to be the scenario of being in a helpless, submissive relationship to someone or something the Devil stood for. The erotic element in this thought was already strongly indicated through the dream material that we had. But Frank's shocked "Are you telling me I want that?" rocked me back on my heels. Perhaps, I thought, I was wrong in spite of all the seeming evidence. It seemed safer to continue to work on what we could secure agreement on while working to broaden and deepen his understanding of himself.

The above reasoning was the process that I went through at the time. In retrospect, it seems to me that my suggestion about the meaning of the Devil fear was much too great a leap from the data of Frank's conscious experience. As I myself had already pointed out to him, the Devil thought had sometimes followed insecurity about being liked or accepted by someone. The incident on the beach that Frank described would have been the perfect opportunity to take this one step further. I could have pointed out that, paradoxically, he had momentarily identified the very person he wanted to like him with the Devil. That would have been progress enough for one session. My interpretation that being possessed by the Devil symbolized being in a relationship of helplessness and submissiveness to someone, and not just to someone, but a man to whom he looked for affection and acceptance, could have followed later. That interpretation would have been emotional dynamite at any time, judging from Frank's reaction.

In any case, I could and did observe that he wanted the admiration, respect, and affection of men (which he could and did readily acknowledge). However, I said, these men could reject and hurt him, as his father had once hurt him by his withdrawal. He himself went on to add that the possibility of being hurt in athletics was very real because you could be rejected if you were not good enough.

The Devil as a Man

In this same session, Frank presented several dreams: The first was, "In an auditorium filled with beautiful women. I was being brought around by someone and introduced to all the women. They were all charmed by me and liked me." The second: "Somewhere, a baby crawling with a diaper . . . wanting to squeeze the child." The third, "My birthday. A friend made a comic book out of *Penthouse* [magazine] leaving in the pictures. One cartoon had a blue Devil in it. I said, 'You know about this.' She said, 'Yes.' I felt very bad but it seemed like no big deal to her." It seems significant that, in a magazine noted for its erotic depictions of women, the sole male figure appears in the guise of the Devil. In the discussion of this dream, I proposed to Frank that the Devil seemed to be a man. He did not seem threatened by this and agreed. As is evident throughout this study, the theme of Frank's needs in relation to women stands side by side with the theme of his needs and feelings in relation to men. The first dream accurately depicts what Frank longed for in relation to women. That could be presented without distortion or disguise in the manifest dream. The second dream, about the baby, is less obvious. He wanted to squeeze the child in order to hurt it. The baby taps into Frank's need to be loved and taken care of, into needs which could be directed toward either sex. The child must have represented the baby brother of his teen years who *was* loved and taken care of at Frank's expense.

While I came to understand that Frank's emotions about men constituted a strand of feeling separate from his emotions about women, there were nevertheless indications that some degree of emotional bouncing back and forth between men and women could have occurred. His need for his mother's nurturing had certainly not been satisfied. Even if it was due to his father's alcoholism, her weakness in facing life and, most poignantly, her turning to him to make up, with his small earnings and gifts, for what her husband threw away on alcohol was embittering. The birth of his brother at a time of his life when he was so vulnerable—early adolescence—must have written a finish to any hope that he would ever be the recipient of that nurturance again. One could imagine that this event must have reinforced the longing for the strong father of the earlier days to take care of him. But this longing, with the sexuality of adolescence, must have taken on a sexual form as well; it was the sexual component of that longing that must have been decisive in the creation of the Devil symbol.

Of course, a question occurs about the birth of the baby brother: What impact on Frank, who had just entered adolescence, did the fact have that it was his *father* who had made his mother pregnant with this child? By then Frank and his mother had lost the man they used to depend on, but this pregnancy showed that his mother still had that man in a sexual sense. Could this have made Frank envious and could this have accounted for the identification with the woman in some of the dreams? Did he wish to have his father as his mother had had him? In consciousness, Frank had always sought to emulate the qualities that he had admired in his father, most notably his strength. But alternatively, and only unconsciously, he seemed to want to be the recipient of that strength in another sense. I am talking about the difference between wanting to *be* the strong man that he saw his father to be and *having* that man. Perhaps the correct interpretation of the dream in which a voice said that Mary Hartman's husband was a "real Devil" was that Mary Hartman—who was the title character of a soap opera—stood for Frank's mother, whose life he might have bitterly characterized in those terms. In that case, Frank's father would be the "Devil" the dream referred to.

Meanwhile, Frank continued to monitor the occurrences of the Devil thought. He noted that it occurred a couple of times when he was with his friend Robert and once when fishing on a beach where there were families. Both times he felt weak and envious. It was in this session that he explained why he continued to cling to his wife even though it was now clear that she was not going to return to him. He said that he felt that no woman could love him . . . because he was weak—that is to say, he needed people. My reply to him at that time was that all men needed people. One can see here the bitterness that accompanied Frank's attempt to relinquish his need to depend on women as he had relinquished his dependency on his weak and overwhelmed mother. His pessimism about women must have added further impetus to turning to his male friends, Robert for example, to have these needs met. The Devil thought had occurred in the presence of this friend to whom Frank had confided that it felt really good to know that he, Robert, would be "there" to back him up if "the shit hit the fan." (Robert had replied that he would *want* to be there.) This conversation took place at a bar, and one of the girls there said she could see the love between them.

Correcting for my earlier oversight, I noted that he nonetheless might fear that allowing Robert to get too close might make him weak and helpless. He answered that he would try it and see what happened. Once again, his association to what the Devil might "do" if he could possess him would be to make him his slave, kick him around, ridicule and mock him—all actions at the farthest remove from his feelings about his relationship with Robert. One could see here how Frank's conscious doubts about women's unwillingness to tolerate his weaknesses contrasted with his firm assertion that he knew he could count on his male friend to be there for him "if the shit hit the fan." And yet, the paradoxical occurrence of the Devil thought in connection with this friend must have symbolized something potentially destructive in this relationship. Undoubtedly, one aspect of this destructive potential must have been the possibility of sex between them which, in spite of Frank's tolerance toward others who were gay, clearly was unacceptable when the notion of homosexuality got too close to home. But the Devil also symbolized something "really evil," a description that seemed to transcend a threat to his masculine self-esteem alone. The idea of love between them was entirely acceptable to Frank, as long as it did not hint at sexual love. When Frank, earlier on, had nervously asserted "You can't love a man," he was consciously referring to the kind of love that would include sex.

Meanwhile, he continued to see his wife toward whom he felt he could not express anger. He felt that then he would really lose her, although he had no more hope of her coming back anyway. He asked, "Why can't I get angry?" He could feel the anger toward her but still could not express it. The following week he had this strange dream: "There was a medieval type of prison and, opposite, across a gulf, there was a cliff. There was a Japanese woman with an infant—a large infant, almost like a midget. While I was looking the woman dropped the infant. I picked it up and thought, "Should I have sex with this child?" Instead, I just squeezed it and handed it back to the woman. She asked what I would like as a reward. I asked her to expose herself. She bent over and then a horde of brigands came riding out of the prison, to rape her. I couldn't protect her." His associations to this dream were an older friend who was married to a Japanese woman who had had a nervous breakdown. He remembered feeling jealous of his family because they took his friend's time away from him. He did not really want to dwell on the fact that the child was a man-child. It was seen from the back only, and was naked, with muscles. As for the question he posed himself in the dream about having sex with the child, he repeated that he had no sexual desires for any male. But, I asked, perhaps he could have the desire to be physically close to or hug a friend, Robert for example? He conceded he might but said that he would never let that happen unless he were drunk.

At the time, I found this dream puzzling. Who or what did the woman in this dream represent? Consciously, while Frank did not seem without some sympathy for his mother, he had little desire to take on the role of protector in her life. When it came to his wife, his jealousy had more accusation in it than it did protection. Yet it could not be overlooked that the dream images had parallels to his family constellation at about the time that his brother was born. The element of this dream, however, that I now think was the most important was the image of the brutish men from whom he could not protect the mother of the child. I feel this must have reflected the poignancy and bitterness of the family situation and that part of his feelings, rarely in awareness, that wanted to protect his mother from his father. In fact, Frank's baby brother had been conceived during the period when his father had already begun his descent into alcoholism. So, while he might indeed have envied his mother his father's sexual love, he might have simultaneously felt it as a crude self-indulgence by a man who no longer was willing to be a responsible husband and father.

The discussion of this last dream, however, brought us one step closer to the idea of the physical expression of his feeling for another man. The qualification that he would have to be drunk to allow himself to be hugged by or to hug Robert was an interesting compromise. He might let himself do it but only in an "altered" state.

Sex and Emotion—Women

Near the end of this first year, Frank said he realized that his wife was not going to come back to him. He did not want to lose her, he said, because of the sex. When he thought of other women, he felt he wanted only sexual involvement and nothing else. The contrast between these feelings and those toward men was striking, in that with men, it was precisely the reverse—he wanted affection and friendship, with sex being unthinkable. Nevertheless, his continuing sexual interest in women signified that he did indeed want something emotional from them. But his anger and pessimism were undoubtedly behind the denial of this need. But only the sexual wishes toward women expressed these needs, symbolizing them in the imagery of sex.

At this point, another anxiety, rather vague and not specifically a "Devil" thought appeared sometimes—the disturbing feeling that there might be some ghostly or supernatural presence in the basement. On one occasion this occurred when his friend Robert wanted Frank to skip a Christmas party and go drinking with him instead. Frank had felt that if he went to the party, he might meet girls, "get laid." In this small vignette, one could see the conflict in his emotions, pulled as they were to both sexes. He wanted Robert's companionship and affection but still wanted to meet a woman, though ostensibly chiefly for sex. In this instance he experienced this ghostly anxiety after consciously feeling pulled between friendship for Robert and a possible sexual opportunity with a woman. The alien feeling of the ghostly presence in the basement must have symbolized the unconscious *sexual* feeling Robert's invitation provoked and which he inwardly fought off. Paradoxically, however, it was women he confessed to being "afraid of." He was shy about looking a woman who was attracted to him in the eye. He did not know what to say to her. These thoughts and feelings were occurring as we got into the second year of the second phase of the analysis and reflected the deep fear of rejection that probably lay behind his professed lack of interest in women emotionally. However, in his dreams, fear was attached to male figures.

Another Key Dream

At this point, he reported a most significant dream: "I came into my house. I saw a man's arm and was frightened. Then I saw that it was my father's—he had passed out." His description of this arm was very striking. He described it as "heavily muscled, with black hair, a killer's arm." The juxtaposition of father and killer seemed most important. For the moment, all I said to him was that there seemed to be some fear connected with his father. The other striking contrast was that between aggressive, lethal strength on the one hand, and total weakness on the other.

This single image of this dream constituted a symbol, heavily saturated with meaning and emotion. The heavily muscled arm was emblematic of male power, a power Frank's father once possessed and that Frank deeply admired. But the *dénouement* of this concentrated and intense vignette, revealing his father in the bitterly familiar state of alcohol-induced impotence, reflected the crushing end of the boy's romantic idealization of the once powerful father. The arm, appearing disembodied, "heavily muscled, with black hair," is strikingly phallic in its evocations. But the owner of this arm, the wielder of this phallus, is a killer—a phallic killer *and* an impotent alcoholic. It was not the Devil himself that Frank confronted in the first image of this dream, but it was pretty close. Frank's father had never been physically harsh to Frank, rather it was through his abandonment that he painfully wounded his son. If I am correct about the meanings of this dream and the dream of the "brigands" just discussed, then one could fairly put them together to form a composite picture of Frank's adolescent experience as his father "raped" the boy's mother, leaving Frank with another competitor for the attention of that overwhelmed woman, and then sank back into alcoholism. In any event, this last dream, with its dark glints of eroticism, set the stage for what happened next.

The Devil and Erotic Symbols

Over the next few weeks, a series of very significant dreams followed: First, "A friend [with whom he played guitar] approached me and showed me a rock magazine with the name of a group, 'Devils,' on it. I was afraid for a second. Then I thought, 'Oh no—not that bullshit again.' And then I had no more fear." Second, "I was being chased by a group of people—Johnny Rotten and the Sex Pistols. They pushed me out the window. When I landed I got into a fight with swords with someone—the other person was like a giant." In this same session, Frank reported yet another dream: "I was being held prisoner by a rock group called "Kiss." They had me on a chain, by a collar around my neck. Every time I tried to get away, they pulled me back, tormenting me. Then I got away and jumped into a deep pool."

Probably relevant to the actual imagery in these dreams was the fact that Frank had begun to take an interest in learning to play the guitar and in writing lyrics for rock songs. He and some friends were contemplating starting a band. The dreams with the names of these rock groups were occurring coincidentally in time with the development of this interest. In fact, he was very close to one of the members of this band, Chuck.

The eroticism of these dreams seemed unmistakable, but there seemed to be a very wide gulf between the erotic symbols of Frank's dream life and those of his waking life. These three dreams formed a meaningful triad of interconnected symbols: "Devils" . . . "Sex Pistols" . . . and "Kiss." Of these three, the Devil was the only symbol that appeared both in his dreams and waking life. His dismissal of his momentary fear of the "Devils" symbol as "bullshit" reflected the conscious conviction that he was able to maintain most of the time—that the fear of demonic possession had no justification in reality. The symbol of the kiss had already appeared in two earlier dreams which, taken together, connected tenderness and sensuality with the Devil. But in those earlier dreams, there had been some sense of a fatherly relationship. In the most recent dream, the symbol of the kiss was associated with a group of younger men who were about the same age as his friends in the band. The "Sex Pistols" were an indisputably phallic reference and also involved a group of men of Frank's age. In both dreams he was trying to escape from these groups of young men whose names advertised their sexuality.

I think it is important to see that Frank's feelings toward *both* sexes were dichotomized. He could consciously feel real emotional need and even love for men. However, he could not allow these emotions to express themselves in sexual imagery or, of course, action. But the pressure to do so was too strong to be entirely suppressed and under the conditions of sleep erotic images were formed that, even in his dreams, he tried to escape. It seems unlikely that these erotic images would have arisen in the absence of the emotional needs that he had toward men, needs that were being progressively uncovered. However, Frank had to maintain his heterosexual identity. In the culture in which he had grown up—and, in fact, the culture in whose context the analysis was being conducted—heterosexual men did *not* entertain sexual images with regard to other men, and if they did it was deemed a problem to be resolved. Conversely, sexual images of women were not only expected but encouraged. When he first began the second phase of the analysis, however, Frank was even worried about his heterosexual fantasies. Well before the end of the first year that anxiety had faded, never to return. What began to surface ever more clearly, however, was his mistrust of women emotionally, mistrust that even led him to deny to himself that he wanted anything *except* sex from them. However, as with men, I am equally certain that he would not have continued to want sex with women if it did not symbolize getting something emotional from them—even if he refused to admit this fact to himself. However, the denial of emotional need with respect to women was rather transparent.

Thus while it seemed that his marriage was over, his wife remained very much in Frank's thoughts. In the session where he said that he only wanted a woman for sex, he was bitter about the fact that he had recently been without electric power for twenty-four hours and that his wife had not even called to ask how he was. After a pause, he said, "I hate her." This was the first time he had said this about her. About two months later, he reported the following dream:

"My mother had to have the seams on her dress fixed. We went to a tailor. My mother thought the price he asked was too high. I argued with my mother, saying it had to be done anyway. Finally, I said to her, 'I hate you.' " He was surprised to discover such intensely angry feelings toward his mother and felt guilty about having them. The anger toward these two significant women in his life was beginning to surface in his feelings.

A New Context for "Devil"

However, at about this time, the Devil thought occurred in a new context. He was watching TV and during a commercial a good-looking, muscular man came on the screen. At that point, the word *Devil* occurred to him. He felt that it would not have occurred if the person on the screen had been ugly. I asked about his association to "Devil" in this context. He could imagine looking in the mirror and perhaps saying to himself, "You're a handsome Devil." He might think this if he were feeling good about himself. Or, this phrase might come to mind in relation to some other person. He showed me a sports magazine with a picture of a black football player who had a tense, piercing look on his face. This was a kind of look he interpreted as "Devilish." He said he knew he was feeling inadequate in that context. I in turn said that we did not know why he could not simply be aware of the feeling of inadequacy without having the idea of the Devil occur to him. He agreed that this remained a mystery. An attempt on my part to pursue the juxtaposition of the Devil thought with the handsomeness of the man drew a blank.

Soon after this session, the following two dreams were reported:

"I was beginning to make love with Anne (his wife) but she stopped me." And "I was held prisoner by first a man, then a woman, then a man. I was being driven around in a car. I tried to escape a number of times but couldn't."

The manifest content of the first dream seemed clearly related to his conscious thoughts about Anne's rejection of him. The man in the second dream was somewhat sinister, like the man in the dream of being kissed. The car was a convertible. The only person he knew with a convertible was the son of an older male friend of his. He was a nice person, but they had no relationship. Shortly after this session, the following two dreams were reported: "Anne was obviously having an affair with Sam and she was cold to me." The second dream was: "I killed two young black men on a subway. They'd touched my hat. Then, I ran, holding two balloons and thought of holding up an Indian jewelry store."

I could not help but notice how these dreams came in pairs. In one of them, there is the theme of rejection by Anne. In the other, some situation of confrontation with males, although in the dream of being held prisoner there was some alternation in the sex of the person holding him.

It seemed striking that the dreams involving men were so much at variance with his conscious feelings about men. In dreams, he was being pursued, held prisoner, actually fighting with them, or seeing them as rivals whom Anne preferred to him. In waking life, he sought their friendship, felt close to some of them, and felt anxiety about not being accepted or liked. None of the dream images concerning men seemed relevant to his current conscious thoughts, with the exception of feeling that Anne must be rejecting him for someone else. It was true, also, that he consciously felt inferior to other men sometimes. But this feeling was evident in dreams largely in the triangular situations with Anne in which she preferred the other man.

Intuitively, I guessed that the holding up of the Indian jewelry store might have some reference to me and asked if he had any anger toward me. After thinking about it for a while, he said the only thing that he could conceive of being angry at me for was the fact that, as summer approached, "You're going to be taking a vacation from my problems." This theme continued in the next session, when the Devil thought occurred in relation to myself. He saw me as "the Devil" for an instant when, in some small talk at the beginning of the hour, I had pronounced the name of the actress Simone Signoret with a French accent. The thought was that I was being a phony, trying to impress him. This led into a discussion of my responsibility toward him and my caring in view of my upcoming vacation. I recalled to him that he had needed more fatherly caring from his father than he had received. I understood that he might feel frustrated that I could not make up for that loss myself, that is, be truly fatherly. He said that sometimes he thought about having a good friend who could give affection and acceptance. Once again, I let the possible pairing of a sexual wish, strongly implied by the thought of the Devil, with the need to have me care about him slip by.

He also reported another occurrence of the Devil thought in the past week. He had been brooding about Anne. Then he saw on television a handsome, muscular man surrounded by girls. He felt envious and thought "Devil."

It seemed important that the two themes of men and women in Frank's feelings both intertwined and yet maintained a certain separateness. Anne had been the person in his life who had been his dependable friend and ally in the period just after the emergence of his obsessional symptom. She was his companion when he explored the house where he needed help in the early dream of this second phase. After his disillusionment with her it seemed that he turned to his older friend Robert for closeness and acceptance. He seemed to rule out other women except for sex. In spite of the many dream indications that erotic feelings about men existed alongside the need for acceptance and affection, consciously Frank responded to another man's sexual attractiveness by envy, never desire. Furthermore, any attempt to gently explore the desire for physical closeness of a kind that could be construed as sexual—even in connotation—seemed to meet with a blank wall. He could accept, quite readily, the observation that the Devil idea sometimes occurred when he wanted the acceptance or admiration of a man who might reject him, but he could not venture beyond this proposition into the physical realm.

It was striking that he kept having dreams in which his wife was involved sexually with a good friend. Thus, he had the following dream: "Anne is involved with someone from my old neighborhood. Later she is with my friend Chuck. I hate them both." It was at Chuck's house, a few weeks later, when he thought "Devil" as he looked at him. However, his conscious thoughts were envious, that Chuck had everything just now, including the immediate prospect of a marriage. I already mentioned that his friend Sam figured in a triangular dream with Anne. Another one of these was, "In my old house—my wife is telling me she had an affair with my friend Sam because he is strong and she needs someone to protect her. I tell her I can protect her, but she says 'no.' " The dreams involving his friend Sam bring together two contexts in which Frank had recently experienced the Devil thought. The first context was when he thought of Anne going out with someone else. But it had also occurred when he had been with his friend Sam. It appeared that he, Sam, and a friend of Sam's were waiting for the other men's wives to come and pick them up. Frank found himself upset about the imminent prospect of losing the company of Sam and the other man. However, even before the wives turned up, Frank had been feeling somewhat left out because of the relationship between Sam and the other friend. The conversation, he recalled, had turned around sex.

It was around this time that he came in one day and said, "Level with me. What's wrong with me?" The night before, Sam and his wife were visiting. After they left, he had to go down into the basement and he found himself fearful that there was something down there. As was my custom, I first asked for some associations. His associations to Sam were "someone big and strong." During the evening, however, he had thought that Sam's wife would be better off with him. Also, he hoped that Sam would not have a child before he did and thus beat him out. His conscious feelings about Sam were competitive, as they had been in the triangular dreams with Anne. I decided to take him up on his invitation to "level" with him and said that perhaps he wanted something from Sam or other men that was similar to what he had wanted from his father. He seemed startled and said that was ridiculous. It would be weak and "fucked up" to want something like that from Sam. From Robert, perhaps, but Sam was younger. He would have to get over any such feelings if he had them. I proposed to him that a negative reaction of that kind might account for having to put the wish into symbolic terms, that is, the Devil, and might account somewhat for the anxiety about being enslaved. His reply was: "The only thing I admire abut Sam is his body." For Frank, Sam was more competitor than caretaker by a long shot, it seemed. Although his statement about Sam's body could be read as an ironic confirmation of erotic feelings, he admired Sam's physique, but could feel no conscious desire for contact with it. What he meant, of course, was that he viewed his friend's physique competitively. This competitive anxiety obviously played a role in his jealousy, as did his feelings of inferiority—of this he was now aware. But what he could not be aware of was that the emotional triangle in his feelings was two edged. The same man who was his potential rival was also his potential lover. The jealousy syndrome seemed to bring these two otherwise compartmentalized aspects of his feelings about men together. His conscious thoughts about Sam were friendly but also competitive. Consciously, he did not imagine that Sam and Anne were having an affair. Unconsciously, it was he and Sam who could have the affair. However, this potential was twisted around and represented in the dream by its opposite, and the man he felt something sexual for became transformed into a sexual rival.

It seems clear that there were now two categories of men that Frank could respond to with a complex of emotional and erotic need. The first was a certain category of fatherly man, a category that both Robert and I as well as a few other older, usually married, men fell into. The other category encompassed younger men, sometimes just appearing on television but also including good friends with whom he wanted to be close and whose looks and physiques he could admire. Although the second phase of the analysis was taking place in the 1970s, when homosexuality was still generally regarded as "pathological," I could not detect anything that deserved such a description in the complex of feelings that seemed to generate the sexual feelings towards men. These feelings: emotional need, feelings of love, and the expression of intimacy would all seem like perfectly normal accompaniments of sexual feeling in the heterosexual mode. So, why should they be considered pathological in the homosexual? On the other hand, the fear of demonic possession *was* a genuinely pathological element—a symptom of obsessional neurosis. It was caused by his fear of where his feelings toward men could take him; yet, this fear was shared not only by most self-identified heterosexual men in the culture, but also by sizeable segments of professionals in the social and health sciences. In that muddled atmosphere, I found myself in some degree of conflict. I was by now completely convinced that the Devil obsession was linked to the urge to express his feelings toward men sexually. Yet, each time I started to broach this with Frank, I could not help but feel that I was about to hurt him.

In retrospect, I think this is one of the reasons I proposed that what he wanted from Sam was like what he wanted from his father. I felt he could more readily accept needing something from a father than from a friend. His reaction showed how mistaken I was in my judgment. In any case, there was ample evidence that his needs for something from his father were themselves pressing toward sexual expression. I now feel that there were at least two elements behind the still-repressed erotic imagery that attached itself to the figures of friends. The first element was, in fact, a transference of need from father to peers—but all adult sexual love has elements of this kind of transference from parents to contemporaries. One does not need to be a psychoanalyst to figure out the meaning of "I want a girl just like the girl that married dear old Dad." But the second element has largely independent origins in the reciprocal affection of peer friendships that can be seen in many children before the age of two and that continues throughout life. Frank's experience of peers had been twofold. There were the warm friendships with peers that had always been important to him. But there also had been the constant threat of humiliation and attack from bigger and more aggressive boys who were more dominant in the pecking order of the adolescent subculture. The memory of those hurtful experiences was a reminder that men could be dangerous just as his father's abandonment was a reminder that they could be emotionally devastating. I think the dualism of his experiences with peers as well as the dualism in his experiences with his father made Frank acutely aware of the two faces of males, the affectionate and the violent. In fact, in one of his earliest dreams of this phase, he related: "I was a cartoon figure, a small body with a large cartoon face, a face full of fear. Then, there was a different face. It was either, 'This is what you'd look like if you had the Devil in you,' or 'This is what the Devil looks like.' *It was a face full of violence and hatred.*"

In the milieu in which Frank grew up, male violence was openly linked to sexual competition. As a young adolescent, he could be attacked by older and stronger boys for even looking at their girlfriends. He would literally have to avert his gaze even though he wanted to look at the girls. And of course the fight incident was the quintessential insult to his masculinity, inflicted by other males. I think the themes of attraction on the one hand and repulsion and competition on the other are vividly demonstrated in the next dream in which male erotic imagery appears in the most undisguised form to date. "I was in bed with Anne. I was naked. Then Anne turned into Brian ______. [a neighbor]. We were both nude. Brian smiled at me. I was repulsed. His smile seemed to say, 'See, you can't have her.' "

He said he could not make much of the dream. He did not even like this man but did envy him his wife. He said he probably ought to be going now, and the session ended.

In his interpretation of this dream, Frank again saw it as a competitive situation between him and the male figure. The implication of a sexual potential between him and the man he was naked with and who had replaced his wife was not grasped. He could acknowledge his need for affection from male friends, but it was these very same friends who would appear in his dreams as sexual rivals in a triangle with his wife. "Devil" also occurred in waking life as a paradoxical thought in the presence of these same friends. In effect, the sexual thought about the friend could not be successfully repressed, but the context could be narrowed so that the friend was seen as a sexual rival, never as sexual object. The dream of the neighbor reflected the repugnance that Frank experienced about the sexual potential between himself and another man. In the dream, the naked man is someone he does not even like, just as he did not like the idea that he could entertain a sexual desire for another man. Under the circumstances, an interpretation of this wish and the defense against it seemed futile. And besides, rather amazingly, I, myself, obsessively kept feeling that I could not be *absolutely* sure that my hypothesis (a homosexual wish) about the origin of the Devil fear, and not Frank's (feelings of inferiority) was correct. I continued to want to find a way around having to accuse him of "homosexuality."

A fascinating dream that seemed relevant to Frank's mechanism of turning desire into competition follows: "I was walking on the street. There were brownstones, both like the Village and my own [old] neighborhood. A man came up to me. Somehow I knew or he said he was, the Devil. I took him into my hand and tried to squeeze more and more and the person became smaller and smaller until he fit into my fist. He was so small that I put it into my mouth, chewed it up and spit it out. Then, I ran down the street shouting ecstatically, 'I'm free.' " In this dream Frank confronts the man he fears in the guise of the Devil and cuts him down to size, as it were. In this instance, antagonism is the mechanism whereby need is combatted. It is quite literally spit out.

This last dream occurred about four months after the dream of being naked in bed with a man. In the intervening months, Frank had made a breakthrough. He had slept with a woman other than Anne. It had been a satisfactory experience and the first of many successful sexual encounters with women. Strikingly, these successful encounters did not prevent the Devil thought from recurring. In fact, the Devil thought had occurred during the same week that he had had the dream of "spitting out" the Devil—a week also marked by his having sex with a young woman who had not had it before. He felt she was glad to be rid of her virginity, and he seemed pleased to have helped her do it.

At about this time, he found that the old worry about not being strong enough had really gradually faded. He no longer worried about fights. The old fear that had haunted him since adolescence seemed much diminished. Perhaps the confirmation of his masculine attractiveness to women helped a process already under way through the gradual discarding of the adolescent values.

While Frank had begun a sexual life with women other than Anne, he nonetheless found himself wondering if he could love any woman and said that he really did not want to get involved with any of them—a fact that he communicated rather openly to the women who were his sexual partners.

At about this time, which was the end of the second year of the second phase of the analysis, Frank reported a dream that he said was one of the most horrifying he had had:

"A man tells a woman something—he's had enough of her—he doesn't want to see her or talk to her or something. The woman begins to 'freak out,' screaming 'I can't stand it anymore.' She is put in a sort of zoolike environment, something like a bear cage. There are bars but they are low (so one could climb out). There are doctors around, Russian doctors (the setting is Russia) but they can't help her." This dream occurred the week following the dream of spitting out the Devil. In his associations to this dream, he felt identified with the woman. The only observation I made was that, whereas in reality he was leaving women, in the dream he is being left by a man.

As much as any other, the timing of this dream seems significant. Even as Frank was getting confirmation of his masculine adequacy and attractiveness to women, he was dreaming about being distraught over the rejection or abandonment by a man. The "Russian doctors" undoubtedly referred to myself. However, what was it that he wondered if I could help him with? There does not seem to be a sexual issue here, but rather one of emotional turmoil. Could I help him to recover from the grief of his loss? That is what he seemed to be asking. There had been ample evidence by now of the sexual component in his feelings toward men. But here was something equally intense but not, strictly speaking, sexual. How were the emotions of grief over loss that this dream expressed related to the sexual feelings of other dreams? In the erotic dreams he was trying to escape from men, as he was in the dream where the rock group Kiss held him by a chain around his neck, but in this dream, he is identified with a woman who does not want to lose a man. It seems, in the end, that getting these positive responses from women did not diminish his need for something from a man. As will be seen, I did not put this interpretation to Frank at that time.

In line with his felt identification with the troubled woman he recently wondered if he was beyond help and if I could help him. He then added that he sometimes wondered if he could really be gay. For the second time a woman had noted how much Robert seemed to love him. And, in a lighter vein, during a football game recently, he was at eye level with someone's crotch. He said, "I could take a bite out of this." The remark drew a laugh. Oddly, my notes reveal that I backed away from Frank's invitation of explore these feelings. I said that heterosexual men sometimes had homosexual fears that were based on their sense of having emotional needs directed to other men, sometimes because men were perceived to be more trustworthy than women. It seems that in spite of all the evidence I still seemed to wish to protect Frank from feelings of unmanliness that the idea of being gay evoked in him. In this, I reflected the temper of the time and the limitations in the understanding of masculine psychology.

The two themes of feelings toward women and feelings toward men did appear to be independent themes, which I did not yet fully realize, although it now seems so apparent. There also seemed to be an alternating between men and women in his feelings sometimes. It was correct, I believe, to say that as Frank found himself despondent over his wife's rejection, he turned, as a reaction, to his male friends to assuage his loneliness, though not altogether successfully. But it would not seem correct to say that turning to his male friends was *only* a reaction to the rejection by his wife. The need for male affection clearly had independent roots as well. Frank agreed with these observations when I put them to him—but with the understanding that we were not talking about sexual feelings.

A dream he had some months later will be cited at this point, because it seemed to incorporate both themes, of men and women, intertwining in complex fashion with references to both present and past.

"I was with Anne at school. But I had to do some errand for Robert or he'd be mad. Chuck was with Anne and I felt jealous. Then I was somewhere else—my old neighborhood. Chuck was there, helping me. His wife was jealous. Anne was naked and talking about her new boyfriend. He was a 'wimp' but he had money. I was on my hands and knees, crying. I wanted to make it with her but she wouldn't have me. Then I was writing something, saying, 'Here's to my father who was always unavailable when I needed him.' Then I was feeling sick and my friend Chuck was there helping me. At the end, I knew things would be okay."

In the discussion that followed his relating this dream, I again noted that men were both competitors and people that he turned to for warmth and friendship. And in this latter instance, a woman, as in the instance of a friend's wife, could be seen as a competitor. I also reminded him that in his life history, there was no prominent prototype of an unavailable woman. Rather, it was his father who had been unavailable. At this, he became visibly upset and said we could end the session right now. To my question about what had made him so upset, he replied, "I'm mad at myself because I want what I can't have."

This dream occurred in July of the third year of this phase. Going back to February of that year, the following two dreams had occurred:

"I was in hell. I and another man were planning to try to escape. To do it, we had to spray some stuff at a TV set and escape through it. This man, who was kind of like an overseer, seemed to turn into the Devil, with smoke and fumes." And, "I was with my father. I said to him that I couldn't take care of him."

In retrospect, the analysis of this pair of dreams seems clear. In the dream with his father, once again the role reversal is striking. Frank's father needs taking care of, but Frank explains that he cannot or will not do this for his father. The omitted part of this explanation is that Frank himself wants and needs to be taken care of by his father. The man in the other dream is undoubtedly myself, "the overseer" who is helping him to escape the "hell" that he had found himself in just before he returned to the analysis. But the overseer turns into the Devil. Or, more precisely, Frank's wish to be in a relationship with this man in which he is taken care of is so frightening that it renders the man himself frightening; in fact, it turns him into the Devil. These interpretations were, however, not made at the time because they simply were not clear to me then as they are now. It was, however, undeniably clear, from ample evidence, that the Devil thought had an association to the erotic component in Frank's feelings toward men. It should have occurred to me that Frank's wish to be taken care of by me, or another potential father surrogate, was so frightening because it carried with it the wish to be loved in a sense that would be complete for an adult, that is, sexually as well. Hence, he feared being "enslaved" in some fearful way by this unacceptable wish to have this man's love. He would in effect become this man's slave, bound by a contemptible need.

It is striking and significant that this intense collection of feelings about his father and the powerful transferences to other men which the unmet needs for this father provoked did not replace or diminish the intense complex of feelings about his mother and women. In one session, in the spring of this third year, he retold, in a long, very emotional monologue how awful it had been to see his mother in such terrible shape and blaming him for adding to her unhappiness during his adolescence and having her not forgive him even when he cried and apologized. These memories constituted the background for the wish he had confessed to a couple of months before: to find an attractive woman who would love him and do anything for him, body, mind, and soul. Anne had originally been that to him, he said, and he hoped to find it again. This time, however, he would not abuse it, as he had with Anne.

At the level of consciousness Frank was concerned for his parents. His father's health was deteriorating, partly as a result of the long years of alcoholism, and at the beginning of the third year he had been admitted to the hospital. Frank had been feeling that he ought to sell his house and move back in with his parents in order to take care of them. He realized, however, that he would not be able to bring himself to do this. Of course, he had never had his own need to be taken care of sufficiently met by either of them.

The issue of dependency came up in another context where women were concerned. He felt he had always been regarded as the "strong, manly" type by women. In contrast, he noted, with a tinge of envy, how women often seemed attracted to "pretty boy" types exemplified by some rock stars. He said that women were not afraid of them, that it was almost like having a girlfriend. I said that perhaps he saw women as being more protective and maternal to that type of man. Yes, he said, if you were the more manly type you were expected to do that for women. It was increasingly clear that he did not want to play that role with women anymore. In a subsequent session not long afterward he readily agreed that he wished that someone—a woman or a man—would look after and take care of him. It was clear that the "macho" image he had been so careful to cultivate over the years had come to be an intolerable burden. It seemed to have been as much a denial of emotional need as it was an affirmation of masculinity. He said that he felt he did need me. He needed someone to whom he could talk about all the things that troubled him. On the other hand, he was wary of looking to women to be cared for because he expected he would have to reciprocate.

It was possible to see a gradual thawing of some of the rigid defenses that Frank had used to defend his consciousness from feelings that he used to think were inappropriate or wrong. This was clearly evident in his coming to accept some wishes to be taken care of as permissible in his makeup. An increased malleability was even evident in the touchy area of homosexual feelings. He spoke about his friend Chuck who, when Frank was visiting him, would ignore his wife and other friends to devote his exclusive attention to Frank. He would jokingly compare the size of his "thing" with Frank's and sometimes call up Frank on the phone while obviously drunk. He wondered about Chuck and said perhaps Chuck's wife thought her husband was bisexual. Significantly, he did not say he himself thought that, but rather attributed his own query to the woman. Sometimes Chuck would make joking references to homosexuality which Frank interpreted as "put-downs." I said that maybe there was an actual homosexual element in Chuck's kidding around, in the context of comradeship. He seemed to accept that possibility and added that we seemed to be in a different stage of therapy at this time—that we were "building." Some weeks later, he asked, bemused, why it was that he believed that gay men found him attractive but not really good-looking women. Although I did not say so at the time, it was possible that he was more deeply mistrustful of women's feelings. He also realized that he had always wanted to be a "pretty boy" type. It became evident that the realization of that wish was partly behind the nose surgery he had had performed. The result was to make him look more boyish. It is possible to see how issues of dependency and love were the emotional substratum upon which the sexual feelings themselves rested. When I had said earlier that there had been no prototype of an unavailable woman, I was not being entirely accurate. Frank's mother, in contrast to his father, was physically present in the home. However, the disappointment with her had been as profound, in its own way, as had that with his father. In the dream where he told her "I hate you," she was being stingy about money which symbolized her emotional unavailability as well as her own dependency. When he said about Anne, "I hate her," it was because she had not been concerned enough about him when he was without electricity. While being with an attractive woman was very important to him, as was sex, his anger in these two instances had nothing to do with sex, but rather with issues of giving and caring. Frank wanted to feel cared about and loved, and that wish energized his sexual feelings—regardless of which gender was involved.

Meanwhile, Frank pursued an active sexual life with women. However, he said that the focus in his sexual relations with women was to please them by his performance. He said that one would think that such a focus would make it harder to perform but in his case that was not true, likening himself to a prostitute who aimed to please. Nonetheless, he tended to fantasize during intercourse and that, at least partially, was what excited him. A common fantasy was having anal intercourse with a woman, not the one he was with, but with some woman from a scene he might have read about in a magazine. He added that he knew that it sounded like a homosexual tendency but he was not attracted to doing it with a man. In any case, he said, although he wanted to prove that he was sexually better than other men and saw his role as giving women sexual pleasure, he felt that they had nothing to offer him. After sex, he always wanted to be distant.

In the next session, Frank asked what I thought about his stopping therapy at this point. For some time, he had been feeling better and had moments when, as he put it, "Now, when I'm happy, I'm really happy." I said I felt there was more that we could do, and the matter was dropped. In this same hour, he mentioned that he had recently seen his mother who said she wished that someone could just take care of her and of everything for her. He felt she would like *him* to do that for her. One could see that his negative reaction to his mother's wish might have something to do with his avoidance of any attachments to the women he had been having sex with. He did not want a repetition of the early role-reversal with his mother in which he became the "parent."

In my experience, patients sometimes raise the question of stopping therapy when they reach a certain threshold in their minds. To step over that threshold would mean getting into waters that are deeper and murkier than anything so far experienced. It means going further into the maze, toward feelings that were hitherto unconscious. If the relationship with the therapist is good, they usually accept the therapist's proposal to continue, as Frank did. What frequently happens then is that within a few weeks the new material begins to come into consciousness or begins to be accessible through dreams. Such proved to be the case here.

The people Frank was in fact close to at this point were his male friends. One particular friend was Nick, who was an actor and very good-looking. He was going out with Nick and some other friends to a bar where they could meet women. Given his intense concern about his own looks he was curious to see how he would react and how he would do with Nick there. As it turned out, he felt that Nick did attract more girls than he did but he himself did not feel that he was failing to attract women. Another of the friends there that evening was a musician in the band which had now been formed and of which Frank was a member. This musician friend had the "new wave" look that he felt he did not. At school, Frank was seen as strong and in his position as dean even able to project an intimidating image. On the bandstand, however, he was the punk rocker. These were two disparate personae. Like his father, he had always projected a strong image. But the beautiful young man did not have to *do* anything to be admired, and he envied that.

The Turning Point

At this point, Frank had a dream the interpretation of which marked the beginning of the dissolution of the Devil obsession:

"Sam, Nick and I were together at some store type of place. There was a homosexual relationship between me and Nick. First, it was a woman bending over; then, it was Nick and I was taking over the male role, having sex with him." In the dream immediately following, he said: "I saw Anne with another man. I beat the shit out of him, but it didn't matter. Anne still didn't want me."

The feeling that pervaded the first dream was the love that Nick and he felt for each other. He said, also, that over the weekend, he had gone out with a girl and the date was not all that he had hoped for. And, at a bar with Nick recently, he had felt that Nick had been more attractive than many of the girls around him. With respect to the imagery of the dream, Frank said that he had no desire to have sex with Nick. I said I believed that but that I also believed the feeling in the dream.

Trying to explain to him why he had turned toward Nick, I said to Frank that he had been disappointed in Anne and that the relationship with her had contained anger and tension. He had turned to his male friends, as he had to his father when his mother had proved inadequate when he was a child. However, the physical and sexual connotations of these needs in relation to his male friends had made him feel seized by an alien feeling, the "Devil." It was this feeling that had been lurking in the shadows. He then said that there had been another feeling "lurking in the shadows." Last week, Nick had stayed overnight at Frank's house. He had slept in another room, and Frank had found himself wishing that Nick could sleep with him in the same bed—but his thought had not contained any sexual content. With regard to the "alien feeling" to which I referred, he said that he had the same feeling when he felt inferior to another man. Yes, I said, either way, he had felt castrated, impotent, and demasculinized. The fact that this same "alien" feeling was present when he had conscious inferiority feelings must have meant that the inferiority feelings themselves were at least partially caused by the sensed emotional momentum toward sexual expression. It supported the idea that the feelings of inferiority, usually coupled with envy in consciousness, functioned as a sort of screen, blocking the recognition of the sexual wish while serving as the surface upon which the emotional reaction accompanying the wish was projected.

Although this session and the dream it was built around constituted a milestone in the analysis, in retrospect, I would question how I handled it. In the first place, I believe I implied that it was the disappointment with his wife that made Frank turn to his male friends. I think now that it was correct to view the feelings that culminated in the dream of sex with Nick as having independent origins, modeled on his need for his father and male intimacy, that even a satisfactory relationship with his wife would not have significantly reduced. The other important point that was overlooked was the triangular dream that immediately followed, in which he is a competitor with another man for Anne. The sequence of dreams was a clue to the link between the feelings underlying the Devil obsession and those underlying the jealousy syndrome. In the jealousy syndrome, the desired man, as I have said, becomes the man with whom he is in competition. There is another element in the reaction to the man, however, which should not be overlooked: that of intense anger. Frank had felt anger with his father only rarely, but one of the times was when his mother cried, while waiting for his father to come home from drinking. Then, Frank cried, too. The father he loved and missed was the father who also hurt him and his mother deeply. In this pair of dreams, the need for love and the bitter anger toward his father were split so that the love went into the dream of sexual intercourse with his good friend and the rage into the physical punishment meted out to the sexual rival. Finally, I soft-pedaled the interpretation about the sexual component in his feelings by referring to the "physical and sexual connotations" of the need directed toward men. I was, in effect, saying that he had mistakenly thought that sex was part of the package in these feelings. I knew that to be a gross understatement, but at the same time I wanted to make the interpretation about sex palatable to Frank. Thus, I really half deceived myself into believing the sexual wish was merely a "connotation."

The dream about Nick came at about the end of the third year of this second phase. As we moved into the fourth year, the theme of women continued to intertwine with the theme of men. In a session several weeks after this dream, he had been complaining about not being able to meet women, which was so obviously ridiculous that he could not help but agree that the real problem was that he did not want any of those that he had been meeting. After some more discussion in which he again mentioned his mother's wish to have him take care of her, I asked what it was he might say that he was seeking in a woman. After a moment's reflection, he answered, "warmth and tenderness." In contrast, he said emphatically that he did not want any woman that he had to feel sorry for, which would constitute a repeat of the experience with his mother. About his mother, he commented bitterly and tellingly that, sometimes, there was not enough milk in the house, but there was always enough for beer, which his mother drank. I was surprised to learn of his mother's drinking since we had only discussed drinking in relation to his father before this. He again recalled how his mother would take the money he got for his birthday, adding that he realized she had had to do that. To that assertion, I simply asked, "Did she?" Suddenly, tears came to his eyes and it was with great difficulty that he did not give way to tears completely. He went on to recall yet again the scenes of her crying and of his crying with her, telling her he was sorry and that he had not meant to hurt her.

As we talked about the sadness of those days, he said he sometimes wondered why he had "made" it. I asked if he had any idea and he said, "My friends—I just stayed out as much as possible." In this remark there lay at least one plausible suggestion about why Frank continued to look to his male friends in adulthood to have his needs met. The need for understanding and support that he could not have met at home he found his friends could, at least to some extent, satisfy. Nonetheless, the wish to have a female relationship was strongly there in adolescence as well. In the "bunker" fantasy of his early adolescence a girlfriend was added to the situation where, previously, he had surrounded himself with all of his favorite foods as he did with weapons. Recalling the anger he now felt toward Anne in their marriage, he said, "It didn't start with her either." About the girls he was meeting in clubs where he and his band were now playing, he observed that, in that milieu, one would only meet girls who wanted to "fuck a band member." About his constant need to have reassurance about women finding him good-looking, it seemed that this concern incorporated the wish to get a response of unconditional acceptance without his having to "do" anything. This theme of deprivation and the yearning to be the recipient of a woman's warmth and tenderness were evident even in his desire to satisfy a woman as completely as possible in sex. He said, "I'm a good lover. I know how to caress and touch because that's what I would like someone to do to me." Of course, Frank meant he would like that done by a woman. However, it is not at all difficult to see that he could also experience the wish to be touched and caressed in such a fashion by a loving man. At the time, I did not make such an explicit interpretation. In fact, the few allusions I did make to his male-directed sexual feelings were too indirect and paradoxically left him feeling, as he put it, "You seem to be saying 'You're really gay and ought to be homosexual.' "

In spite of the dream about having sex with Nick, he was still somewhat hard put to accept the association of homosexual feelings and the Devil idea. Strikingly, less than five weeks later, he no longer recalled what "role" he had played in the sexual act with Nick in the dream. I think that probably signified the irrelevancy of the "active" versus "passive" dimension in his underlying feelings about males—undoubtedly in the unconscious, the distinction was not important. What was important was the transaction of physical intimacy. It was in this same session that he offered the interpretation of the dream of the "stumblebum" of almost three years before. He mentioned "the dream where that man kissed me and then turned into the Devil."

An opportunity soon presented itself to return to the interpretation of the sexual component behind the Devil idea. I very clearly stated that the Devil idea was specifically linked to the sexual aspect of his feelings about men and that it did not result solely from the feelings of inferiority with respect to other men. I also stated that the sexual feeling was linked to the wish for love and affection from men. Frank then said, "So that's why, when I was in a huddle with those guys, I thought 'Devil.' I wanted something that I couldn't get from women." He was echoing the other point I made in this interpretation, namely that his pessimism about women contributed to his turning toward men. In fact, Frank was assimilating the information I was giving him about the meaning of the Devil idea and producing associations to it, but he was by no means giving voice to a conscious sexual wish toward another man. The closest he came was a few weeks later when he said that, while watching the movie *The Anderson Tapes* recently, he was looking at an English actor with classically good looks with such adoration that he wondered if he really *was* gay. But, he added, he thought he really just envied his looks tremendously. He recalled feeling in his adolescent days that really beautiful women would be disgusted at him and ridicule him. He seemed to feel that the classically beautiful women was looking for a male twin. I had earlier suggested to him that he was attributing to women a wish based upon his own envy of the classically good-looking man. This interpretation was correct, but not complete. The other motivation for this conviction lay in another kind of projection, that is, the projection of Frank's desire for such a man onto the woman.

At about this time, a complicated dream caught up many of the themes that swirled around within Frank's feelings.

"I was young—about eighteen—I was with Anne and made it with her several times. Then, I heard that she had another boyfriend, named Halsey, who was an actor. Then, I was in my old neighborhood on a bicycle. There were some tough guys around. One jumped on the back of the bike. I turned around and said something to him. There was a fight. I smashed my fist in the other guy's face and smashed him against a brick wall. Then three of his friends started coming toward me. Three older men with baseball bats motioned me to come over and I did and that put a stop to it."

The actor named Halsey is an interesting element in this dream.

Halsey Street was in his old neighborhood, while the "actor" clearly referred to his friend Nick. The relation between the homosexual component in his feelings and the jealousy syndrome is clear in this dream. Nick, his friend who was an actor, was the man he had sex with in his earlier dream. In this dream, Nick becomes his sexual rival, as Frank attributes to Anne his own sexual wish. But calling Nick by a street name from his old neighborhood, "Halsey," suggests that this complex of feelings about men was already in place by age eighteen. The tough guy who jumps on the bicycle is a reference to a real event that sometimes occurred in those days and in that neighborhood. "When I was a kid, that would happen. Someone would jump on your bike and you couldn't say anything. You just had to keep on riding. They would usually get off after a little ways. They might slap you around a little." As for the men with the baseball bats he recalled that once, after the "punk-out" incident in which he had backed down from the fight, he was challenged by someone that he himself had once beaten up. An older black man—a former athlete whom everyone admired—motioned Frank over and that ended the fight. Frank felt "special" to have been noticed by him.

Three Kinds of Males

In this dream, three types of powerful intrapsychic representations of males appear: the handsome friend he wanted to make love with, transformed into the role of the envied rival; the tough, aggressive competitors who threatened his sense of masculinity by their contemptuous dominance; and the strong and admired father surrogate who would protect and take care of him and in whose presence the young man could feel special and secure. Also making an appearance is the woman he desires and who rejects him.

In the dream, there was no reference to tenderness or warmth from Anne. In this sense, the dream mirrored his feelings about the women who had recently been his sexual partners. He said he still felt emotionally closer to men than he did to these women. In fact, he went so far as to term the relationships with these women "vacant." There were some women that he felt emotionally close to, but he was not sexually attracted to them. As for the women he did have sex with, he continued to take special pride in providing them with sexual pleasure. And, while he was attracted to them during sex, he sometimes would have to conjure up a fantasy in order to have an orgasm.

At about this time, Frank again raised the question of stopping. He seemed upset and exasperated and spoke of wanting to be independent. In any event, he did not stop and several weeks later related an incident that had occurred in his school. He had confronted a troubled boy, a frequent discipline problem, and stopped him from running away from school. It had worked, but he had found himself shaking and he was upset at this. He questioned himself, in a slight resurgence of the old anxiety about not being courageous (and hence manly) enough. He asked: If he were married, would his wife feel he could not handle the job and lose respect for him? I said that the reaction of shaking seemed like a very understandable and normal reaction under the circumstances. As for his concern that his wife would lose respect for him, I said that this anxiety reflected a certain pessimism about women's feelings toward him. I told him that I felt most women would be concerned for his safety, not for a display of machismo. In fact, it is possible that both the shaking reaction and the subsequent self-questioning were also provoked by the complex of feelings about men that we had been scrutinizing recently. Indeed, the incident of the fight at age fourteen which had been so significant and traumatic may have reflected the already existing complex. The unconscious perception of the repressed sexual feelings produced a sense of weakness and self-doubt. In contrast, the compulsive assertion of manly courage served as a reaction against the feelings of unmanliness associated with the homosexual complex. In the analysis we were, in fact, working on two fronts: that of social values having to do with the role definitions of masculinity and that of the unconscious sexual conflicts.

In the same session in which we discussed the shaking episode, he found himself musing about his preoccupation with anal intercourse with women. He said he did not feel that he really desired it with men. Nonetheless, he wondered if it could signify something homosexual. About Nick, with whom he had had just such intercourse in his dream, he related that Nick had told him that one sometimes had to submit to people's homosexual interest in order to get jobs in the acting field. However, he said that he had never done that. Still, Nick had recently broken off his engagement with his girlfriend because she had been angry at his being entertained by a gay director. He said, about Nick, "I think he may be slipping." He then added that he did not really have homosexual feelings for Nick but that it was more than just friendship. I said that there was a blurry area between friendship and erotic or sexual feelings and that his feelings seemed to lie in that area. In retrospect, my remark, while empathic, once again closed off his own exploration of these feelings. Nonetheless, he said he simply felt closer to men. He could express his feelings more honestly with assurance of being understood. In contrast, he was just with women for sex, with the exception of one woman, Beth, to whom he was not attracted.

We were at this time in the spring of the fourth year of this second phase of the analysis. About this time he saw his wife, Anne, again. He remarked that she was no great beauty and he was hard put to understand the hold that she had had over him. He reflected on his feelings about women and said that he had one mother. He did not want a relationship with another woman that would duplicate it. He felt that maybe he wanted a really beautiful woman because she would be totally independent. He added, ironically, "It's not that I don't want to hurt women, it's that I don't want to feel guilty because of it."

In his sexual fantasies, he was dominant, "the king," with the woman being submissive, doing anything for him. This fantasy seemed a corrective for the the experience with his mother. As a child and adolescent, he had had to do things for his mother; in the fantasy, the tables are turned even while in *actual* sexual relationships he strove to please the woman. He said he would go to bed with women, but they should expect nothing more. Ironically, he had recently been talking with his mother about the problems she was having with his brother. After complaining about his brother, his mother added, "And he doesn't even apologize the way you did."

After the dream of sex with Nick and the discussion surrounding it, the Devil thought had virtually stopped occurring. Now, as the summer approached, he said that he had been having a few "Devil" thoughts of late and he was concerned lest he regress to where he had been a year ago. It seemed to me that nothing short of frank recognition of the sexual component in his feelings about men was ever going to dissolve the Devil obsession once and for all, so I finally bluntly said that five years ago the Devil obsession had been caused by a homosexual *wish*, which we had come to have some understanding of. He was startled by the word *wish* and denied it, preferring to view it as only a homosexual fear. I reviewed the material we had covered, including the dreams about men in which sexual feelings and conflicts seemed involved. He then gave what was essentially a supportive association: In the past week he had thought that it would be easier with gay men. At least they knew what they liked about him, and because they were men he could understand them better.

I must confess to being more than a little perplexed by the fact that Frank continued to be unable to feel any conscious wish for a sexual liaison with another man. The closest he had come before this last observation of his was the wish to have Nick in bed with him, which was consciously felt as a wish for his comforting presence rather than as a wish for sex with him. But the dream that provoked even that admission had been a frankly sexual one. In it, Frank was having sexual intercourse with Nick, and the emotional tone was loving. Should I believe the dream or should I believe Frank's words? Through all this, there was a nagging question in the back of my mind: Was it possible for a wish, one that was powerful enough to threaten a man's peace of mind and even make him doubt his sanity, never to attain consciousness at all? Certainly, many case histories of psychotic patients would attest to the fact that powerful unconscious wishes could do more than that—they could actually destroy sanity altogether, while never attaining consciousness. On the other hand, could a wish fade or be somehow resolved *without* ever attaining consciousness? Later in this book, I will return to this issue, but for the moment I will say that an understanding of these problems requires a more thoroughgoing consideration of the role of symbolism in emotional life and how it relates to unconscious and conscious experience. At that time, however, I finally settled my own doubts and decided to proceed under the assumption that there was a true sexual wish involved in Frank's feelings about men and that it could, albeit with great difficulty, be brought into consciousness.

Nevertheless, women continued to be his only sexual partners. And regardless of the wishes towards men, still shrouded in a defensive mist at best, he continued an active sexual life with women. He reported again having sex with a woman co-worker whom he regarded with unconcealed contempt. He permitted himself to do whatever he wanted with her, to put his fantasies into practice, including anal intercourse which he regarded as a form of domination that a woman might love even though it was painful. Finally, he said, "I did it a few more times so she would come back if I need her to maintain my reputation as a superstud." Frank seemed to identify this woman with an image of women that had lain lodged in the back of his mind: woman as grasping, untrustworthy whore. Meanwhile, Frank said that he had not been troubled by thoughts of the Devil during the past week in circumstances that in the past were associated with the idea. Several times, he noticed an attractive man. He said he realized that he could find a man attractive without being gay. He also felt that gay men would find him attractive. However, he continued not to be so sure about attractive women, though he could not explain why. He hazarded the idea that a man would respond to his masculinity whereas a woman would not find that enough. For a woman, clothes, style, a "look" might be equally important.

At this point, he related what appeared to be a significant dream: "I was in a boat with an old man. It was on the ocean. The boat was not going well, and the old man was explaining that the engine was fouled with bird feathers." This dream woke him up. It was very upsetting, and he could not sleep. He kept thinking: What if something happened to his father? He would feel that he had not done enough for him. A

"Devil" type of feeling accompanied this thought—but significantly there was no Devil ideation, just the *feeling* that had accompanied the Devil idea in the past. As the discussion progressed, the wish emerged for someone to care for and look after him and the recognition that there was no one. He did, however, reflect that the only person he could call on to listen to and understand him completely was myself.

Father and the Homosexual Wish

Given the dream, its accompanying "Devil" feeling, and the thoughts that ensued in the discussion around it I felt it was possible to take another interpretive step. I suggested that the wish for his father's love and protection had been behind the homosexual wish. I contrasted this wish with his feelings about women. With a woman he did not care about, he still had to "take care of" her sexually. With a woman that he found really desirable, he still would have to do things for her to justify her accepting him. He said, "I can't win either way." It was, of course, significant that he awoke with the feeling that he had not done enough for his father, when it was he who felt uncared for. The strong father of his preadolescent years was long gone, replaced by a father toward whom he felt responsible, and who could clearly not even care for himself.

The interpretation just described was not incorrect, but it most certainly was incomplete. It left untouched the whole area of attraction to men his own age, except through the implication that the need for the father was transferred to male peers. It also did not deal with all the dimensions of need and dread incorporated in the Devil symbol, which I attributed simply to cultural unacceptability of the sexual wishes toward males. (In Part II of this book, the cultural issue will be examined in much more depth and, as will be seen, the question of cultural unacceptability of homosexuality is, in my opinion, not at all a simple matter.)

The following week he met a girl, Michele, at a friend's party and went to bed with her. She was married but intending to separate. She had been with many men, rarely exclusively with one. He found himself wondering how she would react if she met Nick, which reflected some continuing insecurity that she would prefer someone better-looking than he was. However, this question was also a transformation of an inner comparison he was making in his own mind between Michele and Nick. Within himself, he did not know which one *he* preferred—an uncertainty that then became a conflict he could imagine Michele having between Nick and himself. This was an early signal, barely perceptible at the time and unnoticed by me, that the homosexual feelings—now that the symbolic meaning of the Devil obsession had been at least partially unmasked—were about to continue their underground existence in the jealousy syndrome. These homosexual feelings were far from fully acknowledged by Frank, not to mention being far from worked through.

Sex had not been all that good initially, and he found that he could not really have sex more than once during a given evening with Michele. Within a couple of weeks he was back to his more usual self, able to go more than once, but still found himself fantasizing sometimes in order to come to orgasm. The fantasy consisted of a woman really wanting him. He was concerned about Michele's propensity for using drugs, especially pills, and was not sure he would be able to stick with her because of this habit. Nonetheless he described her, initially, as the kind of woman he had been looking for, and by the second week had declared to her that he thought he loved her. She responded with the same feeling. These feelings stood in contrast to the wariness with which he viewed her rather checkered past and her drug habits. Like Anne, Michele was a few years older than he. His complex of feelings about dependency manifested themselves early on. Michele had the habit of apologizing to him for something she might have done. He told her that he did not want to hear that since it reminded him of himself apologizing to his mother. I believe a more telling motivation was the weakness in her that this implied. In sex, he found it difficult to achieve orgasm when receiving oral sex from her because he had the feeling that he ought to be doing something for her.

On the other hand, when Michele would say "I need you" during sex, it would turn him off. In contrast, he would have been thinking at that moment, "I'm fucking her and I'm doing it good." On the other hand, he would also think such thoughts as, "Did he do this?"—meaning did a previous boyfriend perform the sexual act he was now engaged in as well? The jealousy syndrome was seeping into the actual sexual engagements he had with Michele.

It seemed to me that an interpretation of the projective component in the jealousy syndrome was necessary, and I hazarded the following statements: First, his jealous suspicions reflected his mistrust of women; second, he was projecting his attraction for the man onto the woman, attributing his interest to her; third, Michele's actual infidelities and her multiple sexual experiences contributed to his suspicions. In this connection, he mentioned that she seemed to like sex so much that he wondered if sex was her main interest in him. As a consequence, he could not help worrying if she might drop him if she met someone more attractive. There was something paradoxical about Frank's situation. He very much wanted to be the best sexual partner that a woman had ever had. Yet, if she seemed to respond to him in that way, it would raise the specter of her leaving him for someone who promised to be still more exciting sexually.

In the session following the above interpretation, Frank raised the question of termination. I suppose this should not have come as a great surprise since the sexual component of his feelings about men had never been fully accepted. It remained for him a rather theoretical idea, even though the Devil idea had now stopped occurring. He simply could not give credence to the interpretation of a homosexual wish as an important factor and voiced his wish to take a vacation from therapy and from always analyzing.

As we approached what turned out to be the end of this second phase of the analysis, the Devil idea seemed to have evaporated. It had been revealed to him to symbolize his homosexual fears, if not, from his point of view, his wishes. He could still experience a certain uncanny emotion that had accompanied the Devil idea but the obsessive fear of possession seemed to have reliably left him. I was convinced that the sexual wish that he still could not consciously experience had taken refuge in the jealousy syndrome, but I could not seem to evoke a similar conviction in him. *His* interpretation of his jealous preoccupations was that he feared losing what was his to another. Apropos, he caught Michele in a lie. She had denied accepting an invitation to go aboard a boat owned by another man. When he discovered her lie, he told her he was through with her, but finally relented. But he found himself having thoughts of taking revenge on Michele for her faithlessness to him and to others. Paralleling these developments was his renewed disgust with his mother for her constant self-preoccupation. As for Michele, his ambivalence toward her continued to grow as he saw her as dependent on drugs, clinging desperately to people, and afraid to face her fears.

The issue of dependency seemed every bit as important as gender-related issues of sexuality at this point. I pointed out to him what I felt was a denial of his own dependency in this relationship. There seemed to be a repetition of the pattern with Anne. He became drawn to a dependent woman who would submit herself to him; then he would deny his own feeling of need while accusing her of weakness. He then told of a dream in which he went to Anne's house. She was with a man bigger than he. He pleaded with her, but she would not have him.

He said that he would never behave that way in reality. Nonetheless, I countered, the dream suggested that this was the way he already felt, pleading for acceptance from a woman. Perhaps, he said, but he would never admit it. He would project an image of strength and independence, and people would see him that way. Yes, I said, people had at one time seen his father that way. As tears came to his eyes, I added that this had been his father's tragedy—that he had had to maintain that strong image of himself. Frank repeated then that he felt convinced that a woman would despise him if she saw him as weak or vulnerable. However, as I questioned the realism of this belief, he reflected on the fact that Beth, a woman he really liked and respected, did not regard him that way when he confided his feelings to her—on the contrary, she had seemed to love him for it. In spite of this acknowledgment, in the next session, he remarked bitterly that all women were essentially like Michele.

Added to this perception of Michele as weak was the ongoing suspicion that she was not trustworthy, either. He had been at her house recently and she had wanted to go to sleep and not make love. He thought perhaps she had made love that day already with someone else. I once again interpreted the jealousy syndrome. Reflecting on the last dream in which Anne had rejected him for someone bigger, I said that he seemed to envisage her with someone strong, powerful, possibly older and wealthier, who could take her away from him. But the imagined sexual rival was also, I asserted, someone *he* could love. Surprisingly, he then mused, "I can't win either way. I can't stop him from taking her away and I can't get the guy either."

The above exchange took place in the next-to-last session. Frank did now seem determined to stop, and I felt that it was wise to allow him to do so—considering the fact that we had together accomplished the alleviation of a symptom that threatened to crush every chance of happiness in his life. In the course of this work, many of his energies had become liberated and available to him. Nevertheless, the analysis seemed incomplete in some respects and, as his last remarks show, he himself did not feel that all the major issues in his emotional life had been resolved.

In the last session he reported that he had recently seen his father in whom prolonged alcoholism, coupled with other not clearly diagnosed neurological problems, had produced a condition in which he was unable either to rise from bed or to speak. He was near tears as he described this scene of his father in bed. But he either could not or would not get further into those feelings. He felt he could not tell Michele about his feelings because she would not be able to take it, "like all women." He then said, "You must be thinking: 'With a feeling like that this guy is stopping therapy?' "

Nonetheless, he said he was going to stop worrying about Michele's past. She did seem to care for him and if she could not be trusted, that would be that. He could not see marrying her, but he would stick with her for a while.

Thus ended the second phase of the analysis. Since Frank and I had originally met in a social setting and because we had had a teacher-student relationship at one point, there was always an element in our relationship that was separate from the therapist-patient role. This dimension continued after the end of this phase of the analysis. In the two and a half years that preceded the beginning of the third phase of our work, I saw Frank several times, meeting him for lunch and talking about how things were going in his life. The band had continued to develop, and he and his friends were playing club dates with some regularity. As always, Frank continued to be bemused by and to enjoy the contrast between these two aspects of his life—rock-and-roller versus junior high school dean. At one of these meetings, less than a year after the termination of the second phase, he said, "Do you remember our talking about being attracted to men and I'd say you were wrong? Well, it's there." The experience of being up on stage and being admired and envied was one that he enjoyed, and he seemed able to accept analogous feelings in himself with regard to other men—looking at them with admiration, finding them attractive. However, he said he had no desire to actually do anything with anyone, but he could recognize the attraction. This recognition seemed to be experienced by him as more of a liberation in his personality rather than "proof" of homosexuality.

The relationship with Michele had broken up, at his initiation. Another development, and quite an important one, was a career change. For some time he had been dissatisfied with his public school career and decided to retrain himself in a new professional field. He saved sufficient money to enable him to quit his job and to take an intensive-training course and then undertook the challenging task of finding an entry-level job in his field. After some persistence in the face of initially discouraging results, he found a position. Interestingly, one of the reasons he got the job was his teaching background because he was to play an important role in the corporation's own training and instructional program. His life seemed to be on an upward path.

3
The Third Phase

Two and one half years after the end of the second phase of the analysis had ended I got a call from Frank asking to see me at my office. He had been exhausted and enervated by worry over a relationship with a woman with whom he was intensely involved. Over the weekend he had told Jenny that he wanted to break up but she did not want to lose him. He felt that he was in competition with both her career aspirations to be an actress and with her strong affiliations with her friends. While not working as an actress, she supported herself by working in bar settings until the early-morning hours. A pervasive anxiety was that she was or could be attracted to someone else. He felt she did not want to lose him because no one else had ever been as nice to her. Earlier on in their relationship, she would say things like, "I want to suck your cock—I want you to pour it into me." It disturbed him to think she might have said those things to others as well. He also found he wanted her to be more attentive to him; for example, to kiss him when he came in after work. He related the following dream:

"I was with Jenny. I saw her at the top of hill, surrounded by men—she was in her glory. I couldn't get to her. The only path was a single track surrounded by pillars. To get to her, I had to weave my way through the pillars. I was afraid that I might do something to bring the whole structure down on top of me."

This dream was striking in its resemblance to the theme that had pervaded so many of his dreams about Anne. The situation is essentially triangular. The woman is rejecting, unavailable or, as in this dream, inaccessible to him but not to another man or men. The recurrence of this theme in his dream life and in actual life through his jealous anxieties answered a question that had been in the back of my mind since our termination two and one-half years before. Would the work that we had done in the unraveling of the Devil obsession permit Frank to be free of the complexes that had underlain the development of that symptom? The answer seemed to be in the negative.

Within a week or two of our first meeting of this third phase, Frank said he was feeling better. He said that his whole ego had been given over to Jenny. In an allusion to the old "control" issue, he now felt back in control; the other morning he found himself repeating to himself, with some satisfaction, "I'm me, I'm me." At this point, my vacation intervened and when we resumed, it appeared that he had been doing some thinking. He wondered if the reason he was so attracted to women who drank and took drugs was because there was something of his mother and father in them. He could not help them but somehow he had the conviction that he could help a woman now—but he realized, he said, that he could not. What also emerged was anger at the girls, in his adolescence, who did nothing when the boys teased him about his nose. He felt they were "fucking the guys who made fun of me." He still thought of Michele or Jenny having sex with the kind of guy who would have made fun of him back then. He reflected that some of his sexual practices might express anger. He recalled, when he wanted to have anal intercourse, Anne asked him why he would want to hurt her. In oral sex with Jenny, he would find himself pushing himself down her throat as if to say, "You want it? Okay . . ." He added, with vehemence, that he was through with women. However, he had not broken up with Jenny. Near the end of this session, I observed that he must have envied the boys who had teased and derided him. He said, "I still do."

Another theme that had continued unchanged since two and a half years ago was the desire to prove that he was the best lover that a woman had ever had. I raised the possibility that a woman's having a past with other men might have a certain appeal. He agreed that it did but said that he also hated it. In this same hour he spoke of a couple of male acquaintances who had been "putting him down" in some ways. I took this opportunity to reflect on a certain love/hate dimension with both women and men. The theme of competition with men was apparent, but I recalled that the Devil had had another component—a sexual and affectional component. I also recalled his observation some time ago about the sexual attraction to men "being there." He affirmed that he liked gay men finding him attractive and that he found some of them so. He added that there was a physical side of his relationship with Nick with much touching between them. He felt it had a homosexual element in it on both sides. However, his consciousness continued to be focused on his intense ambivalence toward Jenny, not on men. He said that sometimes he tried to get her to say or do something that would prove she was a "whore." He felt that was rather "sick" of him.

The following week, he related two dreams which together captured the dualism in Frank's emotional life: In the first, "The Devil [a good-looking man] is after me, trying to possess me. He's looking at me, laughing at me, and so are others. I realize that the only way I can get away is by going mad. Then I can destroy him." This dream actually occurred *before* the previous week's session in which I had reintroduced discussions of the Devil idea. The second dream, which he had had in the past week, was "I'm crying because of Jenny. I can't decide what to do about her. She won't do something—give me reassurance, I think."

I interpreted the dream about the Devil as reflecting his anxiety about his feelings toward men which threatened to "possess" him. He responded that he could see living with a man, but only for friendship. As I disputed this interpretation, it emerged that he had difficulty in remembering both the wish to have Nick in bed with him and his observation that Nick was better-looking than most of the girls they had been meeting in bars. The shifts in Frank's responses to the sexual aspect of his feelings toward men could be bewildering. Just after he had rather openly referred to the homosexual component in the relationship between him and Nick, he seemingly denied any possibility of a sexual relationship between himself and a man.

The Theme of Dependency

In a very interesting development Frank, the next week, disclosed that he had been thinking that I had introduced the homosexual idea because I wanted to hurry up the therapy because he was paying me so little. In fact, his fee was about half what I would usually set. When he first saw me this time, he had explained his rather straitened circumstances, which were due to having had to take a salary cut in his new field, after a prolonged period of not working. He had very little cash to spare; nevertheless, given the length and nature of our relationship I was entirely willing to see Frank for a fee that he could afford. Of course, I had no wish to shorten his treatment and said so. However, I emphasized that this fear reflected a lifelong complex of feelings, consisting of the wish to be cared for and the reality of disappointment by his caretakers. He feared that I would disappoint him as had his parents. Money, of course, had been a particularly sensitive focus of these concerns since he was compelled to turn over his earnings and gifts to his mother to make up for his father's alcohol-induced failure to provide for his family.

In an interesting coincidence, some of his friends on the new job had presented Frank with a stuffed bear. This little creature was gotten up in modish fashion including dark glasses and a rakish bandanna. Frank enjoyed this gesture and had taken the bear along when he had gone out, propping him next to himself at the bar. He had named him Aloysius, after a similar bear carried around by one of the protagonists of the British television series, *Brideshead Revisited.* He asked me if I thought it wrong to tote the bear around in public. Of course, it was done in the spirit of good humor and, in the milieu that Frank moved, was regarded in that light. The deeper meaning, of course, was evident in the symbolism. Although it was not a transitional object, it stood for one and the relationship of dependency symbolized by the transitional object. When Frank reflected on whether it was appropriate for a grown man to carry around a stuffed bear, he was asking if it was really permissible for a grown man to have dependency needs. And perhaps significantly, the protagonist of this series had also been homosexual, which signaled that one of the origins of the homosexual feelings was in childhood.

While the obsessional anxiety about demonic possession had evaporated and never returned, Frank was sometimes aware of having feelings of a kind that had accompanied that obsessional thought. The symbol of the Devil had retreated from consciousness and now only appeared in dreams, taking its place, as it were, among the array of symbols in the dream life. Now, when the affect that used to accompany the obsessional thought appeared, it was possible to understand it as having some comprehensible, but not supernatural, connection to a given context. Thus, just such a feeling occurred when Frank was riding on the subway with his now nineteen-year-old brother. He noticed that his brother had become attractive, reminding Frank of himself at that age. He then felt that women would find his brother more attractive than himself. During this sequence of thoughts he had just a flash of the "Devil" *feeling,* that is, the affect, not the thought.

A Pivotal Dream

Before discussing the interpretation of this event, I would like to recount a very significant dream, in some ways pivotally relevant to the understanding of the jealousy syndrome and to the continued exploration of the complex of feelings that had underlain the Devil obsession:

"Jenny and I were in a house, on the first floor or in the basement. On the second floor was a man who was dangerous. We called the police. I wanted to leave, but she wanted to stay because she found his dangerousness exciting. The man was tall, good-looking, there was something Devil-like about him."

A striking aspect of this dream was the following: While Jenny's attraction to the other man was an anxiety that Frank consciously experienced in waking life, his *fear* of the man to whom she was attracted was not. In the dream, this tall, good-looking, "Devil-like" man is dangerous to Frank, while Jenny is oblivious of any danger—in fact finding his dangerousness exciting. However, no interpretation of this dream was made at this point. Rather, we dealt with feelings about Jenny. He felt he did not come first in her feelings, that if she got a call for an acting role in California, she would unquestionably go. However, when he hinted to her that he wanted to break up, she cried. It is interesting to note that, while Jenny was giving him cause to doubt her feelings for him in the dream, the competition he was facing was not her career aspirations, but another man. Further, her crying would have appeared to be a spontaneous expression of her wish not to lose him.

Since the man in the dream had something "Devil-like" about him, and Frank had come to agree that the Devil obsession had sprung from his anxieties about men, I focused on that complex of feelings—not dealing, for the moment, with the triangular feature of the dream. As we discussed the history of the Devil obsession, another recollection that emerged for the first time was that, in the summer when he had experienced the dream that had marked the beginning of the obsessional symptom, he had met Nick for the first time.

I now suggested to Frank that the feeling associated with the Devil idea would not have occurred while in the subway with his brother in the absence of finding his brother attractive. He would have been able to accept such a feeling about his sister. To this he readily agreed. I wanted again to try to bring into consciousness the sexual wish in relation to a man that I felt the fear of the man in the dream was motivated by. But Frank continued to be unable to give conscious utterance to the wish. As we discussed the complex of feelings about men and its history in his life, he said that, yes, he did want a man to take care of him, to want him, and could imagine enjoying being held by a man; nonetheless, the ideal of a sexual liaison seemed inconceivable. He felt that in a sexual relationship, one man would be using the other, exploiting and abusing him. I recalled that this was precisely how he had imagined the Devil would treat him. I recalled the juxtaposition of attractiveness with danger in the dream figure of the man. He then made the observation that, in the dream, it was the *masculinity and power* of the man that was dangerous. He added, however, that he felt all sex was exploitive, no matter whether the context was homosexual or heterosexual. The observation about the man's masculinity and power being dangerous was a candid and sensitive perception on Frank's part and reinforces the belief that the Devil obsession reflected the fear of being degraded and transformed by enslavement to the phallic power of another. The Devil was not just a man, he was an *abusive* man. It is true that the Devil had symbolized the sexual potential in a relationship; and for a long time that was all that I believed it symbolized. But it is evident that the sexuality of the man was also fused with cruelty as well as power. Long ago, in the early part of the second phase of our work, an obsessive suspicion about Anne had flitted through his mind. He thought that, even while she was allowing some greater sexual freedom on his part, she might be having sex with someone else—not for sexual reasons *per se,* but rather because he was "macho," did not need anyone—a sort of sadistic, "kick-them-out" type. In the second phase of our work, I had not really grasped the nature and significance of this image composed of equal parts of sensuality, power, and cruelty. And I still found it perplexing in this third phase.

In the next session, Frank recalled an incident from his adolescence. His father had dropped him off at a place where he was going to play ball. He had no money to get back home, either because his father had not left him any or because he had spent it on a soda—he could not remember. He had to borrow some money from a priest in order to get home. He subsequently lied, saying he had been mugged and so had no money. He then expressed concern that he had not paid me in some time. Perhaps I would expect something else instead? It was not clear to him what that could be—perhaps some kind of aggressive ego satisfaction. Everyone, he observed, expected reciprocation. Both the memory of the incident with his father and his worry about my intentions reflected the deprivation he had had with his father. This history and the pessimism it had generated seemed to contribute to seeing sexual relationships between people as exploitive. Sex was an aggressive form of taking, not an expression of love. Therefore, on the one hand he could imagine wanting affection from a man to the point of being held in his arms; on the other hand accepting a sexual component in a relationship with a man would mean opening oneself up to exploitation and abuse. In one sense, the sexual component symbolized the egocentric, selfish and abusive aspects of a relationship. This seemed paradoxical in view of his wish for male acceptance and love.

At the time, I did not raise it with Frank and I am still not certain that such a feeling was present—even in an unconscious form in his mind. However, it did occur to me that, in some vague way, there was some possibility that Frank might imagine my demanding something like a sexual submission from him in return for my accepting less money. I had not, it is true, ever interpreted occurrences of the Devil thought in relation to myself as having a sexual meaning. Undoubtedly such an interpretation would have been met with incredulity, but might have eventually been experienced in consciousness as a desire for me to like him, care for him, and find him attractive. Any wish for a direct sexual expression of feeling from me would have been buried as deeply as all the other sexual wishes involving men.

At this point, however, an event occurred that changed the immediate focus back to the theme of mistrust of women. Looking through Jenny's dresser one day, while waiting for her in her apartment, Frank happened on a letter she had written to a friend but not yet mailed. In it, Jenny referred to having slept with the very man, a bartender, that Frank had suspected her of being interested in. Frank was enormously upset and felt that this was the end of the relationship. Jenny, however, swore that she had only slept with him once and that it was all over. As he reflected on it, he realized that his constant mistrust of her had been a chronically upsetting factor in their relationship. He also realized, now with regret, that he had always put down her career aspirations. Trying to understand Jenny's motivations, Frank thought she was attracted to two kinds of men: on the one hand, secure, family types; on the other, a kind of man who was flashy, exciting, and handsome. He thought that, for a while, she had seen him as both.

The reality of Jenny's brief affair could be interpreted as lending credence to Frank's jealousies. Therefore, I felt it important that the element of *fear* in the dream of the dangerous man did not correspond to any feeling he had in reality with respect to this bartender and that it was analogous to the kind of fear he had felt in the Devil obsession. I said clearly that his jealousy had been a function of his feelings about other men, as well as reflecting his mistrust of women. Even before the discovery of the letter he characterized Jenny as being primarily interested in her own ego gratification. He felt she was clinging to him for security. He himself wanted to be appreciated and loved for his sensitivity, his loyalty, and warmth on the one hand and to be purely sexually desired ("lust," he interjected) on the other. When he imagined a woman being unfaithful to him with someone else, it was always on the basis of her being more sexually attracted to someone else. The fear was that she would find someone more sexually attractive, not someone more loving or sensitive. In turn he would feel baffled and hurt that a woman would not put the devotion and love he was offering her above everything else.

For a while, Jenny had been calling him every day, which he found a considerable strain. She wanted to continue their relationship but wanted him to accept her reserving to herself the right to see someone else if she chose. As a result, they were at an impasse because he could not really bring himself to go along with this condition. As for the man she had slept with, Frank had noticed her talking to him sometime before and that seemed to mark the beginning of his acute feelings of jealousy. He felt that Jenny was not just drawn to the looks of this man but to his "whole being." At the time, he had begun his new job just a short time before and was feeling insecure. He felt he had been nothing in comparison to this man who seemed so sure of himself.

In sexual fantasies, a woman would be begging him for sex. In his mind's eye, there seemed to be a man who was worshiped by a woman. He wanted to be that man, but his fear was that she would turn to someone else with those feelings. In his own approach to a woman, he could discriminate between a certain kind of accepting, trustworthy woman who wanted to marry and another, more sexually flashy type. He said, with a touch of regret, that he still needed that "flash."

Frank's resistance to the acknowledgment of any wish for a sexual relationship with a man was so persistent that I found it a constant source of reflection on my own part. Of course, there was the abundant dream material and the jealousy syndrome which had been such a powerful and corrosive element in every important relationship he had had with a woman. I persisted in my view that everything pointed to the continuing disruptive influence of a sexual component in his feelings toward men. Once again Frank produced a recent dream which seemingly corroborated this line of reasoning while his conscious mind drew a blank. In my experience, never has the theory of the "censor" been so tantalizingly illustrated. The dream he reported was: "A man in my office—kind of a 'macho' type, was following me down the corridor on the way to the bathroom. He was goosing me and trying to fondle my balls, as if to say, "Come on, you're cute.' " This man was, in reality, a superior and had been somewhat brusque to Frank. As it later emerged, this man was also of similar background and reminiscent of his father.

Identification and Sexual Object Love

It seemed that the most accurate interpretation of this dream was that it incorporated a wish to be sexually desired by a man *and* a desire to get away from this wish. Nonetheless, a complex collection of feelings swirled around this wish. Inwardly, Frank seemed to display both a need for identification and a desire for love in his responses to men. For, in the same session, he revealed that he was having his father's overcoat remodeled so that he could wear it. Virtually simultaneously, one could see the desire to be close to his father through identification with him on the one hand and, on the other, the flight from the wished-for seduction by the father surrogate. In fact, as I reflected on the history of the Devil obsession it was possible to discern how these two modalities intertwined. Frank had always felt that the Devil thought was linked to his feelings of inferiority with respect to other men, particularly in the area of attractiveness. When he could feel masculine, attractive, and adequate the thought seemed less likely to occur. I, on the other hand, pointed out to him that the Devil thought was a reaction to his fear of his desire for a relationship of sexual love. It seemed that a feeling of identification was an alternative to, and defused the need for, love in sexual terms.

In the instance just discussed this dualism of identification and sexual love was seen in the context of his feelings about his father. An analogous dualism was suggested with regard to a certain image or representation of masculine power, virility, and strength. I have already discussed Frank's perception of the bartender with whom Jenny had her brief affair—Frank saw him as self-assured and suavely dominant in his relationships with women, including Jenny. He was the kind of man Frank could imagine enthralling a woman and one whom he could imagine Jenny being drawn to—but on a purely sexual basis, a basis that had nothing to do with the personal qualities of sensitivity, generosity, and warmth that Frank valued in himself. It was all the more ironic, then, that in sexual fantasies, Frank imagined himself as this kind of man, as "boss," master, with the woman totally submissive to him because of his looks and strength. When I questioned his belief that a woman would leave him for sexual reasons alone, he began to muse over the fact that his father had been a strong man, never showing emotion. However, he had been alcoholic and emotionally abusive to his mother. But she stuck to him always, even at the end, before his death, when he lay restrained in bed, regardless of what it did to her. He then recalled the fact that Jenny had had an abortion once, after getting pregnant by an actor who said, when she told him that she had his baby inside her, to get rid of it because it might turn out to have a mind like his. He wondered aloud why women were attracted to men who abused them. That the image of the "other man" had tremendous meaning for Frank was already abundantly evident. Nonetheless, I could not help being struck, as indeed he was, by the answer he had given a friend who asked him which would bother him more, losing Jenny or the thought of her being with someone else. He said that he had to admit that it would be her being with another.

In any case, it began to appear that Frank's fantasy of being the masterful man to whom the woman totally submitted herself might also have a strong element of *defensive* identification. That is to say, he could *be* that man instead of desiring him. If this was the mechanism, it was not entirely successful since the image continued to haunt him in the form of jealousy, as a projection of his own desire for this man as sexual object.

Once again, Frank recalled the history of his jealousy in relation to

Jenny. It began when he was just finishing professional school, thinking that he was not doing all that well, and having trouble finding a job. He began to accuse her of being attracted to bartender types, of preferring to be with her friends, of not wanting to spend enough time with him, and of not caring enough about his feelings. It appeared that he doubted her love for him. He had said earlier that he had loved and continued to love her. It had started by his being attracted to her. Initially she was "promiscuous" with him, which he had liked. After a while, however, he realized that she had been with other men, something that was suggested by some of her sexual techniques. As he learned the nature and extent of these past involvements, this history began to bother him.

Dominance versus Need for Tenderness

Sometimes Jenny would want him to put his head on her breast,but in a tender way. He would do it and then start to turn it into something sexual. He asked, "Why would I want to do that (accept tenderness) with anyone except someone who wanted to marry me? And then, I could do it all night." I was all the more surprised, some time later, when I learned that Frank had never literally asked Jenny to marry him. He just assumed that she would not. In spite of the powerful feelings above love that he expressed, his feelings during sex corresponded more to the fantasies of being brutally dominant than they did to tenderness. I remarked to him that his tender feelings and his need for love seemed rather separate from his feelings during sex. He then said, "I just want someone to hold me, to be as weak as possible and still have someone love me. No woman has ever been as tender and loving to me as I've been with them." I said that he did not seem to think that Jenny was capable of loving him. He replied, "I don't think anyone is." He recalled how, over the years, he had seen his mother beaten down by life and feeling rejected by everyone. She had held on to his sister and him and cried, and they had cried. Clearly he was feeling an empathy and identification with his mother at that moment. He felt that, now, he wanted to "redeem" a certain kind of woman. However, he could not do it now and had not been able to do it for his mother then.

I think Frank's remark that no woman had ever been so tender and loving to him as he had to women is very telling. The almost brutal fantasy of sexual dominance sprang from multiple sources. It was, as I have already said, a form of defensive identification with the person he seemed to want, however repulsive such a wish was to his consciousness. But it was also an attempt to be what he felt a woman *really* wanted from a man. He had an image of the woman as demanding to be satisfied by a man, sometimes through tenderness and sometimes by sexual power, but *selfishly* demanding in either case. In his mind the point was what he could do for a woman, never what she could do for *him*. It seems that since he could not have his own needs for tenderness met in any case, he could at least have the masculine ego satisfaction of being strong and masterful, of being the "best lover she ever had." Hence, tender and loving feelings tended to be banished during sex, because they were signs of weakness unwelcome to the woman who put her own needs first. They were replaced, then, by the fantasies of power and dominance. In my work with men, I have found that they are every bit as likely to feel that they ought to be suitable "sex objects" for women as women do in regard to men. However, whereas the feminist movement has challenged this role for women and helped them to put up some resistance to being "sex objects," men tend to feel ashamed and guilty if they are unable to function as a variety of sex machine. Thus the fantasy of dominance had another defensive function in Frank—it blocked out and substituted for his need for love and tenderness from a woman.

He now reported a dream that went as follows: "I see Jenny. She is lying on top of a black man. I think she is looking at me in a malicious way." He felt like a helpless victim as the onlooker in this dream. He had earlier asked me if I thought his jealousy could destroy a relationship. Although he understood that he, too, had the power to hurt, the perception of the faithless, selfish woman continued as part of a complex of feelings that was latent—always waiting to be evoked, as in this dream.

Dependency needs, broadly conceived as the wish to be loved, were, however, now emerging with powerful emotional accompaniment. He said that he wanted to be held like a baby, loved, and taken care of. As for Jenny, he did not even like the way she was now: working and "hanging out" in bars. I felt and said that he was reliving core, earlier experiences in this complex of feelings about Jenny. Both parents had disappointed him, his mother by her weakness, and her leaning upon him, and putting up with his father's abuse; his father, by leaving him to go to bars (sic!) and no longer being strong for him. At this, he burst out with much emotion, "I can't take it anymore, loving someone, being abused, left, and then not cared about!" I think Frank's feelings make it clear that acceptance of dependency needs is a necessary part of any love relationship; they are not merely a set of "immature" needs sometimes dismissed as "orality" in the analytic literature. And I think it makes sense to say that if one cannot feel dependent upon another, one probably cannot feel love either.

As this third phase of the analysis continued to unfold the various themes from the succeeding phases of development and with respect to male and female appeared, sometimes highlighted singly as in relief, sometimes intertwined and blended. That Frank had felt abandoned by both mother and father in different ways was clear. The theme of not being loved or cared about, of being the victim of egocentrism or selfishness emerged with both women and men, with the gender of the other being in a sense peripheral to this complex of needs and anxieties. In the next session, Frank expressed his disappointment with his friend Nick. He could understand, he said, how people might not like him because of his egocentricity. He also expressed disappointment in the man who was the drummer in their rock band. He was now referring to needing more from some of his male friends than he was getting.

In contrast, the feelings of jealousy and competition flared in another context. Because he lived out of town, he sometimes found it convenient to stay at the apartment of a female friend in Manhattan. Their friendship was a platonic one. However, she lived just a few blocks away from the man with whom Jenny had had her affair. He said he would have to take a tranquilizer to sleep because he would be thinking of her getting "dicked" by this man. This imagery bothered him so much that he had been avoiding staying anywhere in Manhattan because of it. This feeling was reminiscent of his earlier phobic reactions to Manhattan, which he had had when still married to Anne and during the period when the Devil obsession had first emerged. By now, I felt the meaning of this anxiety was clear—it was a fear of the sexuality of the man displaced onto memory of the betrayal. Consciously, Frank wanted to be distant from the place that symbolized Jenny's rejection of him. While that was indeed one of his motivations, the other, unconscious, motivation was the wish to distance himself from the feared sexuality of the seducer, just as in his dream he wanted to get away from the handsome and dangerous criminal. However, rather than repeat this interpretation, I simply asked him why this thought had the power to keep him awake. He simply retorted, "Wouldn't you feel jealous if your wife cheated on you?"

I believe that Frank perceived the implication of my question and his retort was an exasperated denial of the implied interpretation. Nonetheless, he produced an observation that came from his own self-monitoring in the next session. He said that when he watched TV, he always looked at the men, not the women. He compared himself with the men, wishing to be like someone he found attractive so that women would be attracted to him. I believe the wish to be attractive to women, as he perceived these men to be, was quite genuine. In this wish, there was quite probably lodged the memory of the teasing of his peers from his adolescence. However, he had ample and abundant evidence that many women found him attractive since that time and in the present. It was true that he had always retained some ambivalence about the particular way he looked. There was envy and some degree of residual self-rejection in this comparison of himself with another. However, this wish to look like someone else also had a defensive component, something that went like: "If I can be that person, I don't have to want him. I can substitute being the man wanted by a woman for wanting the man myself."

In the same session, he told of receiving a letter from Jenny saying that she would like to see him, even though she would not yield on her wish to be free to see others if she chose. They had not been seeing each other since shortly after the incident of the letter. He was very angry about this insistence of hers. He said he still loved her and would probably be willing to go back to being as they were. But he said, "She's laughing at me." I said that this perception of her seemed like a distortion in view of her letter saying she wanted to see him. It made her out to be cruel and heartless. He then related a dream in which he was beating Jenny up. She was saying all the things that might hurt him, things she had actually said, plus things he had imagined her thinking and feeling.

Again, in this session, one could see the dualism in Frank's emotional life and how it expressed itself in the jealousy syndrome. The woman's betrayal symbolized her heartless rejection of him. This rejection enraged him and was a fear that was quite independent, at one level, from the complex of feelings about men. Those feelings were embedded in the syndrome as well, but as a projection, attributing to the woman the unacceptable needs and feelings toward the man.

However, as we worked, Frank was able to think about these needs and feelings with greater openness of mind. We were talking about a man at work, someone he had described as a "man's man" who seemed to like Frank quite a lot. Frank said he realized that his man's admiration meant as much to him as did that of any woman. An incident that occurred with this man took place in a bar. Frank had lightly said to this man that he regretted being neither Jewish nor beautiful. This acquaintance then replied, "You *are* beautiful." Frank was gratified at this response.

The Priest's Kiss

As we continued to discuss these issues, he conceded that, yes, homosexual feelings were possible. He went on to accept the idea of the projection of the sexual component in these feelings in the jealousy syndrome together with the more readily accepted idea that his jealousy reflected a mistrust of women as well. He asked, somewhat wonderingly, "Why is all this coming out today?" In spite of having gone further in the acknowledgment of these feelings than ever before, he continued to feel that actual actions were unthinkable and disgusting. A memory came back at this time, one that he had mentioned once, years before. When he had been an altar boy, there had been a priest who used to corner the boys behind the altar and kiss them passionately on the mouth. He did this to Frank as well. At the time, he was disgusted but could not tell anyone. Later—and this seemed highly significant—the feeling and texture of the priest's kiss came back when he had the Devil idea. He had not mentioned this before. In reflecting on this, it was possible to perceive the profound ambivalence that the seduction by this priest—and a more literal father surrogate it would be difficult to imagine—had aroused in the boy. The passionate kiss had welded sensuality with love in a way that must have been both arousing and appalling. Now, many years later, as an adult, Frank said that the idea of kissing a man was so disgusting that it literally made any notion of sex with another man out of the question. This seemed like an almost unshakable reaction formation. How eerie that the sensory memory of the "Father" who pressed his sexual advances on the boy should return to haunt the man, riding in, as it were, on the wings of the Devil obsession.

The reader might recall with me now the symbol of the "kiss" as it emerged during the second phase of the analysis. It first appeared as a sensual kiss between a woman and an older man in a dream where there was some vague allusion to the Devil; it next surfaced in the dream of the man who turned into the Devil after imprinting a tender, paternal kiss on the old "stumblebum" who actually represented Frank; finally, Frank was trying to escape from a group of young men called "Kiss" who held him on a chain. In our culture kissing is a modality that expresses a variety of affectionate feelings between people, feelings ranging from parental tenderness to unchecked sexual passion. Quite against any conscious will, then, the imagery of the kiss emerged to express Frank's emotional needs toward certain categories of men. But while in dreams the kiss symbolized what he needed from men, in consciousness it symbolized what he feared from them. The prototype of this conflict must have been the experience of being cornered by the "Father" in church who had overwhelmed the boy as he covered his mouth with his own.

As we discussed these issues, one could again see juxtaposed in Frank's fantasy life two kinds of men: the first included men like a good father, like the older men to whom he was drawn and who took a kindly interest in him. It also included the good friends on whose support he had drawn since boyhood. But the other kind of man was quite the opposite; he was hurtful, selfish, even evil, like the bartender types whom he loathed and the cruel adolescents who had taunted him when he was a youngster. While it was clear that the wish for a loving father or friend was a motive force in originating the Devil obsession, the relationship—if one could use that term in context with the Devil—was conceived as one in which Frank would be the object of derision, scorn, and cruelty rather than love. The Devil image seemed a good deal closer to the cruel or hurtful kind of man than it did to a good father or a friend.

On the other hand, there was a certain dualism in the way in which Frank had experienced his father. In the early part of his life, he had known a strong and at least sometimes attentive father with whom he strongly identified. He both loved and respected that father. Later there was the father who deserted his family and his son, who spent time in bars, who became self-absorbed through his alcoholism. Toward this father, Frank felt anger and disappointment. This image of his father shared something in common with the bartenders whom Frank hated yet envied.

In Frank's culture—and in the culture in which the analysis was taking place—a kiss symbolizing passion between men was a forbidden symbol. To entertain this symbol in consciousness meant transgressing a cultural boundary that Frank was not prepared to do.

But Frank was now in a reflective mood and said that what he sought from men was warmth, friendship, and ease. And, about women, he would feel, "I don't need you." I did not want to leave the sexual component out of our discussion and I therefore reminded him that the sexual part of the feelings toward men had been projected onto the woman in the jealousy syndrome. In fact, I reminded him of the dream in which Jenny lay on top of a black man. The friend who had said to him, "You *are* beautiful," was partly black. Nonetheless, I emphasized that his need for love underlay all his sexual feelings toward either women or men.

I felt this last point was particularly important since it specifically linked the emotional and sexual in a way that could help undo the defensive splitting of Frank's conscious feelings into the realms of the emotional on the one hand and the sexual on the other. While he struggled against the sexual symbols of his feelings toward men, he sometimes struggled against his emotional needs for women. He was angry at Jenny for turning down, as he saw it, his offer of love. On the other hand, he felt weak for not being able to forget her, in other words, for needing her, for being emotionally dependent, for wanting love *from* her, as opposed to offering it to her.

But Frank continued to be unable to put Jenny out of his mind. He was not sleeping well and was always wondering whom she might be with. After some time I commented that he still seemed to be looking for a father. He seemed surprised and asked, "In a woman?" I noted the parallels between his feelings about Jenny and about his father. He was always imagining her in a bar, not caring about him. He said, sometimes he wanted to slap her in the face. How could she refuse what he was offering her? I wanted to pursue the suggested links between Jenny and his father and I recalled that he had not been in therapy at the time of his father's death. "How did I feel about it?" he echoed my implied question. As his father deteriorated he gradually became more and more unable to do things. He could no longer rake the leaves, no longer write his name, and then, in the end, no longer talk. Frank would sometimes try to help, but to no avail. Sometimes, after being with his father, he would cry about it later. During this hour, he also said a number of times that he would like to help Jenny, though he could not.

Frank, at this juncture, moved into Manhattan, renting his house in the suburbs. While still angry at Jenny, he was feeling more self-confidence and felt that he was a worthwhile person who had something to offer that people would want. He wanted to know now what areas I felt he still had to work on. It was evident that he was still occupied with Jenny and bitter over her apparently choosing a life in bars with the kind of people who patronized them to living with him. He still did not like being near the street where the man she had her brief affair with lived. At this point, I felt an interpretation was in order. I said that he seemed to be reexperiencing the anger and hurt he had felt when his mother had stuck with his father (the "guy in the bar"). But, I said, he was also drawn to that person who was seen as vile and hateful but sexually virile. I said that since he felt he had given up a relationship with that man, he wanted Jenny to as well. No, he said, I was wrong. He had stopped admiring that kind of person and wanted her to as well. He repeated his view that he had wanted a close, emotional relationship with a man, but not a physical or sexual one. In reply, I restated what I felt was an inescapable conclusion based on the work we had done and on the evidence of his psychic life: that he had desired a man not just as friend but also as lover and that he had split off the sexual component of this wish and projected it onto the woman.

It was striking how this point represented an impasse in the analysis. I would not accept what I felt was a denial of a set of feelings for which there was ample evidence; Frank, on the other hand, could not permit himself to feel what remained unacceptable to his conscious self. Once again he raised the issue of "taking a break" from therapy and asked if I felt any issues were outstanding. In response I once again raised the question of the feelings toward men that had been embedded in the jealousy syndrome. He had not really let the sexual feelings through the barrier that separated unconscious from conscious. Although he had acknowledged an attraction for men, he seemed quite unable to "go all the way" with an actual sexual fantasy with a man. Rather, I said, he fell back on a second line of defense and projected the sexual component of his feelings onto the woman in the jealousy syndrome.

Once again, Frank produced a supporting association. He said he thought that he moved some feelings from a certain kind of man—the bartender type—onto a certain kind of woman, the kind who hung out in bars. With a woman of this kind, he felt that *he* had the power and he was also very angry. In sex, he would "smash into" them. He could "perform" very well, he said, as could a prostitute. What Frank meant to say was not that he displaced his sexual feelings from such a man to a similar woman, but his angry feelings. Yet in this association, a sexual displacement could be inferred as well.

He still, however, could not feel an explicit sexual wish for a man. As we returned to these issues in the following session, I hazarded the suggestion that the Devil obsession had represented the wish to be made love to by a brutal man. He recalled the sexual dream with Nick, but added the qualification that he, Frank, had been the "man." Yes, I said and his fear was that he could relate to the other person as the "man." The jealousy syndrome, I noted, arose from the fact that he had the girl but not the man. His wish to have him was projected onto the woman. And, I emphasized, as long as he was jealous, he would never feel secure with any woman he cared for. He seemed thoughtful and replied, "When you put it that way, I can accept it."

Ever since the feelings toward men had surfaced in the second phase of the analysis, they had remained the subject of ambivalent reactions on Frank's part. The fact that the Devil obsession did not evaporate until the interpretation of a homosexual wish was explicitly made bolstered my confidence in its reality. But Frank could literally be seen going back and forth in his acceptance of its reality in a sort of intrapsychic tug-of-war. What would be accepted one week would be denied a few weeks later. It was a classic illustration of unconscious resistance. I retained the full, even eager, cooperation of his conscious self throughout. But the resistance to the awareness of the unconscious fantasy was enormous, even though Frank produced one association after another that was consistent with and indirectly corroborated the reality of the unconscious homosexual wish.

Thus, in the next hour Frank reported that he noticed that sometimes, in the past week, when he saw a good-looking man, he found himself thinking, "Jenny would find him attractive." That he had this thought when he was alone supported the hypothesis that I had advanced to him that it was he who created imaginary triangles with his girlfriend because of his interest in the man. One could see the birth of the jealousy syndrome in this vignette. He did not think, "I find him attractive," but rather, "*She* would find him attractive."

At this juncture, a new element was introduced. On a business trip to a midwestern city, Frank met a woman, Katherine, whom he facetiously said he had fallen in love with. He invited her for dinner and knew she would have liked to accept. However, she said that she had a boyfriend and he respected her for that. But, I said, if *his* girlfriend had admitted to wanting to go out with someone, he would have been very upset with her rather than respecting her, even if, like Katherine, she declined the invitation. He seemed struck by this and said, if he were attracted to a man or woman in the street, he would not do anything about it as long as he was in a relationship. I was, in turn, struck by his statement because, as I reminded him, he had not so far actually acknowledged a wish for a sexual relationship with a man. Ambiguously, he replied that he would not want a purely physical relationship with anyone. However, I pointed out, he had felt Jenny as well as other women he had known would. He feared, he said, that she would attach herself to someone abusive, who would use her. He himself would not want that from either a man or a woman. Yes, I agreed, that had been part of the Devil fear.

As we focused on the Devil obsession, Frank referred to that aspect of his feelings about men that he could accept. He said that he had been looking for a fatherly relationship—in contrast, by implication, to a sexual one. Tempting though it was to interpret the sexual imagery as a "cover" for the dependency longings directed toward the father, it was a temptation that I felt it important to resist. While I was completely convinced that no sexual wishes would have emerged in the absence of the emotional needs, the fact was that the sexual component was there, just as it was with regard to women. And here I had a datum from one of Frank's own dreams to offer him. This was the anxiety dream of the "killer's arm" which turned out to belong to his sleeping father. That arm seemed to symbolize an element of cruelty and power, including the implications of sexual power that stood in contradiction to the fatherly love which Frank could acknowledge seeking. The arm would have been more appropriately attached to the dangerous criminal in the dream with Jenny, or to one of the abusive men he feared she might be attracted to or . . . to the Devil himself. In this light, it seemed somehow significant that in sexual fantasy, Frank would imagine himself dominating a completely submissive woman, a scenario in which the focus was on pure lust, mainly hers for him. Rather on intuition, I said it seemed that he was identifying with his partner when he made love and experiencing . . . "myself," he finished thoughtfully. Through identification with his female partner, he could have the sexually charismatic man, whose role he was taking.

Again, Frank was in an open and reflective mood with regard to his feelings about men. The following week he said that he had no further data on what we had talked about the week before. He did say that he enjoyed wrestling with Nick but had no desire for any explicit sexual act with him. I made an interpretation now that followed from the material of the previous week. I said that it seemed to me that he wished to be made love to as he was making love to Jenny, but by someone like himself. On the other hand, sex with a man seemed to be conceived of in destructive terms where he was concerned, not as lovemaking. He told of recently having sex with a woman with whom he had had a friendly but also occasionally erotic relationship. But he was not really involved, he said, observing, "I was a machine." I asked him why he had done it and he replied, "Macho . . . to be the best she ever had, but it's no good unless I'm in love." I said that perhaps it was important to believe that a woman would care for him even if he were not the best lover she had ever had. He said he would have to come to believe that. As for women like Michele and Jenny, his fascination with them was perhaps because of the link they had provided to a certain kind of man. He said that could be.

At this point, Frank reported a short but intriguing dream. In this dream, he met Richard Nixon who recognized him and shook his hand. His association to the dream was that, while Nixon was a scoundrel, he was still a powerful man and it would be an honor to be recognized by him. It struck me that, several years ago, the Devil might have appeared in such a dream instead of Nixon and the meeting might not have been friendly. The dream was rather a compromise in Frank's attempts to deal with his feelings about men. As we discussed these yet again, Frank granted that, yes, he would like an older man to want to make love to him, but only because it would be flattering. He had no actual wish for penetration. As for the suggestion that he could have any desire for anything sexual with one of those "scumbags" who hung out in bars and exploited women, the idea was absurd. That would be like an animal. To this vehement denial, I countered that a desire for such men was precisely what he had nonetheless attributed to Jenny. It was noteworthy that although the former president by no means qualified as a "scumbag," he did combine the two polarities, one of which was acceptable, one of which was not—that is, the wish for a strong, fatherly presence versus the attraction to the scoundrel or "scumbag." Nonetheless, the idea that he could want to submit in any sexual way to the low types that he believed some girls seemed attracted to was simply not a possibility in Frank's mind.

Submission to the image of the cruel or destructive, yet sexually charismatic, man is certainly not unknown. It occurs acknowledgedly in sadomasochistic fantasy which may or may not be played out in reality. The Devil was such a figure and the bartender was his latter-day human incarnation. Although this figure of cruel seduction had stirred a response in Frank's feelings, an actual masochistic submission to such a person was unthinkable, nor would I have thought it a particularly desirable therapeutic outcome. Initially, for Frank, *any* homosexual relationship would have been tantamount to capitulation to such a figure, to a humiliating and masochistic submission. His growing openness to recognizing some sexual feelings toward men was, I think, only possible as he became aware of the links between his positive emotional needs for love and friendship and their previously repressed sexual symbols. Because of Frank's particular life experiences—the abandonment by his father and the adolescent years of fear and humiliation that he had had to negotiate—this menacing male figure had had an especially powerful grip on his imagination. But I think this figure, which the Devil is so eminently well suited to personify, generally imbues male-to-male relationships with a chronic edge of unease. A good deal of the second part of this book will be devoted to trying to cast some light on some of the darker corners of this issue. In the meantime, although this issue could not by any means be completely elucidated, its discussion did seem to help with the forward momentum of the analysis.

His friendships with men continued to be important to him. He was recently disappointed in two of these with whom there had been a falling out of sorts. On the other hand, he recently met an ex-girlfriend of one of his very good friends, went back to her place, accepted some cocaine, and had sex with her. However, he could not have an orgasm because he felt no attraction for her whatever. He was in fact planning a trip abroad with this friend, Colin, who was English. However, he described the ex-girlfriend as a "slut," a word that he bitterly applied to Jenny as well. He recalled waiting at Jenny's apartment for her to return from her job at the bar, where he imagined her talking to men and having a good time. I asked him what model for such a relationship—waiting for the return of someone—there could be in his life history. He answered, certainly not his mother, but rather his father. He remembered, at age eight, asking his mother when his father—who was then in a bar—would return. He was like his mother, he said, waiting. He wished he could beat Jenny up so that she would know what she had done. Now, she could get away without paying, as did his father, until the end, that is, when he paid dearly. When I again reflected on the transfer of feelings about his father to women of a certain type, he agreed. He began to contrast this interpretation with the homosexual interpretation—the resistance was still strong—but I affirmed again that the Devil idea had reflected the transfer of these feelings to males as well.

In heterosexual women, one may frequently see a transference of complexes of feelings originating with the mother onto males. In Frank, an analogous transference could, it seems, be seen from father to women of a certain type, as well as to men.

At this point, vacations intervened. Frank himself went abroad on a two-week trip with Colin and while there experienced some of the old uneasiness. The full story emerged over a period of weeks. Recently, he had had a dream in which an unattractive, dark haired woman was after him. People were laughing at him and this woman seemed to be saying, "You can't get away from me." When he awoke, the light on the TV tape machine was blinking. It was eerie, seemingly reminiscent of the uncanny feelings associated with the Devil idea. On the trip, he found that he was not having much success with the British girls, with whom it seemed difficult to make contact. British men had warned him that American women were freer and more approachable. He spent two quite intense weeks with Colin. He would find himself looking at him with what really felt like love. He did not know when he would see him again, as Colin had now returned to England and Frank felt insecure about himself to boot. One night, in Paris, they had slept in the same bed. At first, he could not sleep but just drank enough until he did.

Since his return, he had been sometimes having the feeling associated with the Devil, though not the idea itself, upon seeing an attractive man. He would tell himself, "He's not more attractive than you. You don't want to make love with him. If a woman you're attracted to is attracted to him, it doesn't mean you're inferior." One could see Frank, in this poignant vignette, struggling to marshal his defenses against the sexual feelings for the man. If he could feel attractive enough himself and not feel inferior it would help to ward off the feeling of the need for the man. This defensive operation was almost conscious. In the same hour, seemingly in corroboration of my suggestion that a reactivation of the feelings associated with the Devil idea was probably a result of the feelings stirred up in him by his friend Colin, he recalled another fact from the summer when the Devil obsession had first seized hold of him. He had been working with a cousin whom he idolized. His cousin, he felt, had strong feelings for him as well. After Frank moved to his new house, they were out of touch. Again, in a reflective and wistful afterthought, he said, "I want a connection with a beautiful woman and a beautiful man. But I'll never have the beautiful person I want." What he meant by this was that he was pessimistic about this happening whether he was heterosexual or gay.

Meanwhile, in what had now been established as the norm for Frank, the side of his feelings drawn to women continued to churn. Katherine, the woman he had met on his business trip to the Midwest, came into New York and came to the club where he and the band were playing. For some reason, he drank a pint of bourbon that evening and his playing was consequently far from its best. He recently called up Jenny on the telephone to see if she was "still alive." When she answered, he hung up. He now felt real hatred for her, feeling like beating her up, wanting to say to her, "Whose dick have you been sucking?" As for Katherine, she had told him that she had never known anyone like him. She was fascinated and intrigued. His comment to me about that was, "Who cares? What happens when she meets someone more fascinating? I want someone to love me for myself."

In the light of those feelings, it was something of a turnaround when, the following week, he announced to me that he was in love with Katherine. This sudden declaration of love was reminiscent of the plunge into the relationship with Michele. I made this observation and asked why he did not wait for her to prove herself before he, in a sense, offered her his love. The week after this, he said that he had been thinking about ending therapy. Katherine had said that her ex-boyfriend had told her he would change and had asked her to marry him. Frank told her he would wait. As for ending therapy, Frank felt he wanted to feel that he could "do it" on his own now. As it was, he looked forward to our sessions and had depended on being able to talk to me about anything. He felt that if we ended, he would like to see me informally twice a month but he doubted if I could take that much time away from my family. He did not think that I could be only a friend even though he thought of me as a friend. When I raised the question of the paternal component in our relationship, he said he had never thought of me as someone older, in spite of the differences in our ages. But, on reflection, he guessed that I had nurtured certain things in him and he was a different person because of that.

The juxtaposition of a new relationship with a woman and his proposing to end the analysis, which had occurred when he met Michele and which had led to ending the second phase of the analysis, could not be overlooked. This time, I was prepared to be fairly strong in pushing for an exploration of this juxtaposition. However, things were now moving rapidly and Frank's feelings were changing week by week. An extraneous but rather important variable that entered into the equation now was the job situation. He had been shuttling back and forth to the

Midwest on his firm's business, and the office out there had expressed an interest in having Frank on their full-time staff. The move presented an intriguing career opportunity. He felt he would have a chance to learn new skills in what was still a new field and to undertake responsibilities that would put him in a more competitive position with respect to his peers. The first flush of romance also quickly faded. Katherine said now that she was not prepared to move as fast as he seemed to want to. His conclusion was that perhaps the whole thing would prove to be only a romantic interlude. Nevertheless, moving out there would give him the opportunity to explore the possibilities of this relationship. The issues of dependency, giving, and getting were raised in this new context. He said he could not understand how a woman could refuse his offer of complete love. He felt she needed much reassurance and if he were out there he could give it to her. But then, he asked, "Why doesn't someone reassure me?"

Some weeks before, I had asserted to Frank what had become more and more obvious in the time that I worked with him: that all the sexual feelings we had discussed had been related to the wish to have something essential in him loved. While there was some oversimplification in this, I believe it was essentially true with regard to his feelings with respect both to women and men. In the course of our work, Frank had come more and more to express these feelings. Now he said that he wanted to be desired physically but that this was not enough. He had felt so betrayed by Jenny because he had given so much of himself to her. Now he felt, if a woman related mainly to the physical in him, why wouldn't she with someone else? There seemed to have been some genuine shift in the balances of Frank's inner feelings. When he first began to like Katherine, he said he liked her very much without caring who she had slept with. This was something of a "first" for him. As their relationship became more involving, the jealousy syndrome did not show any signs of returning.

The focus now shifted to the real possibility of the analysis ending because of what began to appear like an imminent move by Frank to the Midwest. The motivation for the move seemed to be twofold: first, a genuine attempt to enhance his career prospects without which he was quite insistent he would not make the move, regardless of his interest in Katherine. The second motivation was to see if that relationship might be furthered. In any event, the prospect of termination occasioned some further consideration of our relationship.

The New Relationship versus the Therapeutic Relationship

One day, our session had to be shortened by a few minutes so that Frank could go to the airport to meet Katherine, who was arriving for a weekend visit. The following week he revealed to me the reason for his early departure—he had made some other rather more vague excuse on that day. He had not told me, he said, because, in the "mood" that I was in, I would not have accepted it. He was referring to my interpretation, made several weeks before, that his raising the idea of termination was related to the imminence of the new relationship with Katherine, a connection he had denied. I said that he seemed to feel as if there were some competition between me and Katherine. I suggested that these feelings of competition were within himself and reflected the oscillations of his feelings between men and women. There was also the relationship of dependency to me, about which he was experiencing some ambivalence.

The following week, Frank said he had been having some second thoughts about his desire to terminate. Still, one thing that he was somewhat bothered about was the inequality of our relationship in the sense that I knew much about him whereas he knew very little of me. On the other hand, he was somewhat concerned that he might need my help in the future if the Devil thought were to return, or if he had problems on the job, or if a relationship with a woman—perhaps Katherine—did not work out. In the face of these concerns, I said that his wish to terminate seemed to reflect the fact that I was the last reminder of how he had turned to men . . . "to take care of me," he finished. Yes, I agreed, I was the man who had taken care of him and now he wanted to shift that dependency to a woman. But, he said, it could not be enough with me. I agreed, of course. It seemed to me, I said, that the decision to terminate should be made on the grounds of whether the work we had set out to do had been completed. Frank did now disagree but it was becoming apparent that another factor would now intervene—his job relocation. We would indeed terminate and soon.

At the eleventh hour, however, Katherine introduced a complicating factor. She proposed moving east and taking a job in a suburban area near New York. She thought it would be responsive to his wish to remain in New York and it would bring them closer. Frank was angry and exasperated with this example of what he had begun to think was her unpredictability. Such a move would not bring them closer since a car would be absolutely necessary for them to see each other. Let her relocate to the city itself, he said, if closeness was her aim. He did not want to be involved with another "child-woman," he said, and he had begun to fear that she had some of that characteristic. In any case, his own decision to go to the city where Katherine lived was almost finalized. Accordingly, we set a termination date which would be very soon since he would probably be leaving within little more than a month.

In our last session, he said he was a bit concerned about going out there and having the relationship founder, which it could do given the volatility of Katherine's feelings. He was worried about dealing with the stress of the new job, feeling that he would not be able to afford even two sleepless nights. I myself was somewhat concerned. Some issues had been raised in the last couple of months which, while not new, had occurred in the context of the transference which I was prepared to tackle more thoroughly than I had in the second phase of our work. While interpretations had been made, I certainly was not confident that they had been worked through very thoroughly. To the very end, the sexual component of the feelings toward men had not been without controversy. In any case, Frank promised to keep in touch and so we parted on very good terms.

Frank did indeed keep in touch. He wrote a number of times and also called me on his visits to New York and we met informally. The job proved not to be all that he had hoped, but was still useful as a learning experience. He experienced social success and was comfortable with his work colleagues. The relationship with Katherine was rocky. He cared for her but was prepared to leave the relationship if she could not make up her mind. After a while, he was quite certain that he did not want to stay in that midwestern city and began to make plans to return to the New York area, where he still owned his house. In the meantime, there was no question of being troubled by the Devil obsession; also, his feelings about Katherine, though not unmixed, were untroubled by jealousy.

The most recent postscript was the following: Frank moved back to New York, leaving Katherine with the thought that he would no longer wait around for her to make up her mind, even though he still cared for her. Shortly after his return, she told him she did not want to lose him and she would marry him and live with him in New York. He was happy about this, and the marriage took place. Katherine recently gave birth, and Frank is very happy about being the father of a son. He recently saw his friend Nick and spoke of the special bond that continued to exist between them, quoting Nick as saying, "We're more than brothers—it's physical."

Frank referred in an easy manner to "the homosexual feelings," seemingly recognizing them as implicitly integrated in a number of his male relationships, the one with Nick being the most obvious. He mentioned another, younger, man in the Midwest, with whom there had been this special quality. It seemed to be something that added to the pleasure of a relationship with another man, something of which he seemed easily accepting. It seemed to be incorporated into a complex of feelings that included camaraderie, respect, and affection rather than having to be split off and either repressed or projected. He remarked, with a certain wryness, on how terrified he had once been of those feelings, and having utterly to deny them. There was no indication that he felt the need to consummate a sexual relationship with any of these friends, however. I did not ask him outright, but given the degree of awareness and acceptance that he seemed to have, if the wish should arise at some future time, I felt that chances would be good that—whether he acted upon it or not—it would be understood for what it was rather than having to be cloaked in symptomatic disguise.

Part II
Theoretical Considerations

The ultimate testing ground for psychological theory is the individual case. When a general theory does not adequately explain the outcomes in the life of an individual, then the theory needs modification. However, an alternative to modifying the theory is modifying the perception of the individual so that he no longer appears to be an exception to the rules of the theory. The latter alternative is a danger in psychoanalytic work. Initially, I found myself trying to fit my understanding of Frank into the framework of analytic theory as I understood it in the mid-1970's. I have tried, in Part I, to convey some of the ways in which I began to question those theoretical assumptions. In particular, the viewpoint that homosexual feelings were "pathological" and represented a retreat from heterosexuality did not fit. In Frank, there was no retreat from heterosexuality. And as I came to understand the feelings that were behind the homosexual pressures he was battling, they seemed to have much more to do with normal human feeling than they did with anything deformed or diseased.

I wanted to present the case of Frank in detail in order to provide the reader with much of the "data base" that prompted me to propose the theoretical formulations of Part II. I expect professional readers to bring to the data of Part I their own fund of clinical experience and introspection. It is against that experience that the utility of my proposals can also be tested. Nonprofessional readers will, I trust, bring their own life experience and observations to the same task.

In our century, discourse about sexuality has taken place primarily within two frameworks. The first is the religious/moral framework, which is an aspect of the wider culture. The second is the biological/medical framework. This framework has aspired to operate independently from the religious/moral framework, and practitioners of psychotherapy from all disciplines, behavioral as well as medical, have tended to operate in their culturally defined roles as healers of the sick. Nevertheless, analytic theorists, particularly since the death of Freud, had to some extent also been operating as representatives of the religious/moral viewpoint. In this context, they spearheaded a revision of one of Freud's basic tenets—the theory of universal bisexual predisposition. Under the aegis of the "adaptational" school especially, they reconfirmed heterosexuality as the biologically determined, "normal" sexual modality, and redefined homosexuality as a psychologically determined and pathological deviation.

The facts of Frank's life could not be satisfactorily explained by the revisionists' monosexual hypothesis. Instead they call for the recognition that, in men, emotional needs in relation to men and emotional needs in relation to women operate with considerable independence from each other. Sexual experience that satisfies emotional need with respect to one sex will not necessarily have the effect of reducing the desire for sexually mediated emotional experience with the other. These and other facts call for an approach to sexuality in terms of theoretical frameworks other than the religious/moral and biological/medical. One of these frameworks is the framework of historical/anthropological analysis. The other framework is the artistic/symbolic.

A central thesis of this book is that sexual action and imagery function in a symbolic sense to enable people to experience and express complexes of ideas and feelings which can only be mediated through symbols. At the center of the analysis described in Part I was the powerful, millennia-old cultural symbol of the Devil. The symbol of the Devil rose up in Frank's consciousness because the homosexual symbols that would otherwise have mediated the complex of ideas and feelings whose repudiation was incorporated in the symbol of the Devil were not available to him. The homosexual symbols were prohibited by the culture, but the feelings expressed by these symbols were too powerful to remain entirely in repression. The case of Frank illustrates the fact that culture exerts powerful controls over consciousness by determining which symbols are permissible to mediate thinking and feeling.

Part II of this book will deal with sexuality as it functions symbolically in ritual, art, religion and—of course—Frank's life.

The symbol of the Devil was particularly well suited to express the complex of wishes and fears that so deeply troubled Frank. It emerged into his consciousness precisely because it has served as a historical and cultural repository for feared and repudiated elements of psychological experience which have also been symbolized in the revulsion against homosexuality.

I think the case of Frank illustrates the fact that the outcome of analysis has to be viewed in cultural perspective. The therapeutic process takes place in a cultural context that can be understood but never entirely transcended. Even such basic elements of psychological experience as wishes and defenses seem susceptible to shaping by culture. Later in this book I will have occasion to repeat what I think is a basic truth: that a person is both an exponent of his culture and, at the same time, an individual in a dynamic and potentially confrontational relationship to it. This was the truth that created Frank's dilemma. The resolution of that dilemma through the help of analytic therapy may illustrate another "truth"—that the outcome to an analysis is virtually sure to have elements of compromise between what is individually necessary and what is culturally possible.

4

Bisexuality Theory and the Biological/Medical Framework

In his paper "Analysis Terminable and Interminable" Freud (1937) expressed some views on the nature of human sexuality. He observed, ". . . we have come to know that all human beings are bisexual . . . and that their libido is distributed between objects of both sexes, either in manifest or latent form" (p. 347).

I think it is important to see that, in this paper, one of the last of his works to be published, Freud restated his bisexuality theory in these unequivocal terms. As I think an unprejudiced consideration of the data in Frank's case shows, the homosexual and heterosexual themes coexisted in his feelings and both reflected important complexes of feelings in relation to people of both sexes. These facts were certainly consistent with the observation by Freud that I have just quoted. Nonetheless, after his death, a process of revision of this basic tenet got under way. It was led by medical analysts who used a medical model of health and sickness to repudiate Freud's bisexuality theory. In their revision, heterosexuality was biologically normal and healthy and homosexuality was psychologically determined and pathological. I am going to try to show how the arguments they used were specious and had as an unacknowledged aim the reinstatement of the sexual morality that psychoanalytic theory under Freud's leadership had challenged.

Earlier, in his 1915 footnote to his *Three Essays on the Theory of Sexuality* (1905), he had stated, "Psycho-analytic research is most decidedly opposed to any attempt at separating off homosexuals from the rest of mankind as a group of special character. By studying sexual excitations other than those that are manifestly displayed, it has found that all human beings are capable of making a homosexual object choice and have in fact made one in their unconscious. Indeed, libidinal attachments to persons of the same sex play no less a part as factors in normal mental life, and a greater part as a motive force for illness, than do similar attachments to the opposite sex. On the contrary, psycho-analysis considers that a choice of an object independently of its sex—

freedom to range equally over male and female objects—as it is found in childhood, in primitive states of society and early periods of history, is the original basis from which, as a result of restriction in one direction or the other, both the normal and the inverted types develop. Thus from the point of view of psychoanalysis the exclusive sexual interest felt by men for women is also a problem that needs elucidating and is not a self-evident fact based upon an attraction that is ultimately of a chemical nature" (pp. 11–12).

Chronology is significant and should be taken into account in assessing Freud's views because, over his long career, his thinking and theories evolved and changed in some respects. His writings are voluminous and complex enough to lend themselves to finding just the "right" quotation to back up the point one wants to make. In this sense, they are similar to the Scriptures, from which a quote can be extracted to justify almost any moral position. As the founder of psychoanalysis, Freud continues, through his reputation and his writings, to exercise tremendous charisma and one might quite naturally want to have him on one's side in an argument.

In his book on Leonardo, however, Freud quotes that artist as saying, "He who appeals to authority when there is a difference of opinion works with his memory rather than with his reason" (Freud, 1910, p. 72). Rather than using Freud in that manner, my intent is to try to show how the data of this case are supportive of important elements of one of Freud's theories—a theory that, unlike many others, has suffered from neglect and even repudiation by many who would describe themselves as Freudian in their orientation. I refer to the theory of universal bisexual predisposition. He held to this theory consistently, even though his theories about the causation of homosexuality *per se* seem to me to have had several different strands, indicating that he never subscribed to one single model to explain all homosexual outcomes in life. Still, the one element that he almost never failed to mention was the idea of the tendency to bisexuality present in everyone. *This element in their makeup was one that both homosexual and heterosexual men had in common.*

After some initial remarks on differences between the two, he returns to the theme of essential similarities between them. "In inverted types, a predominance of archaic constitutions and primitive psychical mechanisms is regularly to be found. Their most essential characteristics seem to be a coming into operation of narcissistic object-choice and a retention of the erotic significance of the anal zone. There is nothing to be gained, however, by separating the most extreme types of inversion from the rest on the basis of constitutional peculiarities of this kind. What we find as an apparently sufficient explanation of these types can be equally shown to be present, though less strongly, in the constitution of transitional types, and of those whose manifest attitude is normal. The differences in the end-products may be of a *qualitative* nature, but analysis shows that the differences between their determinants are only *quantitative*" (Freud, 1905, p. 12).

I think it is important to realize that, in those days, Freud was not a conservative with regard to attitudes about homosexuality. On the contrary, the prevalent attitude that he was actually repudiating was likely to equate homosexuality with degeneracy. The "degeneracy" theory that psychoanalysis, under Freud's leadership, refuted was in fact elaborated by the medical profession. Greenberg (1988) discusses in some detail the process by which the previously moral and religious prohibitions against homosexuality were reinforced and rationalized on medical grounds. Thus, Freud says, in opening his discussion of "inversion": "The earliest assessments regarded inversion as an innate indication of nervous degeneracy." He adds, "Several facts go to show that . . . inverts cannot be regarded as degenerate . . ." (Freud, 1905, p. 4). He goes on to say that "inversion" is found not only in people who exhibit no other deviations from the normal but that it is also found in people of high intellectual and cultural accomplishment. He was well acquainted with the fact that homosexuality was both frequent and even had important institutional status in the civilized ancient world as well as being prevalent in many cultures termed "primitive" in the world contemporary with his own.

What comes through in Freud's views with respect to homosexuality is that, although it differed from heterosexuality in the choice of object, the personalities of both homosexuals and heterosexuals were mosaics composed of the same elements, differing somewhat in their arrangement, but in the end being more alike than different. However, this stance did not necessarily conform with the views of some homosexual people of the period. In *Leonardo* . . . he first states that, ". . . everyone, even the most normal person, is capable of making a homosexual object-choice, and has done so at some time in his life, and either still adheres to it in his unconscious or else protects himself against it by vigorous counter-attitudes. These two discoveries [the other being the intense erotic attachment to the mother Freud had seen in all his own analytic cases of homosexual men] put an end both to the claim of homosexuals to be regarded as a 'third sex' and to what has been believed to be the important distinction between innate and acquired homosexuality" (Freud, 1910, p. 49). Freud was unequivocally asserting by 1910, not only that homosexual men had a history of heterosexual object choice in their own lives but that heterosexual men had made an analogous choice which was kept in repression by "vigorous counter-attitudes."

Even in the 1905 edition of the *Three Essays* . . . when Freud acknowledged that one of the tasks implicit in object choice was that it should find its way to the opposite sex, he thought it reasonable to speculate on the factors that worked against a homosexual outcome. He first noted the effect of attraction of the "other" sex on both men and women. Yet, he felt, that factor alone would probably not be enough. As for other factors militating against inversion, he observed, "Chief among these is its authoritative prohibition by society. Where inversion is not regarded as a crime it will be found that it answers fully to the sexual inclinations of no small number of people" (p. 95).

It seems clear that a major component of the bisexuality that Freud spoke of had to do with dualism in *sexual object choice,* not overt traits of "femininity" or "masculinity." An issue that has attracted the interest of researchers in recent years—the acquisition of character traits that are "masculine" versus varying degrees of effeminacy—did not seem to preoccupy Freud.

In fact, the question of what is "feminine" and what is "masculine" seems to have become less and less important in his thinking. In his *New Introductory Lectures* . . . (1933) in the latter part of his career, he seemed to feel that it was futile to try to define "masculinity" or "femininity" in any objective way. "Active" versus "passive," a rather rough-and-ready distinction that he had, with reservations, used in the past, he now felt to be unhelpful.

In *Civilization and Its Discontents,* published in 1930, he had said, "The theory of bisexuality is still surrounded by many obscurities and we cannot but feel it as a serious impediment in psychoanalysis that it has not yet found any link with the theory of the instincts. However this may be, if we assume it as a fact that each individual seeks to satisfy both male and female wishes in his sexual life, we are prepared for the possibility that those two (sets of) demands are not fulfilled by the same object, and that they interfere with each other unless they can be kept apart and each impulse guided into a particular channel that is suited to it" (Freud, 1930, p. 53). Nonetheless, surrounded by obscurities or not, Freud never saw fit to abandon the theory of bisexuality.

He had earlier, in 1926, shown that he was capable of reversing himself on a major theoretical point when he relinquished the theory that anxiety arose from the libido of a repressed instinctual impulse. Instead, he asserted that it was the ego's perception of danger that both generated anxiety and set repression into motion (Freud, 1926).

However, the concept of bisexuality, in the end, remained rooted in clinical observations and the bedrock of the Oedipus complex. He noted, "Closer study usually discloses the more complete Oedipus complex, which is twofold, positive and negative, and is due to the bisexuality originally present in children: that is to say, a boy has not merely an ambivalent attitude towards his father and an affectionate object-choice towards his mother, but at the same time he also behaves like a girl and displays an affectionate feminine attitude to his father and corresponding jealousy and hostility towards his mother. It is this complicating element introduced by bisexuality that makes it so difficult to obtain a clear view of the facts in connection with the earliest object-choices and identifications, and still more difficult to describe them intelligibly. It may be that the ambivalence displayed in the relations to the parents should be attributed entirely to bisexuality and that it is not, as I have represented above, developed out of identification in consequence of rivalry" (Freud, 1923, p. 23).

The prototype of psychological bisexuality is found, it would seem, in the dualism of the child's affectionate feelings for his parents. The little boy's adoring feelings for his father, in their erotic aspect, are defined as the feminine counterpart of his (masculine) strivings toward his mother. This formulation is repeated in numerous places, and there seems to be little doubt that Freud regarded the boy's negative complex as the prototypical homosexual object choice. It was the child's potential, confirmed through psychoanalytic observation, to respond to *both* parents with affectionate and sensual feelings that seems to have clinched for Freud the credibility of the theory of bisexual predisposition. His anatomical and physiological observations seem to have reflected his interest in establishing links between the psychological and physiological, as well as between the psychological and the historical. Nowhere does he seem to rely on these speculations as persuasive proof for the validity of the theory. The physiological component of the theory was succinctly stated in the 1905 edition of the *Three Essays* . . .: "For it appears that a certain degree of anatomical hermaphroditism occurs normally. In every normal male or female individual, traces are found of the apparatus of the opposite sex. These either persist without function as rudimentary organs or become modified and take on other functions. These long-familiar facts of anatomy lead us to suppose that an originally bisexual physical disposition has, in the course of evolution, become modified into a unisexual one, leaving behind only a few traces of the sex that has become atrophied" (p. 7). However, he rejected outright any attempt to relate homosexuality to actual physical hermaphroditism, contenting himself to observe that ". . . a bisexual disposition is somehow concerned in inversion, though we do not know in what that disposition consists beyond anatomical structure" (pp. 9–10). However, as we have seen, five years later he had arrived at the view of the universality of at least unconscious homosexual object choice, with the notion of a constitutional bisexual predisposition only *one* of the contributing factors. The other and primary factor seems to have been the triangular Oedipal situation, to which other life experience could contribute.

It seems clear that Freud built up psychoanalytic theory on the foundation of clinical observation of psychological events, with physiological data of interest as supporting evidence from an allied field. In his Postscript to a *Discussion on Lay Analysis* (1927), Freud asserted that, ". . . psychoanalysis is not a specialized branch of medicine. I cannot see how it is possible to dispute this. Psychoanalysis falls under the head of psychology; not of medical psychology in the old sense, nor of the psychology of morbid processes, but simply of psychology" (p. 105). In line with this, the theory of bisexuality could not have rested on physiological evidence in any meaningful sense.

In his "Analysis Terminable and Interminable," Freud (1937) alluded to the difficulties that men experienced with the male-to-male side of the bisexual equation. While it is quite true that in the *New Introductory Lectures* (1933) a few years earlier, he had rejected the activity-passivity dimension as having any claim to being a scientific criterion of masculinity and femininity, passivity remained associated with a sense of femininity in men's minds, an association that could be understood to have its origins in the negative Oedipus complex.

Freud remarks, "Both in therapeutic and character-analyses we are struck by the prominence of two themes which give the analyst an extraordinary amount of trouble. It soon becomes clear that some general principle is at work here. These two themes are connected with the difference between the sexes: one is characteristic of men and the other equally characteristic of women. In spite of the difference in their content there is an obvious correspondence between the two. Some factor common to both sexes is forced, by the difference between them, to express itself differently in the one and in the other.

"The two corresponding themes are, in a woman, envy for the penis—the striving after the possession of a male genital—and in men, the struggle against their feminine or passive attitude towards other men. What is common to these two themes was singled out by early psychoanalytic nomenclature as an attitude to the castration complex. Subsequently, Alfred Adler brought the term 'masculine protest' into current use. It fits the case of men perfectly; but I think that, from the first, 'repudiation of femininity' would have been the correct description of this remarkable feature in the psychical life of mankind" (Freud, 1937, p. 354).

Freud makes it clear that it is passivity toward men in particular against which the "masculine protest" is aimed, asserting that ". . . the masculine 'protest' is in fact nothing other than fear of castration." If even an attitude of passivity toward other men generates castration anxiety, what would the presumed effect of a passive sexual wish be when directed toward another man? The obvious answer, of course, is repression and denial. Yet, the concept of the negative Oedipus complex meant that every boy had entertained just such a wish at some point in his life. Such a wish arose from two main sources: the universal bisexual predisposition and the universal dynamics of family life.

Repudiation of the Bisexual Theory

In 1940, very shortly after Freud's death, Sandor Rado (1940) published his paper called "A Critical Examination of the Concept of Bisexuality." Rado's proposals were quite influential on the course of psychoanalytic theorizing about bisexuality and homosexuality for the next thirty years or more. The paper is a curious mixture of a well-argued appeal to abandon a rather outmoded and vague concept of a physiologically based "constitutional bisexuality," followed by a rather contradictory and confusing argument for its replacement by what amounts to an absolutist concept of normality based on biologically determined heterosexuality.

The paper opens with a nod in the direction of historical and anthropological research touching on the concept of bisexuality. However, the course of the ensuing argument is signaled by the comment that "Certain Egyptian gods were *notoriously* bisexual . . ." (Italics added.) After a brief discussion, this section concludes with the observation that ". . . the idea of bisexuality far antedates the scientific era and owes its origin to primeval, emotional needs of animistic man. It is important to bear this in mind in our examination of the part played by the same concept in modern science" (p. 140).

The next section of the paper touches on the nineteenth-century biological finding that the urogenital systems of the two sexes derive from a common embryonic origin and contain cellular material of both gonads. The term "hermaphroditic" was applied to this common embryonic material. Rado then added, "This unfortunate appellation of an undeveloped embryonic structure marked an historical turning point as it opened the door to indiscriminate speculations of man's bisexuality." After a few words on the neuropsychological speculations about male and female brain centers by Krafft-Ebing and others, he turns to Freud himself, rather fairly representing his views as I have also attempted to describe them. Referring to Freud, he noted, ". . . he spoke significantly of 'constitutional bisexuality,' and as he of course always maintained that constitutional factors were beyond the reach of psychoanalytic investigation, the phrase explicitly disclaims for psychoanalysis all responsibility as to the validity of the assumption. Psychological data alone have never been, and could not be, conclusive in this respect. If the hypothesis were abandoned in the field of biology from which it had been taken, the data accumulated by psychoanalysis would have to be reinterpreted. In any case, verification rested, and quite rightly, with biology" (pp. 141–42).

Rado goes on to assert that "a truly enormous amount of relevant data has been assembled leading to new formulations and terminology, and that as a result the old speculative notion of bisexuality is in the process of withering away" (p. 142). In fact, no significant new research is cited in the article. The only difference is one of definition. Essentially, the argument goes that, since humans, like most other species, are specialized, for the purpose of reproduction, into male or female, and no humans are effectively hermaphroditic in the reproductive sense, the concept of bisexuality cannot be a meaningful biological concept. It seems to me doubtful that the force of this argument would have persuaded Freud to abandon his theory.

The article goes on to introduce some confusing language. For example: "At this point there of course arises the question of extra-genital pleasure functions discovered and explored by psychoanalysis: oral, anal, tactile, etc. These are rooted not in the reproductive system but in the alimentary or some other basic biological system. They interact and combine with one another and with the genital pleasure function to make up the individual's entire pleasure organization. The latter is obviously neither sexual nor nonsexual, but an entity of a new order, brought about by integration on a higher level" (p. 146). It is unclear what is meant by "an entity of a new order." More follows, however, and then the statement: "The identification of pleasure and sex made by classical psychoanalysis is at any rate biologically untenable . . .." Rado goes on to assert that ". . . the biological status of the genital pleasure function . . . is definitely established: inseparable from the reproductive action system . . ." (p. 146). In other words, if an act has no reproductive potential, it is not sexual. This proposition is a complete refutation of Freud's unequivocal position that "sexual" was not a term limited to genital pleasure or functions. In addition, Rado was asserting that, while constitutional bisexuality was a fiction, constitutional heterosexuality was fact. The reason for this digression into what I assume Devereux had in mind when he referred to some psychoanalytic colleagues' excursions into "pseudobiologia phantastica" (Devereux, 1978, p. 75) was to discredit not only an overall homosexual adjustment as falling outside the range of normality, but even to assert that there was no such thing as a normal homosexual impulse. The target of this article, in any case, was not really the loose, quasi-philosophical concept of constitutional bisexuality, but rather the concept of a normal *psychological* bisexuality, and hence, nonpathological homosexuality.

This main agenda of the article was stated near its end: "Free from the conception of bisexuality, we must of course take new and more reliable bearings in the field of *genital psychopathology* (italics added) . . . . "The basic problem, to state it briefly, is to determine the factors that cause the individual to apply aberrant forms of stimulation to his standard genital equipment." A question that can be fairly raised is why the application of "aberrant forms of stimulation" to one's "standard" genitals *is* a problem. However, if it *is* a problem, what kind of problem is it? I do not see how the answer could be any other except a moral problem. It seems the wheel had almost come full circle. Freud had used psychoanalysis to repudiate the old "degeneracy" theory of homosexuality, which was seen, in his new formulation, as a universal human potential. Now Rado used the psychoanalytic concept of anxiety ". . . which inhibits standard stimulation . . ." (p. 148) to once again place homosexuality in the realm of the pathological as a "reparative adjustment" necessitated by anxiety about heterosexual performance.

Having completely repudiated one of Freud's major and enduring theoretical tenets, Rado then ended with the following dubious tribute to Freud: "Reconstructive work of this nature is more than an invitation; it is a scientific obligation for psychoanalysis. It is also an obligation to the founder of our science, Sigmund Freud, who left us not a creed but an instrument of research" (p. 149). It is noteworthy that no research data whatever are cited in the article.

In 1949, Rado published another paper that continued the theme of a biologically justified "standard" of sexual behavior. I will not discuss this paper in detail. Suffice it to say that heterosexual intercourse is seen as the standard demanded by what amounts to a biological imperative. "From the physiologic concept of reproductive pair we thus derive the psychodynamic concept of orgastic pleasure pair." This "pleasure pair" is obviously composed of opposite sexes. Rado's arguments are essentially that homosexuality is unnatural.

The 1949 article (updated in 1955) is entitled "An Adaptational View of Sexual Behavior" and continues the theme, first broached in the earlier article, that homosexual behavior is *always* an adaptation to inhibitions that prevent a primary and universal heterosexuality. Thus he stated unequivocally, "Only men incapacitated for the love of women by their unsurmountable fears and resentments become dependent for gratification upon the escape into homogeneous pairs." And, chiding Freud, he observed, "Freud himself discovered the early presence of male-female desire in these individuals who later formed homogeneous pairs. Had he not mistaken bisexuality for a proven biologic tenet, he would not have failed to trace the activities of these homogeneous pairs to an original male-female desire and thus recognize its unbroken continuity. By adopting instead the bisexual interpretation that the formation of homogeneous pairs was prompted by a genuinely 'homosexual desire' he lost the fruits of a great discovery" (p. 206).

The idea that Freud would have reversed his views on bisexuality had he not made the regrettable error of subscribing to a biological theory of bisexuality is faintly ridiculous.

For a long time Frank had no consciousness of any homosexual feelings and later, when he became aware of them, he still tried to deny their meaning. Freud left no doubt that he understood the repression of the homosexual component in the feelings of identifiably heterosexual men to flow from castration anxiety. While a little child might literally fear castration as the price for having the father sexually—and such was the understanding of the Wolf Man (Freud, 1909) when he was a little child—adolescents and adult men fear the loss of their heterosexual identity and masculine status. It is this fear, as it was with Frank, that motivates repression and failing that, denial, projection, isolation, or other mechanisms of defense. Of course, in our history, men have also suffered stigmatization, imprisonment, and even *genuine* castration because of homosexual behavior.

Rado's assertion that there is no such thing as a genuinely homosexual desire is perplexing and flies in the face of the seemingly obvious fact that many men experience just such desires powerfully and with full consciousness. However, his paradoxical assertion can be understood as the theoretical equivalent of the repression or denial of homosexual feelings by men whose *conscious* identities are heterosexual. Just as Frank had originally asserted that he had *no* homosexual feelings, Rado and the adaptational approach of which his theorizing is the basis asserted, in turn, that *no one* has any *genuinely* homosexual desires. The presence of such desires in consciousness—which, after all, cannot be denied—is explained as a defensive adaptation to anxiety with regard to the implementation of heterosexuality. This theory, influential as it was, was profoundly important in that it quite literally deprived homosexual experience of *any* claim to authenticity. Homosexual *feelings,* not to mention acts, were regarded as *always* pathological in origin without any claim to being rooted in the nondefensive, nonpathological components of human nature. That, then, had been Freud's presumed error: the granting to homosexual feelings the possibility of having nondefensive, nonpathological status.

Rado's insistence that only heterosexual intercourse between "reproductive pairs" be granted the status of "normal" is to be contrasted with Freud's much more complex view of the place of sexuality both in the life of the individual and in its relation to civilization and culture. In *Civilization and Its Discontents,* he explains the apparent antagonistic tension between civilization and sexuality in these terms: "The tendency on the part of civilization to restrict sexual life is no less clear than its other tendency to expand the cultural unit . . . . Here . . . civilization is obeying the laws of economic necessity, since a large amount of the psychical energy that it uses for its own purposes has to be withdrawn from sexuality. In this respect civilization behaves toward sexuality as a people or stratum of its population does which has subjected another one to its exploitation. Fear of revolt by the suppressed elements drives it to stricter precautionary measures. A high-water mark in such a development has been reached in our Western European civilization. A cultural community is perfectly justified, psychologically, in starting by proscribing manifestations of the sexual life of children, for there would be no prospect of curbing the sexual lusts of adults if the ground had not been prepared for it in childhood. But such a community cannot in any way be justified in going to the length of actually disavowing such easily demonstrable, and indeed, striking phenomena. As regards the sexually mature individual, the choice of an object is restricted to the opposite sex, and most extragenital satisfactions are forbidden as perversions. The requirement, demonstrated in these prohibitions, that there shall be a single kind of sexual life for everyone, disregards the dissimilarities, *whether innate or acquired,* (italics added), in the sexual constitution of human beings; it cuts off a fair number of them from sexual enjoyment, and so becomes the source of serious injustice. The result of such restrictive measures might be that in people who are normal—who are not prevented by their constitution—the whole of their sexual interests would flow without loss into the channels that are left open. But heterosexual genital love, which has remained exempt from outlawry, is itself restricted by further limitations, in the shape of insistence upon legitimacy and monogamy. Present day civilization makes it plain that it will only permit sexual relationships on the basis of a solitary, indissoluble bond between one man and one woman, and that it does not like sexuality as a source of pleasure in its own right and is only prepared to tolerate it because there is so far no substitute for it as a means of propagating the human race" (Freud, 1930, pp. 51–52).

Freud's broadly humanistic perspective, illustrated in this passage that I have felt important to quote at length, reflected both his bold iconoclasm and his skepticism about the wisdom of cultural institutions. (It is relevant to note that he alludes to sexual constitution as innate *or* acquired. It seems clear that while he increasingly regarded the physiological justification for a theory of bisexuality as cloudy at best, his support for its *psychological* credibility did not seem at all diminished. It seems the physiological basis simply became less and less relevant to the theory.)

But if Freud's ideas were revolutionary and critical of civilization, Rado's attack on those ideas was counterrevolutionary. In fact, it might be fairly entitled "Civilization Strikes Back." He held that ". . . the identification between pleasure and sex made by classical psychoanalysis (Freud, surely) was "untenable." About this identification, he added that, while it was "originally a source of inspiration unparalled in popular appeal . . ." [as revolutionary movements historically are]". . . it led eventually to hopeless confusion and doomed the psychoanalytic study of sex to scientific frustration." In other words, the revolution had gone too far and it was time to reestablish order not, in this instance, by the former ruling classes but rather by the new spokesmen for the old order. Am I putting the matter too strongly? If so, how else is one to explain the following assertion from the 1949/55 paper? "The desire to fulfill the male-female pattern is a sexual characteristic shared by *all members of our civilization*" (p. 206, italics added). Consider, also, the following passage: ". . . the male-female sexual pattern is not only anatomically outlined but, through the marital order, is also culturally ingrained and perpetuated in every individual since early childhood. Those forced to take a mate of their own sex still strive to fulfill this pattern—by approximation. Such is the hold upon the individual of a cultural institution based on biological foundations" (p. 205).

The Biological/Medical Framework

The argument here is that the cultural dictate incorporates the natural order dictated by biology itself. But how can one establish, empirically, this proposed causal sequence—that cultural norms follow upon and reflect an innate tendency to fulfill a reproductive destiny? In the 1940 paper, even the term "negative Oedipus complex" appears in quotes, an implied negation of its reality, since the concept postulates a nondefensive homosexual component in normal development.

And in the later paper, Rado notes that "In 1940 we attempted to show that "bisexuality" and "homosexuality" are deceptive concepts, misleading when applied in medical theory and practice" (Rado, 1949, pp. 209–10.) But in the passage already cited in his discussion of the question of lay analysis, Freud had explicitly asserted that psychoanalysis was *not* a branch of medical science. And the statement by Rado just quoted suggests that Freud's fears were not unfounded when he said, "We might . . . recall the unfriendliness and indeed the animosity with which the medical profession treated analysis from the very first.

That would seem to imply that it can have no claims over analysis today. And though I do not accept that implication, I still feel some doubts as to whether the present wooing of psychoanalysis by the doctors is based, from the point of view of the libido theory, upon the first or second of Abraham's substages—whether they wish to take possession of their object for the purpose of destroying it or preserving it" (Freud, 1927, pp. 105–106.)

I do not think one has to show that the medical profession was any more conservative than any other group of people who occupied a traditional role of established power and prestige in society. Certainly, academic psychology in this country has, in the past, shown a good deal of hostility to psychoanalytic thinking. Nonetheless, the grounds upon which Rado based his rejection of the bisexuality theory were those of a medical doctor giving precedence to physiological over psychological data. It seems to me that psychoanalysis was being put in a biological/medical framework, especially with regard to its theories of sexuality. Judging from the attitudes he expressed in 1927, when he can be thought to have achieved maturity and perspective in the discipline he had himself founded, Freud did not intend that.

It may be that, as psychoanalysis became an established discipline after, and even before, Freud's death, an inevitable conservatism began to overtake it. Freud himself, both as the founder of psychoanalysis and as a man with both genius and restless, inquiring intellect, could allow his thinking to evolve with maturity and experience. The followers of a great man or woman are in a different position. Certain tenets of the leader may become dogma, with more rigid adherence exacted than even the leader himself would have required. On the other hand, those aspects of the leader's vision that are too advanced to be absorbed by the preexisting culture may be downplayed or even repudiated. In any case, the theory of bisexuality appears to me to fall into the latter category of ideas that many adherents were unable to accept because it was too much at variance with deeply held attitudes, some reflecting "vigorous counter-attitudes" and some internalized from the culture. It was Freud's attribution of a homosexual component to everyone that brought on the most vigorous objections, not his explanations of homosexual behavior as a deviation from the norm. To the critics, the latter could be explained as a pathological deviation; furthermore, its exclusive character lent itself to the kind of dichotomous categorization into illness or health that fit neatly into a medical/diagnostic approach to questions of sexuality.

It is not surprising, then, that landmark research by another iconoclast on this side of the Atlantic was greeted with skepticism and its conclusions with objections by some members of what became the medical/psychoanalytic establishment. Alfred Kinsey's (Kinsey et al., 1949) famous research on the sexual behavior of American males was an unprecedented piece of social research but, in this discussion, I will focus on the data and interpretation relevant to the question of bisexuality or duality with respect to sexual object. The often cited statistic from this research was that 37 percent of the sample in this study had at least some overt homosexual experience to the point of orgasm between the onset of adolescence and old age. This incidence, surprisingly high in view of Americans' previously held views of their own sexual behavior, provoked controversy enough. But Kinsey and his associates provoked another kind of controversy by taking a nonjudgmental and dispassionate stance, viewing homosexuality and heterosexuality not as bipolar opposites but rather as traits ranged along a continuum from 0 to 6. Each man in the sample was rated according to degree of conscious arousal in the homosexual modality and to the incidence and exclusivity of homosexual behavior. Psychodynamic factors behind these patterns of arousal and behavior were quite specifically not dealt with. By these ratings, 50 percent of the sample was rated as having some degree—from just a little to a great deal—of arousal or actual experience in the homosexual mode after the onset of adolescence. By the same token, 50 percent reported neither psychological arousal nor experience with respect to other men.

This result strikes me as interesting. Taking only data available to men's consciousness, the study could not confirm the universality of a bisexual predisposition, as Freud proposed. Nor could it confirm, of course, that everyone has, at some point in his life, taken, either consciously or unconsciously, a person of the same sex as a sexual object.

However, the 50-percent figure was high enough to provoke E. Bergler (1969), a psychoanalyst and writer well known for his view of homosexuality as a pathological condition, to write a reply entitled "The Myth of a New National Disease. Homosexuality and the Kinsey Report." In his rebuttal to Kinsey, Bergler asserted that, "Homosexuality is no longer considered the result of the 'Oedipus relation.' " He goes on to say that Freud only discovered the pre-Oedipal phase in 1930 and could not have really understood that homosexuality was a disorder with its origins in that phase. But it is difficult to assess the merits of Bergler's analytic position without taking into account what appears to be his moral stance with respect to homosexuality. Thus, he said, "Perversion homosexuality is characterized by conscious acceptance of sexual gratification derived from a relation with an object of the same sex. Whether feelings of guilt are connected or *cynically discarded* (italics added) is immaterial for the diagnosis, though not for the therapeutic prognosis" (p. 637).

But the words "cynically discarded" with respect to guilt over one's homosexuality must raise a question in the mind of the reader. The only interpretation that can be put on the use of this phase is that the homosexual person *should* feel guilty, that he has done something that indeed warrants guilt. But by what standard other than morality is the homosexual person being judged when he is blamed for *not* feeling guilt? If homosexuality were truly only a disease as the title of the article states, his doctor would not find "cynical" the patient's failure to feel guilt. On the contrary, if a person suffering from tuberculosis or cholera felt guilt because of his condition, his physician would undoubtedly try to reassure him that such a feeling was utterly groundless.

Bergler devotes several paragraphs to what are labeled homosexual "one-timers." These acts, atypical for the individuals in question, are seen as sometimes reflecting oral regression under stress. Another of the motivations ascribed to such atypical acts is the "allure of the forbidden," akin to drinking during Prohibition, that is, looking for adventure in danger. But what are the reasons for assigning an act to the realm of the "forbidden"? I suspect Freud would have proposed that this realm must contain the wishes forbidden by the individual or cultural ego ideal or superego. Bergler also felt that Kinsey's results on homosexuality would prove damaging in a number of ways. These included a "tax free" warrant to homosexuals to maintain and spread their perversion "without guilt"; and borderline cases would be more easily persuaded to enter into homosexual relations. Finally, the United States, with its purportedly high incidence of homosexuality, would be stigmatized abroad in a kind of "whisper campaign." It is difficult not to see these objections as an expression of a moral stance, although the last begins to have an aura of projection. As for bisexuals, they are viewed as homosexuals who have retained some stunted capacity for loveless sex with women.

The McCarthy era descended not long after the publication of the Kinsey report. In that era, not only those coming under suspicion of past or present communist associations were targeted, but also those suspected of being homosexual. I can only feel that Bergler's attack on Kinsey, like Rado's on Freud, reflected a cultural backlash against his unconventional proposals.

Bergler accuses Kinsey of arguing for the normality of homosexuality on biological grounds since Kinsey regarded homosexual behavior as naturally characterizing both humans and other mammalian species without any necessity to resort to psychodynamic explanations. It is interesting to see how the biological standard for normality can cut both ways. In the hands of one theorist (Rado), it rules homosexuality to be pathological. But from the perspective of another theorist (Kinsey) it is self-evidently part of the normal range of variation in sexual behavior of humans and other species. One wonders if judgments of biological normality boil down to "I find this objectionable," or "I don't."

Understandably, Bergler strongly objects to the ratings of the heterosexual-homosexual balance in individual men, to which Kinsey's 0–6 scale lends itself. He says, "The quantitative approach cannot replace the genetic one . . . It omits differentiation of the underlying diseases" (pp. 640–41). In considering these statements, I would ask to what extent one is almost coerced into making judgments of normality when a medical framework is used to deal with sexual issues. In medicine the term "normality" certainly makes sense as connoting freedom from disease with regard to bodily functions that can be reliably related to the survivability of the organism. I do not see how the term "normality" when used with respect to sexual behavior can avoid being contaminated by moral judgments—whether individual or cultural—of good and bad. Further, I simply do not see how homosexuality can be justifiably regarded as a medical problem since the bodies of most homosexual people are structurally sound and their sexual apparatus is in good working order.

Bisexuality and "Situational" Homosexuality

For critics of Freud's concept of bisexuality, so-called "situational homosexuality" poses a problem. The most common example of situational homosexuality is in prison situations. Because these homosexual encounters or interactions are not seen to be the preferred modality of these men, they tend to receive little further theoretical attention. I think this reflects the assumption, paralleling the normal-abnormal dichotomy, that human sexuality is unidimensional, somehow inherently monosexual. But a less rigidly dichotomous model of human sexual potential that did not conceive of the homosexual impulse or response as always a retreat from heterosexuality could allow the capacity for homosexual responsiveness to coexist with heterosexual responsiveness even where the latter was more powerful.

It seems to me that such a model could easily account for Kinsey's results. In fact, Freud's theory of bisexuality states just such a capacity. To consider this issue further, I would like to turn to another analyst of the postwar period, Robert Lindner, and quote some excerpts from his book about men in prison, entitled *Stone Walls and Men* (1946). Lindner credited Freud with overturning ". . . the comfortable applecart atop which Western civilization had been innocently riding in the assurance that all acts were motivated by principles and ideals above the belt" (pp. 454–55). Lindner also observes, echoing Freud, ". . . it is likewise true that in every female there is a male component just as in every male there is a female component" (p. 455). He goes on to deplore, in very compassionate terms, the harsh and punitive sexual deprivations imposed upon prison inmates. Lindner then distinguishes between homosexuality associated with physical abnormalities, which is rare, and the "essential homosexual," in whom the ". . . strivings, and attitudes, occasionally even the habits, are more like those of the opposite sex. His preferences, tastes, inclinations, and wishes are opposed to his visible biology. And these are the individuals who, despite popular opinion are not so readily distinguishable" (p. 457). He goes on to say that when the "true" or "essential" homosexual comes to prison, he plays the same role as he did on the outside, depending on his passive or active inclinations. For him, Lindner says, prison is often a relatively happy place, since he has no competition from females. In fact, his range is broadened because he is not confined in his sexual interactions with other "essential" types like himself.

The reason for these greater opportunities is that, "Under the frustrative and deprivative situation of prison life *the ordinarily effective checks on the latent sexual component disappear in a surprisingly large number of cases* (italics added), and erotic behavior between individuals of the same sex is common. But this does not mean that all who indulge are themselves homosexual; it does mean that the situation has forced a regression to a phallic level, to a level where the urge and not the object is the paramount concern. So we have in places of segregation the curious phenomenon of men and women behaving erotically toward and with members of their own sex, yet themselves not being homosexual. They are merely satisfying a powerful and normal urge in an expedient way, using what material the environment provides" (p. 458).

I have quoted the above passage because it appears to contain a contradiction. Lindner attributes the high incidence of homosexual behavior to the lifting of the "ordinarily effective checks on the latent sexual component"—by which he must mean the homosexual component. In the same paragraph there seems first to be an acknowledgment of the emergence of a previously checked homosexual component followed by a denial that any such component was in fact expressed in the actual homosexual act, which is said simply to reflect expediency.

Lindner goes on to observe that sex is unquestionably the most pertinent issue in prison life. The next section deserves to be quoted at some length.

"Men (and women) from all walks of life are generally imbued against indulgence in homoerotic, perversive behavior, but they find themselves in a situation suffused with it; their bodies yearn for some expression of sexuality and for the relief of accumulated tensions. *At some point they discover that their thoughts and dreams contain foreign elements which they have been taught to deny* [Italics added]. To these they react violently and fearfully, and they strive for the repression of such forbidden elements. With most repression is incomplete and unsuccessful. In disguised form they crop up either physically as complaints referable to any part of the body, or as more direct psychological signs of the neurotic designation. Yet some succumb to the temptations offered, and when they do they are often overwhelmed with terrible and unbearable guilt, manifesting itself also in psychosomatic or neurotic ways (p. 460).

"That prisons precipitate latent homosexuality is undeniable. While this feature may, in and of itself, be a tragic one, it can be argued that in a few cases it may serve to increase the social and psychological adjustment of the personality so affected. This is rare, yet it occasionally transpires that a criminotic loses his criminosis by finding himself in homosexuality. On the whole, however, the salvation of the rare case is no excuse for the disillusionment wrought, the lives ruined, and the shame descending upon the bulk of prisoners who are exposed to the miserable, frustrated unwholesomeness of prison sex life" (p. 462).

Lindner's position seems to fall between Freud's and that of Rado and Bergler. He refers as did Freud to a female component in men and a male component in women. For Lindner as for Freud, a female element in men seemed to generate a movement toward a male sexual object. Further, when he asserts that the resultant potential for homosexual object choice is normally held in abeyance by certain effective checks and balances, he seems to be thoroughly in agreement with Freud's position that libido is always invested in objects of the same as well as the opposite sex, either in manifest or latent form. However, a third point in Lindner's commentary seems to diverge significantly from Freud's position. He maintains that the prison situation has forced a "regression" to a phallic level . . . where the urge and not the object is the paramount concern. The contradiction here is evident: first, the frustrating conditions of prison life are thought to erode the checks against the "latent [homo]sexual component." But the male partner then becomes objectified as "material" upon which the "heterosexual" male satisfies his powerful—but still normal—urges. As "material" neither the partner's maleness nor even his humanity matters.

In his different statements with regard to homosexuality, Freud did not offer the explanation that it represented either a fixation at or a regression to the phallic stage. As a precursor to the Oedipal phase, the phallic stage, like the oral and the anal, was regarded by Freud as having an autoerotic focus rather than being primarily object directed. Lindner's explanation is aimed at defining the homosexual action of the "heterosexual" inmate as essentially autoerotic. The dread of relating to another male as a sexual object—a central fear in the revulsion against homosexuality—is reflected in this denial. For this *is* a denial in the sense of a defense mechanism, a denial at a sophisticated level, to be sure, and well rationalized. But if the object were truly irrelevant, if regression to the autoerotic focus of the phallic level had truly taken place, why would not masturbation suffice? Lindner's position is logically inconsistent and its very inconsistency reflects the eruption into analytic discourse of anxiety, which the defensive denial is aimed at mitigating.

The dichotemization of men into "heterosexual" and "homosexual" also defends against anxiety by removing the homosexual potential from within the self and projecting it onto the person of "the homosexual," the "essential" or "true" 'homosexual, in Lindner's terminology. The theory of bisexuality threatens to undo this mechanism of projection, or perhaps a better term would be ejection—of the unwanted elements from within oneself—and hence becomes the target of repudiation on various grounds, which when subject to close scrutiny, fail to pass muster.

In another book about prison life, published somewhat later, Sykes (1958) cites a figure of about 30 percent for men engaged in homosexual behavior in prison—but with the qualification that, given the difficulties in securing frankness on this subject, the estimate may well be on the conservative side. Sykes, incidentally, seems to have shared Lindner's attitudes toward homosexuality, so he could not have been accused of inflating this estimate. I note the coincidence between this figure and the 37 percent that Kinsey cited for men with some homosexual experience, but without further comment for the moment.

I would like, next, to turn to a consideration of an important study by I. Bieber et al., conducted under the auspices of the Society of Medical Psychoanalysts. This is a well-known study of a comparison of 106 homosexual men and 100 heterosexual men who were in psychoanalysis.

The authors devote a chapter to the concept of latent homosexuality. They point out that this term has not been used consistently by all writers. Nonetheless, there is a serious attempt to address the issue with some interesting results.

A number of indices by which latent homosexuality would be diagnosed were set out and then all the heterosexual patients in the study were rated on the severity of their homosexual "problems." Of the 100 men rated, 41 showed "no problem"; 17 were judged to have a "mild problem"; 15 were said to have a "moderate problem"; and 27 were considered to have a "severe problem." Indices included both evidence of reaction formations of horror or disgust at homosexual advances as well as direct evidence of homosexual erotic feeling such as in dreams. None of the heterosexual patients had an overt homosexual experience in their adult lives. The authors go on to say, "It seemed reasonable to assume that if 'latent' homosexuality and 'overt' homosexuality were comparable entities, heterosexual patients who scored highest on severity [of homosexual problems] would resemble the homosexual patients more closely than would patients with lower scores" (p. 259). The group of men with "no problem" and the group with a "mild problem" were combined into a group of Low Scorers, a total of 56. The men in the "moderate" and "severe problem" category were combined into a group of High Scorers, for a total of 40.

Both groups were then compared on a six-point developmental scale of childhood characteristics on which the homosexual and heterosexual groups had differed substantially (in percentage terms). The authors were struck by the fact that, on this scale, 77.5 percent of the High Scorers and 91 percent of the Low Scorers fell into the low to borderline range of the scale, whereas only 10 percent of the homosexual men fell into this low range. That scale tapped the following items: excessive fearfulness in childhood; avoiding physical fights; playing primarily with girls before puberty; being a "lone wolf" in childhood; participating in competitive group games, playing basketball. The first four items were more characteristic of men in the homosexual group, the latter two of the heterosexual group.

On another scale of 20 questions tapping parent-son relationships, 70 percent of the homosexual men obtained scores above 11, whereas only 40 percent of the High Scorers had scores in that range. Further analysis, however, revealed that a group of nine men in the High Scorers group accounted for the highest scores on the six-point developmental and twenty-question parent-son scales. The authors observed, "It is pertinent to the present study that High Scorers and Low Scorers resembled each other. Both groups tended to have the preadolescent development normative in our culture, unlike the majority of homosexuals whose preadolescence was deviant . . ." (p. 262).

However, the conclusions drawn from these results seem confusing and disappointingly ambiguous: "The authors of this volume have not been able to validate the ubiquity of 'latent' homosexuality. We have psychoanalyzed many males in whom we have been unable to observe any evidence of this 'complex.' In 40% of the comparison group all items tapping this 'complex' were answered in the negative.

"The data included in this chapter tend to preclude simplistic, unidimensional interpretations. The heterogeneity of the High Scorers and the absence of both homosexual arousal and homosexual problems in many heterosexual patients point to a *complex* of experiential and adaptive factors. A constitutional inability to repress and sublimate a *universal perverse impulse* [italics added] is a metapsychological hypothesis that our data cannot support" (p. 274).

The preceding quotation is indicative of the moral stance in the study—homosexual impulse is regarded as "perverse" even if universal. However, the authors seem satisfied with demonstrating that their data do not support Freud's hypothesis of its universality. On the other hand, even by their own criteria, 60 percent of the heterosexual sample give indications of what they refer to as "homosexual problems." This result would suggest the very wide prevalence of the impulse described as "perverse" in men whose identities are "heterosexual," and whose childhoods and adolescence are normative for males in our culture. From this result, one might propose modifying Freud's theory but not infer that the data provide no support for it. The data *could* support the hypothesis of a widespread bisexual potential in men considered normal. However, this inference is not drawn because there is a stake in the refutation of the bisexuality theory. That stake is the reinforcement of the cultural repudiation of feared elements within the self. The insistence of the dichotomization of males into "heterosexual" and "homosexual" assists in maintaining the boundary between one's conscious heterosexual identity and the feared "perverse" impulses. This mechanism is strikingly illustrated by the fact that, of the sample of 106 men categorized as homosexual, 30 were actually described as "bisexual". The quotation marks were the authors' and reflected their apparent refusal to acknowledge that true bisexuality is possible, a refusal reflected in lumping these subjects into the dichotomous "homosexual" category.

In their diverse ways, data from three different population samples—the general population of the Kinsey report, the estimates of incidence in prison populations, and the population of heterosexual men in psychoanalysis in New York City—all point to a capacity for homosexual responsiveness behaviorally, consciously or unconsciously, that is on the order of 30 to 60 percent. While such figures are only suggestive and do not reach the universality proposed by Freud, they are certainly not reconcilable with the denial of the existence of bisexuality as a psychological phenomenon. They do however support Freud's proposal of a capacity for homosexual responsiveness that coexists with heterosexuality.

I think it is fair to say that Freud felt that the data derived from the psychoanalysis of heterosexual men made untenable the degeneracy theory of homosexuality. These data included not only the data of conscious experience, memory, and fantasy, but also dreams, symptoms, and transference phenomena. His bisexual theory—postulating that a tendency to organize emotional and sexual elements along homosexual as well as heterosexual lines characterized men in general, although only a minority made this tendency manifest—was based on this psychoanalytically derived data. He also sought links to biology in the hypothesized constitutional component. As we have seen, Rado initially based his refutation of the bisexuality theory on these biological grounds. However, even if his argument were deemed correct, the psychoanalytic data that provided the psychological basis for the theory were not abolished. These data were there in the records of men's analyses.

The ego, when it begins to feel anxiety, tends to respond by implementing the mechanism of repression—preventing the source of anxiety from reaching awareness or, in rarer instances, by ejecting the memory of a previously conscious thought or action from awareness. However, when the stimulus to anxiety breaks through the barriers to awareness or when it cannot be banished from consciousness, other means of defense must be employed, as was demonstrated in the case of Frank. I have proposed that the revisionist theorists that I have been discussing had a stake in refuting Freud's bisexuality theory and that this stake accounted for the failure to accept the logical inferences from the analytic and behavioral data at their disposal. I have already indicated that this stake included the maintenance of the boundary between men's conscious heterosexual identity and the repudiated "perverse" homosexual impulses. Repression could not abolish from consciousness the psychoanalytic records supportive of the bisexuality theory. Other means were necessary. Prominent among these was the mechanism of denial, which tends to deny the status of reality to factual data or refuses to entertain the possibility of the highly probable. I think there is evidence for this mechanism at work in the arguments of the post-Freudian and—on the issue of bisexuality—anti-Freudian theorists I have so far cited. This mechanism seems to play a role in the next theory I shall discuss, that of "pseudohomosexuality" (Ovesey, 1969), which sought to reinterpret and negate much of the psychoanalytically derived data that had served as the psychological evidence for the bisexuality theory.

Pseudohomosexuality

The concept of pseudohomosexuality often cited in the literature is associated with L. Ovesey (1969). He raises some very interesting issues but I feel that his treatment of these issues is adversely affected by his *a priori* adherence to Rado's theory. Ovesey distinguishes between the *homosexual* motivation, which seeks sexual gratification as an end goal, and the *pseudohomosexual* motivations, which while using the genital organs to achieve their ends, actually comprise two nonsexual goals: dependency and power.

In explaining the *homosexual* motivation, Ovesey says, "Adaptationally, homosexuality is seen as a deviant form of sexual behavior into which a person is driven by the intrusion of fear into the normal heterosexual function. This concept was first proposed by Rado" (p. 102). As with Rado, homosexuality is essentially a result of derailed heterosexuality, an adaptation to crippling castration anxiety.

The first of the *pseudohomosexual* motivations is dependency. Ovesey begins by noting that the unconscious wish for infantile dependency in adulthood is a confession of "adaptive failure." The prototype of the dependent relationship is that between child and mother. The "magical repair" of these failures is through incorporation of the mother's breast, for which, in the pseudohomosexual solution, the father's penis is used. This equation, the author notes, can be used in two ways: "The first conceives of the father's penis as a feeding organ similar to the mother's breast. The reparative fantasy is then of sucking the penis in which the semen is equated with milk. The second involves incorporation of the father's penis, usually by mouth or per anum. In this way the dependent male undoes his castration, and the donor's 'masculine' strength becomes available to him" (p. 104).

The second pseudohomosexual motivation is power, which is achieved through causing another man to submit in a feminine way. The author notes, "This unconscious conception of power struggles between men derives primarily from Oedipal rivalry with the father" (p. 105).

All three of the above motivations may occur in a given overt homosexual act. In the proposed scheme, a *sexual* motivation is one that aims for purely physical satisfaction. This implies that it is possible to conceive of a sexual action that is "pure" in the sense of being uncontaminated by any other motivation except sensations of physical pleasure. In such a conception even the desire to express or receive love through the sexual act would have to be classified as a "pseudosexual" motivation. I think such a narrow conception of sexuality is difficult to justify. Such a conception would make superfluous any means of sexual gratification outside of autoerotic or mechanical stimulation. However, since even masturbation is almost always accompanied by a fantasy, usually involving another person, I think one could justifiably assert that sexuality—whether in fantasy or in action—is never "pure" in this sense. To suggest that it could be reflects viewing sex from a biological perspective so narrow as to be unrealistic. Nevertheless, this narrow biological framework seems to be used because it provides a rationale for the declaration that only reproductive sexuality is "normal." It follows that the drive toward physical gratification through heterosexual interaction requires no psychodynamic explanation. Psychodynamic explanations are reserved for homosexual behavior.

Freud's theory of bisexuality put the homosexual side of human feeling virtually on a par with the heterosexual. Both modalities were based in the biology—the constitution—of the human organism, and both expressed complexes of feelings from various levels of human developmental experience.

The relation between emotions and the physicality of sexual action is complex and the subject of subsequent chapters of this book. However, it surely cannot be a contribution to the understanding of this relationship to claim that when sexuality reflects emotional need it thereby becomes inauthentic—"pseudo."

In the theory of "pseudohomosexuality" sexuality is split off from emotional need and seen as a biological (and heterosexual) imperative. Next there is a denial of the authenticity of homosexual experience in both its physical and emotional aspects. The so-called "homosexual" motivation is seen as a flight from the female by men who delude themselves into believing they really want and prefer sex with men. The emotional needs that press for expression through male-to-male sexual experience—whether accepted or repudiated by consciousness—are denied any legitimate status as components of human sexuality. They become motivations for "pseudosexuality" rather than the real thing. In the end, all homosexuality becomes "pseudohomosexuality," which abolishes any claim to veracity of Freud's bisexuality theory.

I think it fair to say that in Freud's conception, sexuality and feeling—most notably love—were inextricably intertwined. Thus, in *A General Introduction to Psychoanalysis* (1920), there appears the following assertion: "Those who openly call themselves homosexuals are merely those in whom the inversion is conscious and manifest; their number if negligible compared with those whom it is latent. We are bound, in fact, to regard the choice of an object of the same sex as a regular type of offshoot of the *capacity to love,* and are learning every day more and more to recognize it as especially important" (p. 317), (italics added).

In *Group Psychology* . . . (1922), he proposes, "The libido attaches itself to the great vital needs, and chooses as its first objects the people who have a share in that process. And in the development of mankind as a whole, just as in individuals, love alone acts as the civilizing factor in the sense that it brings a change from egoism to altruism. And this is true both of sexual love for women, with all the obligations it involves of not harming the things that are dear to women, and also of desexualized, sublimated homosexual love for other men, which springs from work in common" (p. 44).

For Freud, love tended inexorably to express itself through sexuality, as the above passages indicate. There is a seamless quality to the relation between them, so he could speak of "homosexual love" without insisting that this love had to find explicit physical expression. The concept of "libido" tied together the experiences of love and sexual desire. Ovesey remarks that the adaptational approach had dispensed with the libido theory, which in turn made possible the reclassification of homosexuality as a neurosis. (It also facilitated the conception of sexuality as a purely biological drive whose aim was the purely physical satisfaction derived from orgasm.) In the preface to his book, Ovesey noted that he found that heterosexual men, in the course of analysis, frequently expressed wishes to be loved by men, to be dependent on them, to dominate or be dominated by them, and to establish physical especially genital contact with them. The patient then became afraid that he "was" homosexual. Ovesey next remarked that the analyst had no choice except to confirm the patient's fear if he followed Freud who, he noted, attributed the fantasies to a feminine component in an inherited bisexual constitution, striving for gratification through a homosexual instinct. The patient would then be asked to come to terms with his "homosexuality" since it was constitutional and not alterable. Such a response seems to me to be a caricature of Freud's views and omits entirely the element of love as a motivator of such fantasies. Indeed, in his theory Ovesey does not mention love even as a "pseudohomosexual" motivation. Even dependency which, in my view, is usually intertwined with the need for love, is defined purely in power terms since, "Dependency strivings and power strivings can . . . be considered opposite sides of the same coin" (pp. 25–26). Finally, the homosexual fantasies of heterosexual patients are not regarded as truly sexual but rather as *symbolic* and thus justifiably labeled "pseudohomosexual."

This last point goes to the heart of an issue with which this book is vitally concerned. I am going to argue, in subsequent chapters,that what is *symbolically* sexual is indeed *truly* sexual, and that sex owes most of its incandescence and power to precisely those symbolic aspects dismissed by Ovesey with the prefix "pseudo."

The Biological/Medical Framework and Social Norms

I have tried to show, through the above discussion, that the biological/medical framework cannot provide guidelines for the understanding of the variety and meanings of human sexual life.

Up until the time that I began to work with Frank, however, the biological/medical framework remained, I think, the most influential one in analytic circles, whether by medical doctors or other professionals. I have tried to show that the use of this framework was contaminated by another motivational force, unacknowledged and probably inadmissible: the reinforcement of the cultural norms prohibiting homosexuality as immoral, requiring the refutation of Freud's bisexuality theory. This refutation was aimed at all aspects of his theory that could lend homosexuality in men a legitimate status as a nondefensive, nonpathological response—in other words, a status on a par with heterosexual responsiveness. This refutation began with Freud's proposal that all human beings were endowed with the capacity for sexual responsiveness to both sexes, and was followed by tacit omission of the negative side of the Oedipus complex in discussion of that concept. Finally, homosexuality, whether in feeling or in fact, conscious or unconscious, was interpreted as a retreat from heterosexuality, with different theorists stressing different reasons for this retreat.

The data that emerged in the case of Frank cannot be reconciled with those concepts. Frank was fully capable of psychological arousal and physically adequate performance with women. First, I think it is clear from the presentation of the course of the analysis that the unrecognized but real homosexual pressures by no means diminished as his heterosexual life intensified. The concept of bisexual capacity allows for just this kind of dualism in sexual life. Second, I think the indications of the importance of the negative Oedipus complex as a force behind Frank's sexual feelings were unmistakable and powerful.

I have said that the biological/medical framework became, perhaps without conscious intention, a cover for the moral order with regard to sexuality that Freud had challenged. Stripped of its moral underpinnings what does the biological/medical framework offer to the task of trying to understand human sexuality? I must say that I think the answer is not a great deal, no more than it offers to the understanding of political life, the arts, or even the sciences.

5

The Historical/Anthropological Framework

If it is true that the biological/medical framework has little to offer to understanding of human sexuality, what alternative frameworks are there? I have already alluded to the framework that preceded it, the religious/moral. It was this framework that dominated the approach to sexuality since the displacement by Christianity of the religions of the classical world. I will consider this framework in some depth a bit later in this section, but now I would like to turn to a third framework, the historical/anthropological.

The simple statement that there are societies in which homosexual behavior is permissible alongside heterosexual behavior in men is no longer news. Neither, however, has this fact been treated seriously by those theorists who rejected Freud's bisexuality theory. It seems to be regarded as something of a curiosity, with no more relevance to theories of sexuality than archaeological artifacts of a more tangible kind. On the other hand, C. W. Socarides (1968) says, "The homosexuality practiced in ancient Greece was in all probability situational in type. Its motivation consisted of the social, economic, cultural and prestige advantages which accrued to the young boys who attached themselves to a powerful patron. The motivation of the latter could have been any of the three types here described [reparative, situational, variational]. Such expedient acts 'are the products of conscious deliberation rather than of an unconscious process and as a rule are dropped as soon as the situation changes.' "

"Variational patterns may occur in the individual who yields to the desire for an alteration of sexual excitation. In some cultures such surplus activity was a part of the established social order, e.g., ancient Greece" (p. 19).

I cannot see the above statements as anything other than a refusal to deal with data that do not fit the variant of the adaptational theory held by the author. One might attribute them also simply to not having sufficient data about ancient Greek society, except that Freud, who had no more information at his disposal, remarked in the *Three Essays* . . . "Account must be taken of the fact that inversion was a frequent phenomenon—one might almost say an institution charged with important functions—among the peoples of antiquity at the height of their civilization." He also added, "It is remarkably widespread among many savage and primitive races . . . and even amongst the civilized peoples of Europe, climate and race exercise the most powerful influence on the prevalence of inversion and upon the attitude adopted towards it." To this latter statement was appended a significant footnote, which read, *"The pathological approach to the study of inversion has been displaced by the anthropological* [Italics added]. The merit for bringing about this change is due to Bloch (1902–3), who has also laid stress on the occurrence of inversion among the civilizations of antiquity" (p. 5).

E. F. Greenberg (1988) has provided a sweepingly comprehensive review of homosexuality in a tremendously wide variety of cultural settings, both contemporary and historical. However, I am going to look closely at two cultural settings on which there is a wealth of detailed information reflecting a high order of scholarship. In these settings bisexuality ranges from the widely prevalent and accepted (ancient Greece) to the universal and mandated (the Melanesian societies). In addition to further demonstrating the cultural relativism of sexual norms, this chapter will also provide an introduction to the symbolic function of sexual imagery and behavior. In this connection, I will broach the issue of some fundamental symbolic meanings of the phallus and the ways in which these meanings are reflected in, and influence, sexual practices.

Thanks to K. J. Dover (1978) we now have a very thorough treatment of homosexuality in the ancient Greek world. At the outset, Dover observes, ". . . Greek culture differed from ours in its readiness to recognize the alternation of homosexual and heterosexual preferences in the same individual, its implicit denial that such alternation or coexistence created peculiar problems for the individual or for society, its sympathetic response to the open expression of homosexual desire in words and behavior, and its taste for the uninhibited treatment of homosexual subjects in literature and the visual arts. It, therefore, presents us with a mass of undisguised phenomena, and we have little occasion, in considering the work of any Greek writer, artist or philosopher, to construct arguments in favor of a diagnosis of latent or repressed homosexuality" (p. 1). Dover adds that the Greeks were well aware that individuals differed in their sexual preferences but had no nouns corresponding to the terms "a heterosexual" or "a homosexual" since they assumed that virtually everyone responded at different times to homosexual and heterosexual stimuli. Athenians of the fourth century B.C.

accepted homosexuality so readily, Dover felt, because it was acceptable to their fathers, uncles, and grandfathers, noting that by the sixth century B.C., it was already widely prevalent in the Greek world.

Eros was the divine personification of both homosexual and heterosexual passion. And in considering the material that Dover presents from the written records and the wealth of visual material, most especially vase paintings, one must conclude that it was indeed erotic desire that was the prime motive force in homosexuality especially of man for youth and youth for boy. To use terms such as *situational, variational,* or *reparative* to dismiss this passion is to resort to a conceptual universe that seems quite irrelevant to the ancient Greek world. That world, taken on its own terms was not without its complexities and even its contradictions. These complexities and contradictions, however, must first of all be understood in the context of the culture that was their setting. After that attempt has been made, we can turn to consider how the complexities and contradictions of that civilization might relate to those that exist in ours.

Dover notes that most of the available literary sources are Attic (Athens and its surrounding area) in origin. Both from these and extant vase paintings, however, it is possible to arrive at some of the main features of Greek homosexuality, although precision with regard to variations associated with different regions and cities is not possible. The most prominent pattern for homosexual love seems to have been the relation between the older *erastes*—the lover—and the *eromenos*—the younger beloved. In fact, Dover states that reciprocal desire of partners belonging to the same age category was virtually unknown. The classic *erastes-eromenos* pair were a man and a youth, although often a youth who had attained full height. On the other hand, growth of the full beard seemed to signal the end of the time period during which the *eromenos* role was considered suitable. There were certain stated ideals for this particular relationship. The *erastes* was expected to show himself worthy of the youth's trust and affection and, while motivated by erotic desire himself, to engender *antiphilein*—love—not reciprocal erotic desire in the *eromenos.* Intercourse between men and youths, when depicted on vase paintings, was between the thighs of the youth and only the older man is shown in a fully aroused state. The youth was expected to have a certain modesty and even chastity about his deportment, while passion inflamed the man. In some respects these ideals strike one as analogous to some of the ideals of behavior that are associated with chivalry in our own tradition—ideals that in the last century, particularly, were still widely seen in middle- and upper-class patterns of courtship between men and women. And, in an interesting parallel to those ideals that we now choose to describe with the faintly smug adjective *Victorian*, the *eromenos* was not expected to find enjoyment in submitting to the *erastes;* should he do so, Dover observes, he ran the risk of being considered akin to a *pornos*—prostitute. Herein lies one of the contradictions even in a culture which was, from the point of view of our own society, not only tolerant but even idealizing of homosexual love. Dover points out that, while both homosexual and heterosexual desire were considered entirely natural, the "naturalness" of homosexual desire was without ambiguity only with respect to the partner taking the active or phallic role in the relationship.

The desire for penetration was not approved, whereas the desire to penetrate seemed to be at least understandable. Again, there is a parallel with heterosexual situations in which a young woman's reputation could suffer if she yielded too quickly or too often—judgments that have not entirely faded today even as women have claimed greater degrees of control over their sexuality. The inference one draws is that the homosexual modality in classical Athens was by no means free of the "double standard" familiar in heterosexual relationships in many parts of the world. However, to infer from this that the relationships Dover describes merely mimic or caricature male-female relationships would be a serious misunderstanding. These ideals, however, elastic in practice as they undoubtedly were, seem to be explicitly designed to protect the masculinity of both partners. The older man took the role of pursuer, was active, and phallic in the relationship. In intercourse between the thighs, it was he who was expected to be the active partner, never the reverse, which would be regarded as humiliating. Similarly, the role of *erastes* had seniority as an indispensable component. Submission of an older man to a younger would entail an intolerable, even unthinkable, loss of masculine status. It is clear that there was an uneasy element in these homosexual relationships that smacks of paradox. The masculinity of the erotic object was an indispensable part of the youth's attractiveness. That the younger partner must have felt some erotic stirrings in response to the older partner's masculinity can hardly be doubted. And most certainly a great many of the *eromenoi* went on to become *erastai*. In other words, a reciprocal homosexual current must have existed between the partners.

To be masculine means to be phallic. Yet to accept or in some circumstances even to desire, phallic penetration was clearly a danger to masculinity. These paradoxical elements were dealt with by prescribing that the older—in effect the partner with higher status because of age and position—could not be the recipient of the phallic penetration by the younger, even though he could clearly include the penis of the younger partner as one of his attractive attributes. The masculinity of the younger man was protected by what must have amounted to at least a partial fiction in most cases, that he was not aroused by his acceptance of the submissive role. It would seem that the observations made by Freud, more than two millennia later, about the association between passivity and castration anxiety had force even in a civilization that accepted and celebrated homosexual love. Dover says, "All the evidence which tends to support the hypothesis that the Greeks regarded male homosexual desire as natural concerns the active partner, and we have yet to consider the abundant evidence that for them differentiation between the active and passive role in homosexuality was of profound importance" (pp. 67–68).

There do seem to have been other patterns of homosexual relationships besides that of the grown man pursuing the modest youth. The homosexual ethos sometimes manifested itself in relationships where a greater maturity of the *eromenos* seems to be implied. Dover mentions that in Elis and Boiotia, *erastes* and *eromenos* were posted beside each other in battle. And in Boitia, the "Sacred Band" of Thebes, formed in the first part of the fourth century B.C., was composed entirely of pairs of lovers. Another pair of lovers, Harmodios and Aristogeiton, who killed the brother of the tyrant Hippias, were regarded as having freed Athens from tyranny, although at the cost of their own lives. (The brother of the tyrant had tried to seduce Harmodios, the *eromenos* of Aristogeiton.)

Dover cites some of the proceedings from an interesting trial of a certain Timarkhos, who was accused of having prostituted himself as a youth. In the fourth century, Athens had made a peace treaty with Philip II of Macedon. The envoys who had negotiated with Philip were being charged with responsibility for the unfavorable outcome to these negotiations, the prosecution being handled by Timarkhos. The latter was then charged by one of the threatened envoys with being unqualified, under Athenian law, to hold public office because he had once prostituted himself to another male. Aiskhines, who brought this charge, won his case and Timarkhos was barred from office. It was the charge of prostitution, not the fact of having had male lovers, that was the issue, just as in our own society it is prostitution and not heterosexual intimacy that merits prosecution. As for Aiskhines, he freely admitted to having been "*erastes* of many" nor did he in any way contend that exceptionally good-looking boys automatically prostituted themselves by accepting the attentions and favors of various *erastai*. Socaride's imputation to the youthful partners of advantage-seeking motivation would have been regarded as the equivalent of prostitution and analogous to the way in which we would regard a woman who attached herself to a man solely for those reasons.

I think it is important to touch on another point in this discussion of Greek civilization—their love of beauty. It is hardly necessary for me to propose that their ideals of human beauty remain influential in our own to this very day. Male beauty seems to have been every bit as important to them as female. The story of Zeus descending in the guise of an eagle to snatch away the dazzling Ganymede reflects the impact of visual beauty on Greek sensibilities. It seems to me that the image of the beautiful person—male or female—evoked and brought together a complex of powerful emotions associated with sexual passion. Since we share their ideals, we may not regard the response to beauty as a culturally induced response. However, I am not sure that we can assume that every culture has put such a very high premium on beauty as an element that focuses and arouses erotic passion. In any case, it was a central element in the homosexual relation, though by no means the only one.

The other major element that seemed to be central was the intergenerational one. The analytic concept of the negative Oedipus complex refers, of course, to the boy's sexual feeling for his father. However, in the Greek setting, it is the *older man,* possibly of an age comparable to the youth's father, who is actively and even passionately drawn to the boy.

And now I think it is important to mention a part of the Oedipus legend that has escaped attention in the analytic literature. That Oedipus was fated to commit his tragic deed is the usual understanding. But in the tragedy produced by Euripides an alternative or supplementary explanation is given. This explanation is that Laios, the father of Oedipus, fell in love with Khrysippos, the son of Pelops, himself a king in the Pelopennesos. A sexual relationship followed, in which Laios might have raped the boy, or seduced him, or abducted him. Pelops, his father, cursed Laios: "May you never have a son; if you do may you be destroyed by him" (Edmunds, 1985, p. 7). This curse was sanctioned by Zeus. Although the act was a homosexual one, the crime was a violation of the laws of hospitality, since Laios had been the guest of Pelops. This violation would be equally heinous whether the object of Laios's desire had been female or male.* Dover cites the lines in the Euripides version of this myth in which Laios says helplessly of the rape, "I have understanding but nature forces me." Although Euripides also relates the legend that Laios was the first person to fall in love with someone of the same sex, his reference to Laios's helplessness before the compulsion of nature seems in keeping with Greek consciousness.

*I owe this understanding to Professor Helen Bacon.

Sophocles's *Oedipus the King* is by no means the first telling of the Oedipus story. The prophecies of the Delphic oracle that figure so prominently in his dramatic treatment presuppose the establishment of Apollo's oracle at Delphi. However, L. Edmunds points out that the Oedipus legend antedates that establishment. As a story is told and retold, elements may be rearranged to reflect the particular consciousness of the times. Our own treatment of the legend reflects the concerns of our own time. Even in our response to the treatment by Sophocles, analytic theory has been selective. *Oedipus the King,* in which the now familiar parricide, incest, and self-blinding take place, is the first of three Oedipus plays by Sophocles.

The next two plays deal with other powerful themes—relations between sisters, between brothers, and between brother and sister. Nor does Sophocles's treatment end with Oedipus's blinding and banishment. The last play, *Oedipus at Colonnus,* is a story of redemption, transfiguration, and return. The theme of father-son hostility, however, is unremitting to the end, as Oedipus curses his sons for driving him away from Thebes when, years later, he sought to return there. Rivals for the kingship, the brothers are cursed by Oedipus with the prophecy that each will have no claim to more Theban soil that is required for his burial.

His daughters, on the other hand, are the source of tender support in his suffering and wanderings in his old age. But the theme that emerges with greatest power in the final play is that Oedipus himself was guiltless, and his suffering comes to be regarded with a mixture of dread and awe reserved for the holy victim of fate. In the very end, there is a moving scene of transfiguration in which Oedipus is taken into the earth near the grove, just outside of Athens, that is sacred to the Furies—those chthonic female immortals who were more ancient than any of the gods. It would be difficult not to see in this a redemptive return to the mother, but I would prefer to avoid making interpretations that are overly simplistic when confronting such great themes as are touched in this *dénouement.*

In his very interesting book, *Oedipus: The Ancient Legend and Its Later Analogues,* Edmunds (1985) has collected many different variants of the elemental situation of parricide and maternal incest that are found in different cultures and in different times, attesting to the power and durability of this theme in the human psyche. But recently, the complex theme of the father-son relationship seems to have been reduced to the single component of rivalry and the expression of other parts of this theme neglected or even denied. But a complete understanding of the father-son relationship must, I think, take all the strands and their complex intertwinings into account. The case of Frank demanded this kind of accounting and could not have been understood without it.

Over and over again, what must be understood in this survey is the fact that so many in our own culture find so alien—that homosexual love, eroticism, and imagery were commonplace in Greek culture. I have tried to indicate, however, that Greek homosexuality was not without complexity and the potential for deep contradiction. However, it was critically important that, in spite of these problems, the Greeks permitted the individual the expression of homosexual feeling in conscious thought, imagery, and action without forcing him to relinquish that side of his feelings centered on women. Why were the Greeks able to accept this dualism of sexual feeling in spite of the ambiguities and even problems with which such tolerance can be associated?

The closing lines of Dover's book are relevant to that question: "The Greeks neither inherited nor developed a belief that divine power had revealed to mankind a code of laws for the regulation of sexual behavior; they had no religious institution possessed of the authority to enforce sexual prohibitions. Confronted by cultures older and richer and more elaborate than theirs, cultures which none the less differed greatly from each other, the Greeks felt free to select, to adapt, develop and—above all—innovate. Fragmented as they were into tiny political units, they were constantly aware of the extent to which morals and manners are local. This awareness also disposed them to enjoy the products of their own inventiveness and to attribute a similar enjoyment to their deities and heroes" (p. 203).

Melanesian Culture

I will come back to the Greeks in a little while, but I would like to turn now to another culture area to consider bisexuality in a radically different context. The culture area in question is Melanesia, a string of islands just north of Australia that includes Papua-New Guinea. I will consider aspects of two societies in particular: those of "Sambia"* and the Marind-anim. The "Sambia" have already been brought to the attention of the psychoanalytic community by Robert Stoller in association with Gilbert Herdt (Stoller & Herdt, 1982) following upon the publication of Herdt's in-depth field report *Guardians of the Flutes*, (1981). The culture of the Marind-anim has been the subject of ethno-

---

*Sambia is a pseudonymous tribal name, chosen by Herdt to protect both his informants and, it seems, their culture.

graphic/historical research by J. Van Baal (1966) in his book entitled *Dema*.

These two cultures have a number of characteristics in common. Both were fiercely warlike, with the difference that the Marind-anim were, until the march of European colonization put a stop to this and other practices central to their culture, inveterate headhunters. The other characteristic shared in common was the systematic institutionalization of universal homosexuality that, in effect, made bisexuality—or dualism in sexual experience—a necessary feature of male sexual life.

The meaning of homosexuality in the Melanesian cultures seems to have had a markedly different emphasis from what it had in Greece of the classical period, especially in its Athenian manifestation. In the Melanesian cultures, love, either in the sense of *eros* or any other sense in which the Greeks conceptualized it, did not seem to figure prominently in its justification. Nor was physical beauty understood to be a prime homosexual stimulus. Rather, both among the Sambia and the Marind, homosexuality was part of the elaborate and complicated rituals and prescriptions by which boys were transformed into the kind of men valued in those societies—men who would, according to the differing requirements of the two groups, be prepared to fight and to take heads.

For the Sambia, the first stage of initiation might begin at seven to ten years of age on the average, while for Marind boys, it started with the first signs of puberty. In both societies, however, phallic penetration was an indispensable part of this ritual. Among the Sambia, this took the form of obligatory fellatio, performed by the preadolescent initiates on the older, adolescent boys who could fulfill this function up until the latter began to have regular sexual relations with their wives. This ritual fellatio was part of a complex belief system and in citing the bare facts about this ritual, one risks caricaturing it rather than fairly describing it. Nonetheless, it is important to understand that the Sambia feel that is absolutely essential for the future virility of the boy that he swallow quantities of semen on a daily basis until he himself reaches puberty and takes on the role of supplier of semen to the younger, preadolescent boys.

Semen is necessary to stimulate growth, sexual maturity, and strength; in addition, it was also thought to be essential for the development of the growing fetus. However, semen is a finite substance among adults (whose sexual life is exclusively heterosexual); the depleted supply of semen must be replenished by drinking the milky sap of a number of different trees and vines. It is, I think, important to realize that these practices reflect biological theories of physical growth and development. What, we might ask, would the effect of the diffusion of modern biological science be on the culture of the Sambia? That is a question that neither the Sambia nor we will have to face for some time if their anonymity can continue to preserve them from the incursions of European culture. However, in the meantime, we can ask how they came to hold such extraordinary theories of human development. For, since they hold these beliefs to be literally true, oral insemination to stimulate growth is not, from *their* point of view, a symbolic act.

The belief in the growth-stimulating power of semen is widely held in the Melanesian cultural region. I do not think it is possible to explain why this particular belief took root in New Guinea, as opposed to much of the rest of the world. However, to explain why it took hold even there, I think we do have to turn to a consideration of symbolism. I would propose that the biological theory originates in the *symbolic meaning* of the phenomena of erection, penetration, and ejaculation of semen. These phenomena can be described, in physical terms. But I think I can say without fear of contradiction that the physiological description of these phenomena is far from summing up the totality of the impact these experiences have on men.

A far greater proportion of this impact can be accounted for by the *meaning* that erection, penetration, and ejaculation have and by the *emotions* that they evoke and arouse.

The phrase "symbolic meaning" refers to this complex of meanings and emotions. The terms *symbol* and *symbolism* have been variously defined, in ways that overlap, and sometimes coincide. My definition of *symbolic* is, I believe, consistent with this loose consensus of usage without being either overly narrow or overly vague. I will trust to the discussion that follows to clarify further my usage of the term.

To return to the question of why the Sambia developed their extraordinary beliefs about the properties of semen in the face of ample opportunity to test and discard the theory, I would turn to Herdt's analysis of the culture in which this belief system operated. It was a culture that, like most of the tribal societies in New Guinea, placed great value upon male strength channeled into fierce and often brutal warfare. At the same time, a curious thread of fear of women and a sense of male vulnerability also seem pervasive. In taking boys away from their mothers and beginning their assimilation to the male warrior cult boys are, Herdt points out, eventually turned into men who can defend their village and attack others.

One of the most important means by which men accomplish these ends is oral insemination. I propose that it is because of the symbolic meanings of the penis in erection and ejaculation that insemination can be endowed with the power to effectuate growth and sexual maturity.

Much that maleness means and some of the most powerful emotions associated with being male are, for the Sambia, evoked by the actions involved in rites of fellatio. That is why the belief in their efficacy can be sustained. The meaning of these acts and the feelings they evoke—which comprise their symbolic aspect—make the biological fiction credible. The central instrument in the rites of masculinization undergone by Sambia boys is the penis, more significantly, the erect penis which, following T. Vanggard (1972). I will refer to simply as the phallus. It was Vanggard who first drew attention to the symbolic meaning of the phallus itself. In traditional psychoanalytic writing a "phallic symbol" had been something—a tower, an umbrella, a tree—that stood *for* the phallus. But that is not at all what Vanggard meant. And that is not what I mean when I refer to the phallus as a symbol. I mean that the phallus *itself* evokes in men a complex of thoughts and powerful feelings; and I would say that a central component of this complex is the feeling of *power* with its manifold meanings. It is *because* the phallus symbolizes male power that it can be credited as the means through which power, strength, and maleness are transmitted to still-weak and powerless boys, newly wrenched from the feminizing influence of their mothers.

Symbolism in Anthropology

Anthropologists have, for some time, taken an interest in the concept of the symbol as a critical focus in the attempt to do justice to the task of understanding alien cultures. The symbolic image or act—and both symbolic images and acts are involved in ritual—is a link between the shared and public aspects of cultural life and the subjective and private world of the individual.

V. Turner (1977), in discussing symbols in African ritual, conceives of their action in ways that reflect my own notions as well. He says "A simple vehicle, exhibiting some color, shape, texture, or contrast commonly found in one's experience. . . . can literally or metaphorically connect a great range of phenomena and ideas. . . . This is probably why the great religious symbol vehicles such as the cross, the lotus, the crescent moon, the ark, and so on are relatively simple, although their significata constitute whole theological systems and control liturgical and architectural structures of immense complexity.

"The second characteristic of ritual condensation, which compensates for semantic obscurity, is its efficacy. Ritual is not just a concentration of referents, of messages about values or norms; nor is it simply a set of practical guidelines and a set of symbolic paradigms for everyday action. . . . It is also a fusion of the powers believed to be inherent in the persons, objects, relationships, events and histories represented by ritual symbols. It is a mobilization of energies as well as messages. In this respect, the objects and activities in point are not merely things that stand for other things or something abstract, they participate in the powers and virtues they represent."

"Each symbol expresses many themes and each theme is expressed by many symbols. The cultural weave is made up of symbolic warp and thematic weft" (pp. 188–189).

I would like to stress the phrase "mobilization of energies" in the quotations cited above, because that touches on the essential element in symbolic action: its evocative power, its emotional impact. Without emotional impact at the level of *individual, subjective,* experience, the symbol remains ineffective. If the cross is simply reacted to as a sign that distinguishes a church from a mosque, its effect is purely semantic, not symbolic. Therefore, when I use the phrase "symbolic meaning," the term always implies emotional impact.

The phallus, like the cross, symbolizes much, much more than can be expressed in a few words or even in consciousness. In contrast to our own civilization, these Melanesian peoples have not suppressed the image and action of the phallus or its acknowledged equivalents in their conscious cultural life. It is not that they themselves endow the phallus with symbolic meaning—it has symbolic meaning quite independently of any such decision by any individual or group—rather they are more willing or able to acknowledge its meanings in word and deed than we can in our civilization. This excursion into Melanesian cultural life is partly intended as a voyage of discovery, discovery of the symbolic meanings of the phallus. These are most certainly discoverable in our own culture as well, and I will try to show how these meanings were operative in Frank, as I believe them to be in most men in our culture. However, our cultural defenses are so powerful and well rationalized that one would become enmeshed in endless argumentation about "pathology" of the kind I alluded to in Chapter 4 if one tried to rely on data from our culture alone. In effect, the phallus has, for us, become a forbidden symbol.

I would like now to turn to another Melanesian culture, the Marind-anim, the "Marind people," as they call themselves. Van Baal first knew the Marind-anim as an administrator for the Dutch before World War II. He returned after the war to serve in the government of Netherlands New Guinea, holding the post of governor from 1953 to 1958. His methods are historical more than field based, and he depended heavily on several other sources—most notably the ethnographer Wirz, who studied the Marind between the wars, and Father Jan Verschueren, active in the field both as a missionary and ethnographer since 1931. I mention these facts because his work cannot offer as many of the direct, on-site, and close-up observations as Herdt's field-based work.

I would like to start by noting some important similarities between the Marind and the Sambia, the most striking being that homosexuality was an integral part of the steps that were taken on the way from boyhood to manhood. The Marind waited a little longer than did the Sambia to begin the initiation rites, readiness for which was signaled by the first signs of puberty. (I should note that the Marind were characterized not only by a social structure divided into clans and sub-clans, which were themselves sub-groups of larger classifications, but different groups also adhered to somewhat different ritual practices or, as Van Baal calls them, cults. Since the aim of this work is psychological rather than ethnographic, I will concentrate on the psychological aspects of these rituals, while trying not to do violence to important ethnographic distinctions. Thus the rite I am about to describe belonged to the Mayo cult, to which most of the coastal dwelling Marind belonged.)

This rite had an important mythological component in the person of a *déma* called Sosom. The *déma* were the ancestors of the clans and sub-clans and associated with their totems. They usually took the forms of humans but could also take animal or predominantly animal forms. Sometimes they were identified with the particular thing they represented. For example, Yorma, the female sea *déma,* also *was* the sea. From one point of view, the *déma* belonged to the mythical past, from another, they were still active and the places where they dwelt were sometimes known and respected.

Sosom then was a *déma,* a giant who came from the east once a year when the east monsoon caused the swamps to dry up. The occasion of his visit to the village could coincide with certain initiation rites, which did not, however, have to take place at every visit. The story of Sosom is interesting in its own right. Sosom, the legend goes, was a giant who could not stop copulating with a certain girl. Finally, the mother of the girl cut off his penis. It remained stuck inside the girl, but a stork got it out. With his cut off penis, he could only "sodomize." Therefore, he is called *Tepo-anem,* "buttock-man."

Among other signs of his arrival for the initiation, a large pole, painted red, is erected in the special place reserved for Sosom. The initiation lasts a single night. The boys are presented by their "*binahor*-fathers," usually one of their mother's brothers. Sosom is represented by a man dressed as the *déma,* then: "After nightfall, the men, with Sosom in their midst, go to the *sosom-mirav,* making a thundering noise and singing the *bandra,* the sacred song of the sosom rites, on their way. . . . On their arrival at the *sosom-mirav* a few of the men tear down the fence and now Sosom enters, slowly approaching the neophytes. In the meantime, the men accompanying him are beating the boys with burning torches and wooden clubs. . . . After the boys have met Sosom, they are presented by the initiates with the bull-roarer of their clan, which they must keep in the men's house under the supervision of their *binahor*-fathers. After having instructed them never to talk to the women about anything connected with the ritual, the *binahor*-fathers bring the boys to the edge of the bush outside the enclosure, where each of them is allocated a place of his own. For the rest of the night the boys are subjected to promiscuous homosexual intercourse. When the boys are taken into the bush, the men tune up the *bandra* and go on singing until daybreak, all the time dancing around the pole in the centre" (p. 479).

In this instance, the pole is a phallic symbol in Freud's sense of a surrogate object standing for the phallus. In fact, the whole ritual just described appears to be a celebration of the phallus. In this instance, the neophytes are introduced to its power through anal intercourse rather than fellatio. The newly initiated boys are then secluded in a special place, the *gotad,* and for the next three years or so, they must avoid women, cannot go to the beach, or enter the village for any feasts or celebrations. However, the boy will also have a special homosexual relationship with his *binahor*-father, in most cases a mother's brother, with whom he sleeps at night in the latter's home. This is a special relationship, in which the boy obeys his uncle and helps him, calling him "father." In turn, his uncle calls him "son," instructs him, and is the only adult who has the right to have sexual intercourse with the boy. This special relationship has some similarities to that between man and youth among the Greeks, but there are no data on the emotional aspects of this relationship.

It seems important that, before a young man's marriage, the Marind created an institution, of a sexual "father-son" relationship. (In the mythology of the Keraki, another Melanesian people, [Williams, 1936, pp. 308–309] the prime originator first utilized anal intercourse on his son to promote his growth.) Certainly such an institution would call to mind the concept of the negative Oedipus complex. However, that concept seems almost jarring in this exotic context. It is this sort of wide disparity in the way individual life experience is organized by different cultures that calls into question the utility or even validity of describing the psychodynamics of "normal" developmental stages based on one culture alone. How can one pretend to describe the dynamics of "normal" adolescent development based on our own culture, in which adolescent boys are powerfully motivated to prove their masculinity to themselves and to others by the complete *suppression* of homosexual thought and action, while Sambia and Marind boys are *required* to traverse a homosexual phase on their way to manhood?

Are we then stuck, as an alternative to an untenable ethnocentric theory of human development and "normality," with a cultural relativism so complete that it implies there is *no* psychological common ground in humankind?

I think there is a way out of this dilemma and C. Geertz (1973) points to it, I believe, in the following assertion: "If we want to discover what man amounts to, we can only find it in what men are: and what men are, above all things, is various. It is in understanding that variousness—its range, its nature, its basis, and its implications—that we shall come to construct a concept of human nature that, more than a statistical shadow and less than a primitivist dream, has both substance and truth" (p. 52).

From that perspective, we can discern certain *themes* that are present in various cultures. One that we are confronting in our consideration of these Melanesian cultures is that of male power and its premier symbol, the phallus. Another theme that seems to thread its way through our considerations is that of an erotic intergenerational relationship that has something of an aura of a father-son relationship. It is explicitly present in Freud's concept of the little boy's "negative" Oedipal feelings for his father. It seems present in the erotic relationship between men and youths in Greek civilization, and it seems to be present in the relationship of the Marind adolescent to his *binahor*-father, his maternal uncle. This particular relation occurs in our contemporary culture as well, and it remains one of the most strongly disapproved forms of sexuality. One theme, three treatments: the Marind required it; the Greeks permitted and even idealized it; we execrate and forbid it.

I would like to return again to the symbolic aspect of the phallus. Herdt tells that, in the creation myth that Sambia men recount, there were two primordial, hermaphroditic beings. One performed fellatio upon the other. The being upon whom it was performed became masculinized, while the being who performed it became feminized. In their contemporary rituals, of course, the boys who perform fellatio are believed to acquire masculinity through this act. Herdt points out the paradox that, in this system of thought,the two outcomes of homosexual action exist side by side in the belief system. They illustrate in their unquestioned coexistence, two opposite symbolic meanings of phallic action.

Herdt mentions that some boys were, in fact, fearful of pregnancy but were reassured by their elders on this score. Williams (1936) tells us that among the Keraki people of New Guinea, pregnancy through anal intercourse was entertained even among the adults as a real possibility. Among them, after a year during which initiates had submitted to it, a ceremony is performed in which lime that blisters the youth's mouth and throat is poured down his throat. It has the express purpose of ensuring that young men do not become pregnant. As with the Sambia, the Keraki men keep their homosexual practices secret from the women and Williams relates that it was feared that, should a man actually deliver a baby, the women would discover the secret of their homosexuality, to their extreme shame. These people believed, as did the Sambia, that repeated injections of semen were necessary during pregnancy to build up the fetus, and they also shared the belief that homosexual intercourse promoted growth. Thus, insemination is understood to make a potent contribution to fetal development, which is clearly desired when a woman is carrying a child. However, to impregnate a man is to feminize him, while giving away a secret that would, paradoxically, shame the men. These contradictory attitudes suggest that for males contact with the phallus through penetration and insemination has profoundly contradictory symbolic meanings. On the one hand, it can reinforce or even create desired male characteristics in the male recipient or, on the other, it can feminize him. Its power to create is matched by its power to destroy. The Melanesians concretize these symbolic meanings of the phallus because there is no competing scientific system of knowledge to contradict their beliefs. In our culture, however, we must make do without any concretizations because we do have a scientific understanding of biological facts. Nonetheless, the symbolic meaning of phallic penetration, instead of giving way to scientific understanding, tends to assimilate science to itself. Hence, the "biological" proofs by Rado and the adaptational school that there is no such thing as a genuine homosexual desire in its own right reflect our cultural fear of feminization through phallic penetration. For the Melanesians, the *act* of phallic penetration can endanger masculinity. For us, the *wish* for it will suffice.

The fear was dramatically seen in Frank and contributed heavily to the formation of the Devil obsession, because of our intense emphasis on the feminizing meanings of phallic penetration.

The Greeks were not insensitive to the paradoxes posed by this dualism in the symbolic meaning of phallic penetration. Passivity—receiving the phallus of another into oneself—could definitively compromise an older man's masculine integrity and had to be handled with great care so that it not compromise that of the youth.

The Phallus and Headhunting

I would like to come back to look at one more feature of Marind life—headhunting. Van Baal observes, "A headhunting expedition is a glorious event in the life of every Marind, in which he participates with all his soul, without needing any reasonable argument, because his disposition is bellicose. If ever one should feel the need to demonstrate the irrationality of war, here is a case in point, provided by people who succeed in mustering the wisdom and restraint to keep peace with the neighbors they distrust . . ." (p. 720). Their expeditions were, in fact, launched against more remote people who would not have the means to retaliate.

The Marind use a ceremonial implement in the hunt, a custom that seems prevalent among the headhunting tribes of the region. The Marind called it *pahui,* while the Boadzi, a tribe with very similar customs to the Marind, call it *bagwa,* literally meaning "his penis," a secret name that must not be used in public. The Boadzi myth relates how the first *bagwa* was made by old Anésaké, a giant.

"Old Anésaké had two sons. The younger one died and was buried. After three days his father visited his grave. A fruit-bearing coconut had grown from the grave and the father concluded that his dead son had turned into a coconut tree. Later, Anésaké with his wives and elder son went to Ienga. Here Anésaké made a gigantic garden. One night Anésaké had a dream. The next morning he said to his son: 'Last night I heard the sound of drums near the river Tamu. Go there and have a look.' The son went and returned, reporting that he had not found anything. The father sent him off again and this time the boy caught a fish, cut off its head, prepared it in the same way as a human head, and brought it to his father. The old man said, 'No, this is our food, go once more.' And the son went a third time, and he prepared a different kind of fish, but still his father was not satisfied, and so he tried again, this time with a pig. The father, however, would not accept this either, saying, 'No, this is an animal.' Finally Anésaké took pity on the boy and ordered him to chop some wood, of which he could make a *bagwa.* Then Anésaké made a *bagwa* and painted it, as is the custom. He suspended the *bagwa* from a pole. That night Anésaké sang *kiw ah,* the headhunters' song. He sang till daybreak and then ordered his son to pass a *kupa,* a stone disc, round the shaft of the *bagwa.* He now gave the *bagwa* to his son, who instantly killed him with it and cut off his father's head. The head, however, went on speaking and instructed the son how it should be prepared. From Anésaké's dead body worms emerged which turned into human beings. . . ." (Van Baal, p. 729).

The implement described in this story is used in a special fashion. Just before the captured victim is killed, the *bagwa* or *pahui* must be shattered over the victim's back. *Then,* the victim must be asked for his name, and then a leader, usually an older man, the *samb-anem,* must come to do the actual beheading, beginning by cutting the throat. The stone disc fitted around the shaft of the implement—*pahui* or *bagwa*—is an acknowledged female symbol. In fact, headhunting seems suffused with sexual, and especially phallic, symbolism. Before a headhunting expedition, the men sing the headhunting song all night long, and during the accompanying dance, have promiscuous intercourse with the women in order to become "hot," that is to say, courageous. When singing the song, the men gather around a carved stick, (usually the *pahui* or *bagwa*).A headhunting expedition was also often timed to follow upon initiation ceremonies. In fact, the last-stage initiates, the *éwati*, were often the prime warmongers, further associating headhunting with a *rite de passage* of masculinity.

Finally, and quite extraordinarily, the most important stimulus for the hunt was to bring back the names of the deceased to bestow upon their children, since each child had to have a "head name," as well as his or her own given name. After the return from the hunt, there is a celebration. The following scene is described: "Then one of the men in the front row seizes the head he has captured and, holding it in both hands, rushes down the beach again, crying out: 'Here, here I will keep you for myself forever,' and 'from there you came, here you stay.' This continues until all the men have had their turn" (pp. 749–50).

There are clear suggestions of an intergenerational component in headhunting, seen in the Boadzi myth of old Anésaké and his son who kills him with the *bagwa*, ("his penis"). In this myth, the Oedipal triangle is suggested by the sequence of events in which the son first passes the penis surrogate—the *bagwa*—through the *kupa*, the female symbol at his father's behest. After that has been done the father turns over the *bagwa* to his son who then kills his father. In this myth, the father seems to be giving his son the phallus, showing him how to use it, and then willing his own sacrifice. But from the father's body worms that turned into human beings emerged; even from the corpse of the father a new generation is born, seemingly undoing his death. In the ritual of the headhunt, the surrogate for the phallus—the *pahui* or *bagwa*—is ceremonially used to symbolize killing the victim, just as in the myth the son kills his father with it. The bestowing upon one's child of a "head name" belonging to the victim has an obvious analogy in the familiar custom of naming one's child after one's own father or ancestor. However, a point I do not want to lose track of in all this is the lethal aspect of the phallic surrogate. It reflects, I believe, one of the symbolic meanings of the phallus—its meaning as an instrument of destruction.

Headhunting and Fertility

Headhunting was a motif that pervaded the culture region of which the Marind-anim, were a part. An important nutriment of the region, especially along the coast where the Marind were concentrated, was the coconut. The Marind associated headhunting with the promotion of the growth of the coconut. Further, in various myths of the Marind themselves and other tribes of the region, there was a connection between the coconut, a human head, and life. In the myth of the old giant, Anésaké, a coconut tree sprouted from the burial site of his son who had died. Van Baal refers to a myth of the Wiram people as related by F. F. Williams (Williams, 1936, pp. 387–88) in which the dog belonging to an important ancestral figure bites off the head of an enemy tribesman, buries it, and unsuccessfully tries to get his master to dig it up for skinning and stuffing. In the meantime, a coconut tree bearing nuts sprouts from the head. Later in the account, these coconuts turn into human beings.

In a reversal of the father-son theme of the Anésaké story, another myth describes how yet another primeval figure, Aramemb, steals a handsome boy who has been born to a snake. However, when this boy, Yawi, is grown up, he commits adultery with his foster mother. Arememb has him killed, regrets the deed, and wants to restore him to life with a certain medicine. It is, however, too late because Yawi has been buried. Aramemb pours the medicine over a snake, which thereupon peels off its skin. Henceforward, snakes do not die when they are sick, but slough off and live. If Aramemb had arrived in time to restore Yawi, human beings would have been immortal, too, merely peeling when ill. However, from Yawi's head, there sprouts a coconut tree (Van Baal, pp. 249–50). Finally, when the successful raiders return from a headhunt, the heads are hung from a special forked pole that then takes on the aspect of a fruit-bearing coconut tree. The theme of intergenerational killing is striking in the Aramemb/Yawi legend, with new life symbolized by the coconut tree coming forth from the head of the son, instead of life emerging from the body of the father as in the Anésaké legend.

The relationship of headhunting to fertility is described in a completely different culture area, Sarawak in Borneo. Freeman (1979) reports that the cult of headhunting was still of passionate concern to the Iban, who had taken numerous Japanese heads near the end of the war. In their myth, when the Iban god of war split open a head, seeds spilled out that grew into a human crop. Traditionally, heads were believed to make rice grow well, cause the forest to abound with game, and to ensure the fertility of women. In fact, an infertile woman was sometimes treated by having a head placed between her thighs. Freeman proposes that the head has phallic significance. Freud (1916) also suggests that the head can stand for the male genitals.

I would suggest a slightly different formulation by proposing that both the head and the phallus symbolize a complex of meanings having to do with fertility, while not denying that the head itself can sometimes be a surrogate for the phallus. (In fact, LaBarre (1984) has proposed that the association of the head with fertility is based on an ancient—but erroneous—belief that the head was the chief locus and source of semen, itself necessary to give life and sustain vigor. He cites the widespread occurrence of this association.) In the case of the Marind, however, I can think of no reason why, had they felt it was the genitals that they wanted, they would have stopped short of collecting those. However, nowhere does Van Baal suggest that only male heads were taken; in fact, Williams (1936) explicitly remarks on the indiscriminate taking of heads regardless of sex or age among the Keraki.

One could interpret much in the headhunt as supportive of Freud's theory of the phylogenetic memory of the killing of the primeval father, with its associated guilt, as he elaborated it in *Totem and Taboo* (1918) and *Moses and Monotheism* (1939). The killing of the victim replicates the murder of the father; the *pahui* or *bagwa* is the surrogate for the son's phallus with which he smites the father. However, the necessity that it be shattered reflects the son's guilt and is a symbol of self-castration that expiates the castration of the father that is to follow when the victim's head is severed. The taking of the victim's name to bestow on one's own child is a remembrance of the murdered father's generative power and a symbolic undoing of the lethal deed. The passionate speech to the severed head after the celebration following the war party's return is a symbolic reunion with the father. Finally, one detail that I have not yet mentioned can be fit into this scheme. The victims' children were kidnapped by the Marind, brought back and raised as their own children, paralleling the generation of new humans from the father's body. Could the above interpretations be true or are they merely "clever"? Personally, I had been inclined to take a rather patronizing attitude toward the theory of the primal horde and father, regarding it as a rather anachronistic nineteenth-century romance that was in any case unverifiable. But the headhunting motifs give one pause. Still, it is useless to regard the practices involved in headhunting and the legends surrounding it as support for an unverifiable historical event, however striking the parallels. Rather, I would prefer to say that Freud focused on elements of father-son relationships that are both powerful and paradoxical, elements that touch on tyranny, rebellion, guilt, love, and expiation. He then cast this father-son complex into a speculative, almost mythical form that was more congenial to the intellectual conventions of his day than it is to ours.

Although the practice of headhunting must, for us, seem brutal in the extreme, we might still admit to a certain thrill accompanying the reaction of horror. Williams, however, recorded some eyewitness accounts of what a headhunting raid was like in the words of some of its survivors. One cannot read these accounts without feeling a profoundly empathic pity. That the Marind themselves were not immune to such feelings as well as to guilt is seen in an anecdote that reveals how they warded off guilt and a legend that illustrates the warded-off capacity for empathic identification with the victim.

They called the prospective victims *ikom-anim,* "the strangers." The Marind themselves were the "real" humans, to whom these strangers were clearly inferior. Addressing one of the European missionaries, they explained, "They are not human beings, sir, let us go and take their heads. That is what they are made for" (Van Baal, 1966, p. 696). The same missionary telling this anecdote also reports the legend in which the moon is depicted as an inveterate headhunter who wanted to cut off the heads of all the people he saw lying on the beach, as they slept covered with mats that left only their heads showing. In the legend, the sun says to the moon, "Moon, you should not do that. The things you see there are men, real humans. You do not know that because you shine only by night, seeing nothing but heads, but I know because I see them at work in the daytime. Then are men. Do not hurt them" (p. 228).

To try fully to explicate the meanings and motivations of headhunting would, I think, entail the same problems as the interpretation of symptoms or dreams. Headhunting is a symbolic act that organizes meanings and evokes emotion as do other ritual acts, as well as symptoms, dreams, and indeed, works of art. Symbols do not depend for their effect on an intellectual grasp of their meanings. The Marind could not explain why they felt it so imperative to procure "head names" for their children, but it was important nonetheless. The Keraki people that Williams studied also hunted heads, though in less dedicated fashion than the Marind. They felt it necessary to shatter the *parasi,* their equivalent of the *pahui,* over their prospective victim's head, but could not explain why. They also addressed this *parasi* by the name of some prominent member of the village they were about to attack and attempt to destroy.

We are then left with a situation in which neither participants nor observers can offer a complete and unambiguous explanation for acts saturated with meaning and emotion. Postponing any further exploration of this apparent paradox for the moment, I do think that a myth—such as that about old Anésaké and his son—that is associated with a ritual act such as headhunting might justifiably be treated like an association to a dream, which offers a clue to an interpretation but usually not certainly. The father-son element is thus strongly suggested but not proved.

Returning again to the themes of male sexuality and symbolism that run through this discussion of Melanesian ritual life, I would like to cite some data offered by Williams on the bull-roarer among the Keraki. There were two classes of these objects which are swung through the air to make the peculiar roaring sound that gives them their name. One class consisted of those actually used in their rituals, while another class was much more elaborate, carefully stored, and seldom if ever swung. These more important ones had names. One of these, *Tokujenjeni,* was also the name of the veritable first bull-roarer, obtained by the mythological originator, from his wife's vagina. The legend goes that he heard a strange noise, which his wife denied hearing but which he realized came from within her body. He got a bird to snatch the bull-roarer out of her vagina, causing her to bleed in the first menstruation. Her husband then declares that, henceforth, it would belong to men only and showed it to his son at the first initiation ceremony. It is added that the first bull-roarer, obtained in this way, was hairy.

Williams notes that raiders would address their weapons—arrows, clubs, beheading knives—by the name of this first bull-roarer, saying, "*Tokujenjeni,* tomorrow go fast and get your man!" Or, as the victim is killed by one of these implements, he might cry, "*Toukujenjeni* is copulating with you" (p. 183). The implications of the act of taking the first bull-roarer from the woman and appropriating it for the men—and it is everywhere a male-cult object taboo to women—are certainly intriguing. I will refrain from exploring that theme except to say that there is more than a hint in this part of the legend that there was a struggle between the primal male and female ancestors over the women's right to possession of a penis. In any case, if the bull-roarer is indeed a phallic object, then it seems that the phallus can be conceived of as lethal in the act of copulation.

This aspect of the symbolic meaning of the phallus seems to be involved in a punishment that Williams mentions for a wife who refuses to stay with her husband, one rarely applied to be sure. At her husband's instigation, the recalcitrant wife is raped by a number of his friends in order to tame her spirit. On the other hand, among the Marind, on the first night after a wedding ceremony of a young couple, the new wife must have intercourse with members of her husband's clan before she has it with him. And, to stimulate a wife's fertility if the need should arise, it may be arranged that she have intercourse with many men in rapid succession. Again one sees that phallic power can be used to help in killing one's enemies, punishing a rejecting woman, or in the creation of new life. In the punishment scenario, male solidarity is utilized against the female. But among the Marind, the same act of multiple intercourse has a radically different assigned meaning.

6
The Artistic/Symbolic Framework

Two themes emerged from consideration of sexuality in the historical/anthropological framework in the previous chapter. The first was the demonstrated occurrence of the coexistence of heterosexual and homosexual responsiveness and behavior in males in widely varying cultural settings. These facts are supportive of Freud's view that a *capacity* for bisexuality—dualism with regard to object choice—is part of the normal male constitution, together with his clearly stated but rarely cited assertions about the extremely important role that culture plays in determining the acceptance and expression of homosexual feeling and behavior. The facts do not support the rejection of Freud's bisexuality theory by Rado and adherents of his "adaptational" theory which regarded homosexual feeling as *always* belonging to the realm of the pathological, and never part of normal male psychology.

The second theme that emerged in the last chapter was that exercise of the sexual function had a symbolic dimension. Further, this symbolic dimension was of such breadth and depth as to raise the question of whether it makes sense to say that a sexual act can ever occur *without* a symbolic dimension. The symbolic meaning of sexual action appears to be complex, rather than simple, and potentially contradictory. The penis seemed to carry the symbolic meaning of power: in erection, penetration, and ejaculation. However, when the object of phallic power is another male, this power had several meanings. It could enhance the recipient's masculinity or it could feminize him and damage his masculinity. With respect to women, it could be used to punish, and dominate or to promote fertility. In headhunting, where the club that was the surrogate for the phallus struck the first blow in ritual murder, the symbolic meaning seemed to be pure destructiveness.

However, among the Greeks, phallic action had quite another symbolic meaning that existed side by side with the power dimension—it was the expression of love, of *eros.* The man was highly motivated to bring his penis into contact with the beloved youth. However, there was evident concern that the youth's masculinity not be damaged by this phallic contact. The "ideal" solution of intercourse between the youth's thighs appears to have been a compromise between the man's desire to penetrate the object of his love and the culturally and probably personally felt necessity to preserve the younger partner's masculinity from damage by the feminizing or destructive meaning of phallic action. However, deviations from this "ideal" must have occurred with appropriate emotional safeguards against a sense of demasculinization or, in the parlance of psychoanalytic theory, castration anxiety.

The historical and anthropological data lend weight to an inference suggested by the data of Frank's life, from psychoanalytic observation in general, and the arts. *This inference is that meanings are the prime motivators of sexual action and imagery.* The physical sensations accompanying excitement and orgasm explain very little of what human sexuality is about. Masturbation, the simplest and most direct means to physical gratification, is very rarely the preferred sexual modality. In the great majority of cases, sex is preferentially interpersonal whether in reality or in fantasy. To deny that this interpersonal experience has multiple dimensions of meaning for each partner would be to repudiate the fundamental tenets and assumptions of psychoanalytic theory. To ignore these dimensions of meaning would be so incomplete that any theory failing to take them into account would run the risk of being incorrect.

Symbolic Experience

I am going to propose that it is in the nature of the human mind to create symbols and in the nature of the human personality to desire and seek experiences mediated by symbols. The pursuit of symbolic experience through sexual imagery and action is a particular instance—though one of the most important—of the general need for symbolic experience.

Devereux (1979) comments on the importance of the symbolic component in human experience: "My basic position is that there is no wholly non-symbolic human activity whatever. Our most basic activities, quite as much as our most recondite ones, always have an operative symbolic significance of one kind or another" (p. 20).

Devereux goes on to advance a very interesting reason for the operation of the symbolic in human activity. He says, "I propose to advance a hypothesis concerning, not the origins of symbols or of man's capacity to devise, use and decode symbols, but some psychological advantages of that capacity. Man is not only an extremely complexly organized creature, capable of highly specific and narrowly segmental acts but, perhaps precisely because such is his nature, also a being experiencing great difficulties in, so to speak, keeping himself together in one piece: in getting totally involved, in responding to specific stimuli not only segmentally, but wholly" (p. 27).

He adds, ". . . man's great capacity for segmentalization, for functional specificity, enables him to get fully involved with persons, things and time only by means of his complementary capacity to make reality highly multidimensional. This in turn, permits a richer, broader, more fully involved response to reality, by means of a perception of and response to, each item of reality, both as concrete and symbolic" (p. 29).

Devereaux notes that one can choose to strip experience down to its bare, concrete, and literal essentials in an effort to keep one's whole self uninvolved. But he adds an interesting cautionary note as well. If the above should be attempted, "The uninvolved (or theoretically uninvolved) portion of one's self does not cease to operate. It simply splits off from reality and goes off on a 'bender' . . . into a dreamlike and almost schizophrenoid state, operating apart from external stimuli which, as noted, become constricted to a point of unidimensionality" (p. 28).

This understanding of symbolism goes beyond Freud's conception while not contradicting it. In Freud, symbolism was essentially the language of the unconscious and, more precisely, of the primary process mode of thought characterizing the unconscious. As such, it was seen both in dreams and in symptoms. What was symbolized was unconscious, usually repressed, material that could not be put into the language of secondary process thinking and thus escaped correction by the ego's experience with reality. There is nothing in Devereux's conception or my own that would be inconsistent with Freud's.

Rather, the theory of symbolism is extended to many aspects of normal—as opposed to neurotic or psychotic—living, and to waking life as well as dreams, and to elements of experience other than those that are repressed.

Symbolism and Sexual Excitement

A point of view that, I think, supports what I am saying about the symbolic meaning and power of sexual imagery and behavior is that put forward by R. J. Stoller who has remarked on the dearth of professional literature on what causes sexual excitement (Stoller, 1979). Stoller's view is that *all* sexual excitement is meaningful, and its meanings are encapsulated and referred to in the conscious imagery and imagined scenarios that spur and accompany excitement. However, he is quite clear about his skepticism toward the meaningfulness of the traditional boundaries drawn between "normal" and "abnormal" in sexual life, proposing that "Maybe we approximate the truth better if, in regard to erotic behavior, we assume that most people are abnormal. At least, then, we shall be less polemical" (p. 103). There are two aspects to Stoller's theory. One aspect touches on the actual meanings of most people's erotic scenarios: his view is that the desire to harm one's object, to degrade, hurt, or humiliate another is a widely prevalent and important element in these scenarios. However, I will focus on the aspect of his theory that has to do with the *way* in which the imagery and action of sexual excitement work, regardless of their precise meanings.

He says, ". . . the construction of erotic excitement is every bit as subtle, complex, inspired, profound, tidal, fascinating, awesome, problematical, unconscious-soaked, and genius haunted as the creations of dreams or art" (Stoller, 1985, p. 47). "The dynamics that underlie aesthetics may be the same whatever field you study: Painting, sculpture, poetry, novels, theater productions . . . or erotic excitement" (p. 45). His concept of the "microdot" (Stoller, 1979) seems very close to that of certain cultural symbols, of a kind Turner (1977) discussed which, while simple in form—for example, the cross or the crescent—have rich meanings as well as evocative power. Stoller's concept of the microdot is explained in the following passage: "During World War II, the Nazis devised a system for hiding messages: the microdot, 'a photograph the size of a printed period that reproduced with perfect clarity a standard-sized typewritten letter.' Most human behavior—the functioning of the mind—works the same way; . . . In a process comparable to the miniaturization that allows stupendous amounts of information to be stored, arranged, rearranged, and transmitted within so small an apparatus as the brain, we—our minds—use psychic mechanisms that work at high speed to compress great masses of data into amazingly small 'space' in a purposeful, organized way. . . . Sexual excitement is a microdot. . . . 'Microdot,' more than 'fantasy,' implies all at the same instant: an ability to condense masses of data. . . ." (Stoller, 1979, pp. 165–66). The "microdot" seems equivalent to a symbol, in that it refers to ". . . a mass of memories, scripts, themes, fantasies, affect, all tremendously packed and purposefully organized" (p. 174).

The relation between meaning in sexual fantasy and meaning in artistic productions is again emphasized: "To repeat, sexual excitement depends on a scenario. The person to be aroused is the 'writer,' who has been at work on the story line since childhood" (p. 31). The conscious "script" carries—or, in the framework of this book—symbolizes, the underlying dynamics and it is in these that the excitement originates. The parallel between an exciting erotic fantasy and experience in the theater is drawn in Stoller's observation that "One part of oneself must know this script is illusion and thus under control, while another, saying it does not know this secret, convinces the genitals that the story is real—and the reality of tumescence momentarily make the story convincing" (p. 19). My purpose in pointing up the parallel between fantasy and theatrical experience, of course, is to emphasize that both are symbolic in their operation and effects, not to denigrate or trivialize either.

About anthropological approaches to sexuality, Stoller notes that most anthropological works stop their investigations at the point where the individual's excitement begins. "The missing link, the essential clue, lies in the detailed study of erotic fantasy, the conscious daydreams people tell themselves or live in the real world, plus unconscious fantasy, the private, idiosyncratic, unrecognized meanings people attach to their behavior and to the objects on whom their behavior is worked out" (p. 25). In the above description, the conscious fantasy corresponds to the symbol—which *is* conscious—and the unconscious fantasy, those parts of its meaning that are not grasped within awareness, but that are mobilized by the symbol.

Symbolism and Psychoanalytic Theory of Art

R. Kuhns (1983) has provided a framework for an extension of the theory of symbolism in his *Psychoanalytic Theory of Art.* While Freud took a vivid interest in the relation between the artist's productions and the life history and psychodynamics of the artist, as in his *Leonardo* . . . (1910), Kuhns's focus is a psychoanalytic understanding of the work of art, of the object itself, not the artist. While it would be difficult to find any society in which artistic activity was entirely lacking—the artistic tradition, after all, is seen in the Lascaux cave paintings of 15,000 B.C.—technology has made artistic experience available to anyone with a television set, the price of a movie, or of a record, tape, or compact disc. It is unnecessary to list all the forms of artistic experience and the associated media to which we have access. The point I want to make is the high degree of motivation on the part of masses of people to experience art, particularly dramatic art as presented on television which, while it may not be the highest expression of drama, is nonetheless art.

In experiencing a dramatic enactment, we temporarily withdraw our attention from the demands of reality, and allow ourselves to be drawn into the symbolic world the dramatist has created. If the dramatist has succeeded, the drama becomes for a while the only "reality" of which we are aware. One's total being can be engaged and the emotions experienced more vivid, more focused, and more intense than anything experienced in much of "real" life. Paradoxically, one might find oneself caring deeply about the outcome of the story and the fate of its protagonists. Other artistic experiences—painting, sculpture, music—can be deeply engrossing in different ways. Naturally, there are plenty of examples of works in all media that elicit only mild interest. However, when a work of art has an effect on the spectator, its effect can be said to be symbolic in the sense that it both organizes and evokes meaning and emotion. But in common with other symbolic experience, it may be difficult to specify in words, and in "secondary" thought processes, precisely what these meanings and emotions are.

Kuhns has presented an analysis of the nature of the artistic experience utilizing psychoanalytic concepts in a way that usefully extends psychoanalytic theory. Kuhns asserts, "The experiences we have with art are surprising because they permit often unavailable thought to suddenly occupy our consciousness. It is as if works of art have the power to transport certain thoughts from the unconscious to the preconscious through their having been, as it were 'aestheticized.' The whole complex activity of art-making and art-using can be understood as a cultural loosening of the ordinarily rigid boundaries of the unconscious and conscious" (p. 18).

Kuhns conceives of the work of art as a cultural object that has a past in a tradition of other objects to which it is related and which, in turn, serve as a background of references and associations for it. The response of the audience to the object reflects its own training and experience in this tradition. Thus, a painting of the Madonna and the infant Jesus by, let us say, Botticelli would be one painting in a tradition of paintings with this theme. However, Kuhns utilizes the psychoanalytic concept of transference to refer to the peculiar treatment of this traditional theme by an individual artist. The artist's own life history and emotional makeup infuse his particular treatment of a familiar theme with certain deeply emotional resonances. Freud (1910) asserted that the smile of the *Mona Lisa* reflected Leonardo's childhood unconscious memory of the smile of the mother he had lost. This infusion of a traditional portrait of a beautiful and aristocratic lady with that unconscious memory is what Kuhns refers to as transference.

The audience to this portrait responds with "counter-transference": ". . . the beholder . . . responds to all the layers with an accumulation of conscious and unconscious associations which include deeply private nodal points in the unique developmental experience to which there are correspondences, but not identities, in others" (p. 21). It is this response in the beholder, which the portrait has so successfully evoked, that accounts for the enduring fascination with which it has for centuries been regarded. The portrait is capable of eliciting this response even if the viewer knew nothing of Leonardo's life history or even of the Renaissance.

Kuhns's description of the "countertransference" response of the beholder rather closely corresponds with what I would term the symbolic effect of this work. It has an impact on the viewer, though it may by no means be possible to put into words the precise nature of that impact or the reasons for it. The *Mona Lisa* is a particularly apt and justly famous example of the symbolic aspect of art, which organizes and evokes meaning and emotion. To her celebrated smile, the adjective *mysterious* is one of the most frequently applied. Freud himself applied it when he suggested ". . . we suspect the possibility that it was his mother who possessed the mysterious smile—the smile that he had lost and that fascinated him so much when he found it again in the Florentine lady" (Freud, 1910, p. 61).

Kuhns also points to one of the motives that impel people to seek artistic experience: "Enactments [works of art that have culturally recognized status] are the cultural means we have to combine the rational and irrational achievements of psychic life, for they take as one of their central concerns the struggle over integration" (p. 77).

The Symbolist Movement

The fact that we in modern Western civilization are such avid consumers of art, even art that aspires to no more than mediocre standards, attests to a thirst for the symbolic dimension of experience, perhaps because the conditions of living in such a complex and segmented society tend to be disintegrative. The idea that artistic experience can open up to the individual areas of the unconscious that he could not touch without its aid will serve as an introduction to the next subject I wish to consider, the symbolist movement in art. I will draw on R. Goldwater's *Symbolism* (1979) for the material cited on the subject of the symbolists and the symbolist movement.

While psychoanalysis has traditionally undertaken the task of interpreting symbols, the artists of the symbolist movement would have rejected the very notion of interpretation as deeply antithetical to their vision of art. Symbolism was a movement in both poetry and the visual arts in the last quarter of the nineteenth century, and many of its leading proponents were French. Their approach was to an inner reality that went beyond the superficial realities which they charged the impressionists with being concerned about. Of the impressionists, Paul Gauguin said that "... they neglected the mysterious centres of thought" (p. 116).

Although Goldwater's book deals with the symbolist movement in the visual arts, the ethos of the movement seemed identical in both literary and visual spheres. Thus the poet Stéphane Mallarmé said, "To *name* an object is to suppress three-fourths of the enjoyment. . . . to *suggest* it, that is the dream." Emile Bernard noted, ". . . symbolism did not paint things, but the 'idea of things' " (p. 95). The symbolists, Goldwater points out, believed ". . . in the reality of an unseen world" (p. 142). The purpose of a work of art was to hint at and evoke that world, its aura, and its moods through artistic symbols. The self-conscious use of symbolism as in allegory was dismissed. Thus, Odilon Redon said, ". . . nothing in art is done by will alone, everything is done by docile submission to the arrival of the unconscious" (p. 118). While Freud undertook the scientific exploration of the unconscious, the concept of the unconscious antedated psychoanalysis. The following paragraph (by Gerhardt Gran) was written in 1893, before Freud's work was well known: "Beneath consciousness lies that great area of the soul (subconscious) which is still a total mystery, but which demonstrates its workings in dreams, in the somnambulistic state under hypnosis and which existed before one's earthly life and which will exist after death. From there arise . . . [anxiety], the passions, love, hate, and all that which occurs without reflection" (Goldwater, p. 216).

Goldwater cites Gustave Kahn's definition of symbolism: ". . . it objectifies the subjective." The *Mona Lisa,* in fact, would undoubtedly qualify as a symbolist work precisely because of the mystery of her smile. In fact, the symbolist view of the unconscious inner reality that could only be alluded to through the symbolic modality was not far removed from Freud's who proposed that the unconscious was not, in fact, directly cognizable except in dreams or symptoms (Freud, 1915b, p. 120). On the other hand, Freud clearly felt that it was possible to learn about both the contents and the operations of the unconscious.

While the symbolists had not the slightest interest in the question of interpretation, I do not think that the concept would be inapplicable to symbolist works, with the proviso that, as with almost all works of art, there is no assurance of the correctness or completeness of a given interpretation. However, the symbolist creed does, I believe, point to a fundamentally important point that applies to art as well as to the operation of symbols in any other realm. This point is: an *interpretation* of a work of art is vastly different, in its effect, from the impact of directly experiencing the work itself.

I have repeatedly stressed that symbolic action has two aspects: the aspect of meaning and the aspect of emotional evocativeness. Interpretation of meaning, even when correct, does not have the evocative power of the symbol itself. *The symbol organizes a complex of experiences that it may not be possible to have any other way.*

To demonstrate this point, I will cite the last stanza from Matthew Arnold's "Dover Beach." I do not think it requires much interpretation as the poet says what he means fairly clearly.

> Ah, love, let us be true
> To one another! for the world, which seems
> To lie before us like a land of dreams,
> So various, so beautiful, so new,
> Hath really neither joy, nor love, nor light,
> Nor certitude, nor peace, nor help for pain;
> And we are here as on a darkling plain
> Swept with confused alarms of struggle and flight,
> Where ignorant armies clash by night!

The sentiments expressed in the poem could easily be transposed into prose. However, such a transposition would be tantamount to a dissolution of the symbol—which is the poem itself. A prose rendition might be understood to state a certain existential point of view that might elicit agreement. However, it would no longer have the evocative power of the poem, that is to say, of the symbol itself. The action of the symbol upon the reader is to produce a state of feeling, in which his own developmental and life history can resonate. Agreement with the sentiments of the poem that follows this kind of symbolically induced resonance is of a different order than agreement with a prosaically expressed philosophical point. Kuhns (unpublished manuscript) makes a similar point in his discussion of the effects of tragedy in the theater. He notes, "To grasp the truth of tragedy the audience must have a certain set of emotional responses in a certain sequence, and these responses are stimulated by a complex set of represented events." He adds, ". . . within the theatrical experience we undergo a developmental maturation in the life of feeling.

"And that brings us now to the basic difference between objects philosophically considered and objects in tragedy. In the arts generally, and in tragic drama in particular, the relationship between perceiver and object is a dynamic, developmental, ever changing relationship in which both object and perceiver travel through, as it were, stages of 'growing up,' of becoming mature in the cultural reality that we inhabit as human beings. In contrast, the philosophical way of treating objects is as static, fixed, "out-there" and always the same external realities; while the perceiver perceives from a fixed point at an unchanging time. There is no 'growing up' in modern philosophy; only being-there-forever as a perceiver stuck in time."

In a theatrical performance, the "complex set of represented events" constitutes the play's symbols and it is these that stimulate the emotional responses of the audience and with which the perceiver is in "a dynamic, developmental, and ever changing relationship." If a theatrical performance fails to stimulate emotional response, then the symbols of the play have not been effective. And even if the meaning of the play is made perfectly clear, one will have remained unchanged by the experience. In fact, people go to the theater in search of emotional experience, and other forms of symbolic experience are sought for the same reason.

The Body as Symbolic

It will be useful now to turn to one of the best-known artists in our own recent artistic tradition, Auguste Rodin. He did not accept the label of symbolist, yet his works have considerable symbolic power in their evocativeness. Of his sculptures, Goldwater (1979) notes, ". . . through the entirety of bodily pose, they embody states of feeling." And Rodin himself said, "The sculpture of antiquity sought the logic of the human body, I seek its psychology" (p. 166). In Rodin's hands, the human body becomes symbolic; yet there is little distortion of the human form in his works, to the extent that some of his critics, Goldwater reports, insinuated that *The Age of Bronze* had been made from casts of the living model. However, even in a photograph, this piece exudes a striking dynamic tension and makes an impression that could be described in words with only partial success.

In his search for the "psychology" of the human body, Rodin conceived of the body, one infers, as an expressive and natural modality of human thought and feeling. *It follows that the imagery and action of the body can function symbolically.* In his determination to seek beauty in life's *natural* forms, Rodin, as he himself suggested, was working in a "tradition of objects" that stretched back to the Greek Archaic period. A recent exhibition on the human figure in early Greek art was a testimony to the intense interest that the body held for both the artists and audiences of antiquity. Included in the exhibition which traced the evolution of the treatment of the figure from the tenth to the fifth centuries B.C. there are works of surpassing beauty whose effect on the viewer would certainly deserve the description of symbolic. Harrison (1988) points out that the *kouros,* the sculpture of a naked youth, for which the period under consideration is well known, commonly commemorated the memory of a son, or in the case of the female equivalent, the *kore,* a daughter. Of the *kouros* she says, "As the image of a young male on the threshold of sexual maturity, the *kouros* represents human generative power in pure, undiminished form. For one who died before he could marry and have children, the statue constituted immortality in the memory of survivors. To his family, it gave a kind of continuity. The epigrams inscribed in the bases of Attic funerary stelai are those of funerary *kouroi* or *korai,* and indicated that these monuments in the Archaic period were mostly dedicated for young people by their grieving parents" (p. 52).

The image of the body in its youthful beauty seems unmistakably symbolic of idealizing parental love, with the nudity and acknowledged sexuality of the body of the loved child as integral parts of this symbol. (In contrast, the depiction of one's son or daughter in a state of nudity, even in stylized or abstract form, as a memorial seems scarcely possible in our own time.) The beauty of the human form seems to have been symbolically meaningful to the Greeks. Although that tradition seems to me never to have been lost in Western civilization, it has been the subject of profound ambivalence at different times and, in fact, remains so to this day.

Ganymede as a Symbol

In a very interesting study of the object of just such ambivalence, J. M. Saslow (1986) has traced the theme of Ganymede in Renaissance painting and its relation to sexuality. Ganymede, of course, was the Trojan prince of such dazzling beauty that Zeus himself fell in love with him and, swooping down on the youth in the form of an eagle, carried him off to serve as his cupbearer. To prevent his suffering the common fate of old age and death, Zeus eventually granted him immortality. Long before the Renaissance and after the decline of classical civilization, the figure of Ganymede remained associated with homosexual love.

Saslow points out that a sexual relationship between men and youths was the most prevalent form of homosexual love during the Renaissance, which made the Ganymede legend a particularly apt representation of that love. Different treatments of the figure of Ganymede from classical times onward would constitute a "tradition of objects" in Kuhns's sense, with the artist's particular treatment of the theme constituting the "transference" and the response of the audience the "counter-transference." In the case of Michelangelo, his drawing of the *Rape of Ganymede* was executed as a gift to Tomasso de'Cavalieri, a young aristocrat with whom he had fallen in love, though this love could not be openly acknowledged or consummated. The artist's own homosexual feeling could be seen to have contributed to his treatment of the theme. On the other hand, Correggio did a similarly entitled work, and in his case there was no reason to assume that his own inclinations were other than essentially heterosexual. However, Saslow observes, the painting would be expected to include among its wealthy and privileged audience men for whom the sexual theme would be more directly relevant. What emerges from this contrast is the fact that, a work of art once executed, stands as a symbolic entity in its own right capable of organizing and eliciting a complex of meanings and feelings independently from the personality of its creator.

Michangelo first met the young Cavalieri in 1532. The remainder of the century saw a gradual tightening of the moral strictures against homosexuality in the Italian principalities, paralleling a conservative reaction in general. Saslow notes, "A decade after Michangelo's love-gifts, the Council of Trent began its work of proscribing classical references in religious art—in effect banishing all pretext for incorporating non-Christian notions of sensuality, however elevated, within a positive spiritual context" (p. 62). As the form of love that the Ganymede theme symbolized came under more severe sanctions, the symbol itself began to decline in popularity and even came to symbolize that disapproval. Under Charles I of England (1625–49) there was a reaction against the open homosexuality of his father, James I. In a court masque produced in 1634, the following lines proclaimed, "Ganymede is forbidden the bedchamber, and must only minister in publique. The gods must keep no Pages, nor Groomes of their chamber under the age of 25, and those provided of competent stock of bearde" (Saslow, p. 194).

Ganymede symbolized not only homosexual love, but also the continuity of the world view and values of the pre-Christian world which gave birth to the legend. Although depictions of classical themes continued in secular art after the Council of Trent, its excision from religious work reflects, I think, a theme of continuing struggle between the symbols of the classical world—which the Renaissance rediscovered in some respects—and Christianity which had suppressed those symbols. Figuratively, even symbolically, the threat of contamination by the suppressed sensibilities was fought.

The suppression of symbolic representations of reprobated themes is understandable from the perspective of the psychology of symbolic action. Symbols act to evoke feelings as well as meanings. Homosexual symbols, will, then, be effective in evoking complexes of homosexual meanings and, if the symbols are effective, feelings as well. If these feelings are acceptable to the viewer, there is likely to be an openness to the symbolically evoked experience. However, where homosexual feelings would provoke anxiety, then the symbols evoking them will arouse discomfort or even condemnation. Suppression of the symbols themselves is likely to follow.

I do not think I would be risking disagreement by asserting that the body and its sexuality have been the subject of ambivalence since the beginning of the Christian era. P. Brown (1988) demonstrates that the body's sexuality was in a state of chronic oppositional tension with the deepest Christian conceptions of the ideal relation to God. This tension was evident from the start in the views of Saint Paul himself and the views attributed to him. It eventually culminated, in the Latin Church, in the forced renunciation of sexuality by the Christian clergy, an event I will discuss in more detail in the next chapter. To this day, it remains true that, in American culture at least, the best organized and most vocal sources of opposition to the removal of restrictions against sexual imagery and behavior are religious, across a broad spectrum of denominations. It is difficult then to reconcile, with the religious frame of reference to which we have become accustomed, another religious tradition that found a place in its sacred precincts for sexual imagery of the most explicit kind.

Symbolic Aspects of Sexuality in Religion

The tradition to which I refer is that of erotic sculpture in the temple art of India. It is particularly evident in temples built between 900 to 1400 A.D., although erotic motifs were plentiful before this period. As was the case with the gods and goddesses of the Greek pantheon, Indian deities were—and—are emphatically sexual. This sexuality found expression in the sculptural depiction of the deities. One of the premier deities of the Hindu pantheon is Shiva, whose symbol is the *linga*—the phallus. In one collection of ninth-century depictions (Danielou, 1973) Shiva is shown, with erect phallus, in a number of different contexts. In one, Shiva the creator is shown in the dance, while the bull, his customary mount, licks his testicles. In another he is shown seated on a lotus in a yoga posture, and in a third, he is shown with erect phallus seated with his wife Parvati. And in the eighth century A.D. sculpture, his semen is shown spurting into the cupped hands of Agni, the fire god.

Temple art, particularly in the time span from the tenth to the fifteenth centuries A.D., not only depicted the gods in sexual postures, but human beings as well, and in the most explicit and imaginative postures and groupings, at that. A. Watts (1971) says that many modern Indians have felt ashamed of the frankness of the depictions in these sculptures. It appears that Indian culture has undergone changes in the direction of muting the overt sexuality of an earlier period. Yet, Devangana Desai

(1975) in her socio-cultural approach to an understanding of the earlier tradition, concluded, "Far from being an anomaly in Hindu culture, erotic motifs were in harmony with the religious environment to which they belonged and with the majestic, courtly, and artistic temples they decorated. . . . Such widespread and riotous sexual depiction throughout India could not obviously be the creation of the whims and caprices of a few individuals but must be the reflection of the social reality of the period" (p. 203). In fact, Desai finds evidence of an extraordinary openness in sexual matters in the literature of the period as well. And M. P. Fouchet (1959) notes that although various explanations have been offered for this remarkable tradition he feels that they all show that the "iconography of love" could not be divorced from the spiritual as well as the everyday life of the people who created these temples and who worshiped in them.

And it is precisely this iconography that I feel is relevant to the concerns of this book. It is found in profusion in carvings of extraordinary excellence in the group of temples at Khajuraho, in north-central India, in a group of temples built in the tenth and eleventh centuries by the Chandella dynasty. These carvings would be described as pornographic in our culture's terms. A perusal of the photographs of the works in this group of temples alone (Danielou, 1973)—and there are many others all over India, though few so profusely decorated with sculpture of this quality—testifies to their power, even in two dimensions on a printed page, to beguile and arouse. It would be hard to believe that this effect was not the intention of those who planned and executed these works.

The imagery of these works of art and their power constitute a further extension of the symbolism of the body as it is depicted in sexual action. The sexuality adds a powerful, supplementary dimension to the meanings of bodily action and this sexuality evokes emotional reactions unique to itself—shaded, in turn, by the different groupings and pairings, the different varieties of postures and contacts.

At about the time the manuscript for this book was being prepared I was able to visit Khajuraho and so to see these sculptures, not only in three dimensions, but integrated into their architectural and spiritual context. I think it is fair to say that their symbolic impact cannot be separated from this context. Images of sexual intercourse, sculpted with consummate skill, in a monumental setting to which one has come to worship deities whose idealized images, whether alone or with their consorts, adorn the same walls must have an altogether different impact from viewing identical images in the squalid and furtive surroundings so often associated with pornography in our own culture. Images of loving couples, not in any sexual posture, also decorate the walls, on which are also found scenes that include musicians, dancers, warriors, and elephants. Sexuality, then, stands out as one of the prime elements in a sculpted tapestry whose other constituents are divinity, love, and the pageantry of life.

The implied participation of human sexuality in the aura of divinity seems clearly delineated by the architectural features of temples in Nepal where, as in India, the Hindu tradition is dominant. I was able to visit a number of those temples in the main cities of the Kathmandu valley. A typical feature of these temples is that the roofs overhang the walls and this overhang is supported by angled wooden struts. Usually, these struts bear the carved effigy of a deity, much like the carvings integrated into the prow of a sailing ship. At the base of this strut, there is often a small carving depicting an explicit erotic scene, not necessarily aesthetically remarkable or depicting persons of any particular distinction. In Nepal, although these temples are of more recent origin—many were built in the eighteenth century—the reasons for the erotic elements are no longer known to many of the population today. But the juxtaposition of divinity and sexuality, of divine energy and human clay, symbolically speaks for itself.

Krishna Deva (1986)—formerly director of the Archaeological Survey of India—has observed that the erotic motif in the religious art of India touches the roots of Indian culture as reflected in the creation myths from the Vedic period onwards which stress the polarity between the sexes as the source of creation. He says, "The Supreme Being impregnates nature through His longing for the opposite, symbolizing the union of Siva and Sakti or Purusha and Prakriti, and the pull between the two principles becomes the source of all life and creation. The joy of physical union thus symbolically reflects the infinite joy of Divinity in creation" (p. 106). This formulation seems entirely consistent with the mood evoked by viewing these sculptures, but this mood is not dependent upon the intellectual understanding of philosophical concepts.

In illustration of this last point, I will mention a fortuitous occurrence. One of my students was telling some friends that her husband, as a young man, had been stationed in India during World War II and near a beach there was a temple in which there were erotic sculptures. He and his friends concluded that the people of the region "worshiped the human body." And some of his friends went back again and again to look, even in preference to going to the beautiful beach nearby. I think it is striking that these young Americans from a culture in which sacred precincts would be the last place to house such depictions, found themselves drawn to a place where the human body seemed to be the object of veneration in a way so alien to their own tradition. It is a testimony to the symbolic power of the sexuality with which the ancient sculptors infused those carvings.

Sexual Imagery and Action as Symbolic

I have tried to show that depictions of the human body can be fairly regarded as symbolic. I have added to this proposition that depictions of sexuality in action can be reasonably regarded in the same light. I would like now to add a third proposition, namely, that *sexual behavior itself is symbolic.* In a manner analogous to the way in which the artist invests meaning and feeling into an artistic object, *a person invests meaning and feeling into the actions, gestures, and movements of his body.* As Kuhns (1983) pointed out, generations of artists can place their own individual stamp on the working of a familiar theme which itself has a history in the works by other artists. The meaning at all levels—conscious and unconscious—which the individual artist brings to his work Kuhns described as the artist's "transference" to this theme. The human body and its sexual action provide the theme and the medium within which the individual who inhabits it works. The meanings and feelings he expresses through his body and its actions are his "transferences." Just as the work of art evokes reactions at conscious and unconscious levels in the audience, an individual's sexual behavior has an impact on others at both conscious and unconscious levels. In Kuhns's sense, the reaction of others constitute the "counter-transference." In this sense, *sexual behavior is symbolically expressive and symbolically evocative—it has meaning and emotional impact.*

It is this symbolic power inherent in the body and its sexuality that makes its depiction such a universal subject for the attention of the artist. The sexual images one is drawn to are compelling because they have symbolic power, because they are meaningful. As the young Americans were drawn to the exotic symbols of another cultural tradition, men and women are sexually drawn to people and situations because they have certain important, emotionally saturated meanings for them. The artistic/symbolic framework must be used alongside the historical/anthropological framework. It adds a dimension of individuality and personal meaning to the understanding afforded by the historical/anthropological framework. Both these frameworks must be used to understand what happened to Frank and why. In the remainder of this chapter I will begin to look at Frank's sexual imagery and behavior in symbolic terms as part of my effort to show how the themes of symbolism and male sexuality are interwoven with each other.

Frank's Sexual Symbols

One of the reasons I have presented the story of Frank in such detail is because a man's sexuality is only comprehensible as a feature—a central feature—of the interconnected web of his life. Sexuality resonates through all the layers of male developmental experience while encompassing the entire range of emotional responsiveness. It may be impossible really to articulate in consciousness the depth and breadth of meaning of a single act of sexual intercourse. But a description of it in purely physical terms is analogous to describing the *Mona Lisa* in words. The description may be correct, but almost everything of real importance is left out.

I would like now to consider some of the facts of Frank's sexual life from a symbolic perspective. We can begin with the fact that there was a dualism in sexual imagery for Frank, a dualism that was first denied but eventually admitted to consciousness and tolerated. This dualism was seen in response to both male and female beauty. Beauty was a particularly potent symbolic image for him. At one point he despaired of ever having the connection he longed for with the beautiful person he sought, regardless of gender. For Frank, male beauty was as important as female beauty, and he himself wanted to be beautiful.

The general human response to beauty is a fascinating and challenging subject. It obviously plays a major and often decisive role in sexual desire. But for Frank beauty also had a particularly important meaning. It was what he so painfully felt he lacked in adolescence. The "classic" beauty of the face, whether in a male or female, symbolized something he would have very much liked for himself and which he very much admired in others. To be with a beautiful other—of either sex—seemed like something of a corrective for the grievous injury to his self-esteem that he had suffered in adolescence.

However, I think there is sufficient evidence in the material of the analysis that it was his need for a loving connection with a male as well as a female person that transformed his aesthetic appreciation of male as well as female faces and forms into incandescent symbolic images, that is, sexually compelling ones. The Greeks, whose standards of beauty were also Frank's, sanctioned and even celebrated male beauty as a symbol expressive of their feelings toward males. But, when in the context of his culture, this symbol began to seep into Frank's consciousness, it was accompanied by another of that culture's symbols—the Devil. The one—the man's beauty—symbolized what Frank longed for. The other—the Devil—what he feared.

The symbol of the "kiss" was particularly potent as an organizer of deeply felt and conflicting emotions toward men. It appeared in three consecutive dreams: The first was the dream in which an actress said something about the Devil and then gave an older man a sensual kiss. The actress might fairly be understood to represent Frank himself. The sensuality of the kiss expressed deeply passionate feelings toward the man of a kind that Frank could not yet admit to as part of his own identity as a man; hence, it had to be symbolized in the dream in heterosexual terms. However, in the next dream, a kiss did take place between two men. It was like a kiss that a parent might brush on a child's forehead to check for a fever. This meaning was acceptable to Frank's conscious mind, and the symbol—the gentle kiss—mirrored this meaning. The passion that had imbued the kiss between the heterosexual couple, however, could not be recognizably expressed in a kiss between two men. Yet, it could not be entirely suppressed. The transformation of the man doing the kissing into a Devil-like being symbolized the feared and suppressed passion. The first dream symbolized elements of a parent-child relationship as well.

In the next dream Frank appeared as himself, struggling to get away from a group of young men who formed a rock group called Kiss. The name of the group signaled that this was not merely a dream in which he was trying to avoid male aggression. Rather it was the symbol of the kiss that was the focus of intense conflict. His struggle to escape from the chain on which the men held him graphically symbolized the struggle to escape from the wish for the male kiss. All these dreams occurred during the second phase of the analysis. It was in the third phase—roughly five years later—that Frank, recalling how he was forced to submit to the priest's kiss when he was an altar boy, said he could never imagine sex with a man because the thought of kissing him was so disgusting. The symbol of the kiss was rejected because what it symbolized—passion between men—remained unacceptable to Frank's consciousness.

I was, therefore, quite struck by what Frank said when, after he had read an earlier draft of this book, I asked him if he had ever had a conscious fantasy about sex with a man. His answer was revealing. He said that he had never had a visual fantasy of this kind, but he could *feel* it. The way in which he could imagine or feel it especially would be in *kissing* another man. What had caused the change in the conscious emotional accompaniment of this symbol? Obviously, he could now accept its meaning as part of himself. Perhaps it was having become the father of a baby boy and the freedom to express his tenderness in a physical way to him that had thawed the earlier defenses. Or perhaps it was another instance of that capacity to reflect on his experience and to open himself up to his feelings that had helped to make our collaborative work a success.

As the analysis unfolded over the course of its three phases, the complex mosaic that was Frank's feelings about women was gradually laid bare. It will be recalled that, at one point in the second phase, he disclaimed wanting anything from or with women except sex. Explaining the desire for sex with women as merely the expression of a biological urge would entail, at the theoretical level, the same kind of denial of its meaning that Frank was attempting at a subjective level. Contact with the body of another is a fundamental human, even mammalian need. Research, including controlled experiments, clinical observations, and naturalistic data, has shown the need for physical contact between the child and his caretakers in infancy and early childhood for proper emotional and even physical development. The evidence is summarized in any child-development textbook. The emotional bonding of infant with mother is virtually impossible in the absence of physical contact, and it is through the universal experiences of physical contact that some of the deepest transactions of tenderness and expressions of need take place between infant and mother.

That powerful emotional needs in later life should seek to find expression through physical contact seems "natural" in the sense of being utterly in conformity with the nature of the human organism as it begins to unfold immediately after birth. And although intense genital pleasure can be and is experienced in solitude, it seems to be a fact of human nature that this pleasure is preferentially joined to the experience of intimate contact with the body of another. Frank did not have to admit that he needed women emotionally. His longing to be in touch with their bodies and to experience the intensity of genital pleasure with and through them was more than ample proof. Similarly, the repressed images of physical contact, including genital contact, with men showed that he needed something from men, too.

Earlier in this chapter, I mentioned the trip to Nepal and India that I took while this book was in preparation. During this journey, I never once saw a young man and woman in the kind of casually intimate physical contact that is seen everywhere in this country. There were no young men and women walking arm in arm or even hand in hand. Nowhere did I see a young woman resting her head on her boyfriend's shoulder or a young man lying with his head in his girlfriend's lap, scenes so common here as hardly to merit comment. However, it frequently happened that two young men walked hand in hand or with arms about each other. Pairs of young men would be seated leaning against each other, even in ways that we only see in mixed couples, for example, one friend sitting between the other's legs with the latter's arms wrapped around him. These scenes of male intimacy would have provoked notice in many parts of our own country, even in cities where people pride themselves on their sophistication. I am not proposing that these young men were "lovers," which these gestures might signal in our culture. In those countries, however, these were permissible symbols of emotional bonding between men.

In contrast, at one point during the second phase, when Frank began to be more aware of his emotional needs toward men, he could only grant himself license to symbolize these needs toward his older friend Robert in a loving hug if he were drunk. It was after the party with Robert that he awoke in the middle of the night, haunted suddenly by the Devil thought. Athletics in our culture are accepted as a legitimate avenue of male physical contact. But this contact is in the context of competition rather than affection. Nonetheless, the physicality of athletics can express and evoke a desired closeness as well, although its recognition may be disquieting. An adolescent boy I used to see remarked that he sometimes wondered if he could be gay because, during his school wrestling matches, he sometimes felt a kind of liking for contact with his opponent's skin.

Much earlier, when the meaning of the Devil obsession was still shrouded in mystery, Frank had exasperatedly told how, during a football game, with "everything so beautiful," he had paradoxically thought, "You'll be thinking of the Devil later on." While physical contact in sports is a culturally acceptable symbol, for Frank at that point, it symbolized the same forbidden meaning that was attached to sexual intercourse—love with a man. But Frank was later to say, "You can't love a man," hence the imposition of the Devil thought.

In the third phase, when Frank was far more aware of his feelings for and about men, he could acknowledge the pleasure he took in wrestling with Nick, not for the competition but for the contact. He did not think it meant he wanted anything more explicitly sexual with him, however, and there is no reason to suppose, on an *a priori* basis, that he did. The point is rather that he could now accept a meaning of the symbol that he could not before—an intimate and affectionate transaction between himself and a male person important to him.

While a culture may abhor what certain symbols mean, its prohibitions operate most readily on the public display of the symbols themselves. However, while the public display of forbidden symbols is relatively controllable by authority, their experience in the mind's eye is not. But forbidden symbols, even when they take shape in individual consciousness, are likely to be accompanied by painful feelings of guilt or shame. It is hardly necessary to point out that the mechanism of repression aims to circumvent such pain. Homosexual symbols are forbidden by our dominant culture. Television, which mirrors and probably reinforces our cultural values, offers almost no scenes of physicality between males that are as overt and open as the scenes of sexual passion between men and women. The tacit omission of sexual symbols between even acknowledgedly gay characters from the most popular medium of our time seems both a reflection of and model for its treatment in the private world of conscious sexual imagery. Insofar as the cultural prohibition against male-to-male physical images is internalized the individual will unconsciously resist symbolizing feelings through homosexual imagery. Freud describes this abortive process succinctly when he notes that in the realm of fantasy, repression can bring about the inhibition of ideas in *statu nascendi,* before they can be consciously noticed, if their cathexix is likely to cause pain (Freud, 1911). It is particularly in the realm of sexual symbols that public and private intersect. For Frank, the pressure against allowing the nascent tendency toward homosexual symbolization to proceed where Nick was concerned was strong. The symbolic image that Frank did permit into consciousness the night he actually had the dream of making love to Nick was having Nick sleep in the same bed with him. With the cultural constraints less in control of the dream than of his conscious thoughts, the nascent tendency proceeded to unfold in the full-blown symbol of sexual intercourse. An important meaning of this symbol was clarified by the emotional accompaniment of this act in the dream itself. It was bathed in a loving feeling. However, Frank could not yet permit himself a conscious fantasy of that kind much less an overt action.

He could, of course, allow his emotional needs toward women to be expressed in these terms. It is interesting that, in the opening of the dream with Nick, it was at first a woman who was bending over, then Nick. This suggests that the symbol of anal intercourse might indeed have had, as one of its meanings, making love to a man—perhaps to Nick. Sometimes when Frank was having sex with a woman he would fantasize anal intercourse with her or another woman in order to excite himself to orgasm. The "unconscious fantasy," that is, the unconscious meaning of the symbol might, as he sometimes suspected, have been homosexual while its other, heterosexual meaning was conscious. This conscious meaning seemed to be his unquestioned dominance of a woman who would do anything for him, a dominance that included a certain amount of anger and contempt.

In the course of the analysis it became increasingly clear that Frank's feelings about women were complex and contradictory, with the themes of intense need and deep anger intertwined. Part of the work of the analysis consisted of the discovery of how these feelings were expressed and experienced—that is to say, symbolized—in his sexual encounters with woman. Stoller (1979) has tried to show the ways in which sexual *fantasy* symbolizes the deepest emotional currents in a person's life. I am arguing for including the sheer physicality of sex, including physical attraction—uncomplicated by any organized and articulated fantasy—in the category of the symbolic. Even before Frank began to be aware of what his sexual behavior with women meant, he was implementing a certain scenario that reflected both sides of his feelings about women. He would deliberately concentrate on giving a woman as much pleasure as possible during prolonged intercourse in order to feel appreciated and wanted. His anger at subordinating his own emotional needs for tenderness and understanding from a woman was simultaneously seen in the violence of the very same sexual act, in which he described himself as "smashing" into her. The very physicality of these actions mirrored the ones he could have attributed to the brutal, sexually charismatic man that was the ever-present rival in his mind's eye. I have already discussed possible meanings of this kind of identification between himself and this figure and will return to this question in Chapter 8. For the moment, however, I will simply say that this violent sex also symbolized a set of meanings that concerned his feelings about males that quite excluded the woman he was with at the moment.

However, as we got deeper into the complexity of his feelings about women in the third phase, the pleasure he experienced in power and dominance became more and more hollow. Sometimes he was unable even to come to orgasm while trying to fulfill the "macho" role of being the best lover a woman ever had. And he now declared, "It's no good unless I'm in love." He wanted to be able to express and to receive love through sexual intercourse as well. I am not proposing that the feeling of masculine power was no longer important to him, but rather that it was no longer enough.

Much of the work of the third phase had to do with uncovering the poignancy of his need to be loved and the layers of reaction formation against that need where women were concerned. As these reaction formations were gradually undone and the anger that had accompanied their construction over the years began to dissipate, he could turn to a woman whom he could believe in—Katherine—and experience feelings of need and love with her that were less alloyed with denial and anger. At the height of the Devil obsession, his needs where men were concerned were so powerful that they pressed forward, in spite of his most strenuous attempts to suppress this movement, toward symbolization in terms of sexual intercourse. By the time that he had become more genuinely open to the possibility of symbolizing his needs toward men in physical terms, the shift in the inner balances of his feelings seemed to have rendered the symbol of sexual intercourse with them obsolete and perhaps needlessly complicating. Rather, at this point the kiss—once even more feared than the image of intercourse—seems to symbolize a rich current of sensual feeling retained, but no longer compulsively experienced, in his relations with men.

7
The Symbol of the Devil

One of the reasons I have come to feel that the concept of symbolism is central to an understanding of sexuality is that at the center of the analysis that this book has described and traced was a powerful, millennia-old symbol—the Devil. I have been fortunate in being able to draw upon four excellent volumes tracing the evolution of this symbol by the historian Jeffrey Burton Russel. His first volume (Russel, 1977) deals with the period from antiquity to primitive Christianity. The second (Russel, 1981) treats the Devil in the early Christian tradition. The third (Russel, 1984) takes the Devil in the Middle Ages as the focus. And the fourth (Russel, 1986) deals with the Devil in the modern world.

I think it is clear that, for Frank, the Devil symbolized the complex of wishes and fears around his sexual feelings about men. The symbol of the Devil rose up in Frank's consciousness because certain symbols which would otherwise have expressed the complex of ideas and feelings—whose repudiation was incorporated in the symbol of the Devil—were not available to him. These were homosexual symbols, which invaded the consciousness of his dream life but not of his waking life, in which the symbol of the Devil appeared instead.

The Devil is a cultural symbol with a long and complex tradition that easily absorbs the attention to it reflected in Russel's four volumes. Yet, for Frank, the Devil was also for a time an intensely personal symbol. So, a question worth asking is: Why did the Devil take the place, in Frank's consciousness, of the repressed homosexual symbols? Why did this young man, in the latter part of the twentieth century—a time when the reality of the Devil had for a very long time been only a shadow in people's minds, more theatrical than frightening—become possessed by this ancient symbol? Why was the Devil equated with homosexuality? To try to suggest answers to this question requires touching on some other questions that go beyond the ability of psychoanalysis to answer though not to contemplate.

Let me begin by quoting the opening paragraph in Russel's last volume (Russel, 1986): "The Devil is the best-known symbol of radical evil. The existence of radical evil is clear to anyone not blinded by current relativism. On the world level it expresses itself in the willingness to put the entire planet at nuclear risk. At present, with arsenals of nuclear weapons estimated at seventy times the quantity needed to kill every living vertebrate on earth, we are stubbornly making preparations for a war that will profit no individual nation, or ideology but will condemn thousands of millions to a horrible death. What force urges us down a path that is daily more dangerous? To whose advantage is the nuclear destruction of the planet? Only that force which from the beginning has with infinite cruelty and malice willed the destruction of the cosmos" (p. 17).

At the end of the third volume (Russel, 1984), he notes, "The Devil is a metaphor. Even as such he is not to be dismissed, for we have no access to absolute reality and must always rely upon the metaphors that our minds manufacture from sense observations, reason, and unconscious elements. The idea of the Devil is a metaphor; so is the idea of God, in the sense that anyone's view of God—Christian, Muslim, Hindu, or whatever—is a metaphor for that which passes understanding. Physics, too, is a metaphor. If we transcend the metaphor of the Devil we may arrive at an understanding that is still a metaphor but a metaphor at a deeper level of understanding.

"The most poignant aspect of the problem of evil for Judaism, Christianity, Islam, and all monotheist religions is the reconciliation of God's power and goodness with the existence of evil" (p. 307).

Russel closes this volume with the following: "The Devil is a metaphor for the evil in the cosmos, an evil that is both in God and opposed by God; he represents the transconscious, transpersonal evil that exceeds the individual human evil will; he is the sign of the radical, unmanageable, yet ultimately transcendable evil in the cosmos. We may now be in need of another name for this force. Let it be so, if one can be found. But let it be one that does not evade, blur, or trivialize human suffering" (p. 311).

Almost fifty years ago, on the brink of World War II and the holocaust, Freud, in *Civilization and Its Discontents,* asked if cultural life would yet succeed in mastering the instinct of aggression and self-destruction. He had, by then, formally proposed a dual-instinct theory: Eros, the creative life force, and the destructive instinct. Paradoxically, in spite of witnessing this century of holocausts, people have been reluctant to accept the metaphor of the death instinct, which implies a force for destruction—of self and others—that transcends consciousness.

It must seem strange that a person would attribute to the Devil the responsibility for his sexual wishes. How we might ask, does the symbol for transcendent evil in the universe come to be associated with a person's sexual feelings, which are deeply individual, often not acted out, or even conscious, and not apparently destructive? Years later, when Frank recalled the terror the homosexual feelings had held for him, he wondered at their power to elicit such strong inner condemnation, remarking that, after all, he had done nothing wrong.

Remote as it may appear to be from Frank's problem, the question of the problem of evil for monotheism needs to be considered. This problem was not so deeply troubling for the nonmonotheistic religions of antiquity. Their gods retained more of the moral ambivalence that is characteristically human, while some deities could embody the darker sides of the divine—or human—spirit and some be identified with more benevolent aspects. But even in these religions, the problem of divinely willed evil existed and one response to this problem seemed to be the concept of the "doublet." Russel notes, "The coincidence of opposites, of good and evil, in the God is frequently perceived as necessary. The basic postulate is that all things, good and evil alike, come from the God. But to the extent that people feel that the God is good and do not wish to ascribe evil to him, they postulate an opposition of forces within the godhead. The god principle is still the source of evil, but it is now twinned (literally or figuratively) into a principle of good and a principle of evil—the former usually being identified with the High God, the latter becoming the God's adversary. Such pairs are called 'doublets' " (pp. 57–58). Psychoanalytic theory incorporates precisely such a process in the concept of splitting.

One of many examples that Russel cites is the pair of Egyptian deities, Seth and Horus, who in some versions of the myth were brothers. In the earlier dynasties they were worshiped together and strikingly, sometimes represented as one two-headed deity. Seth tries to kill his brother (also called Osiris) by locking him in a chest and sinking it in the Nile. Isis, however, bears Osiris a son and eventually there is a confrontation between Seth and Horus the Younger. As the myth aged with time, it also changed to the point where the confrontation between Horus and Seth became one between sheer good and sheer evil (Russel, 1977, pp. 81–82).

In his first volume, Russel examines the evolution toward dualism in ancient Hebrew thought. He points out that in the earliest tradition obedience to God's will is the paramount good. God—Yahweh—is depicted as capable of utter mercilessness in his commandments, willing entire populations to be put to the sword. And he could punish transgressions by his own people with equal severity. However a movement toward identifying God with the more benevolent aspects of divine nature, and splitting off the darker side, is seen in the concept of the *mal'ak Yahweh,* the emissary or messenger of God (Russel, 1977, p. 197). That the *mal'ak* is God himself is evident, Russel points out, in the fact that in Exodus, Moses is addressed from the thornbush both by the *mal'ak* and by Yahweh himself, at different times. It is the *mal'ak* who slays the firstborn of Egypt. In 1 Samuel, God sends an "evil spirit" to incite Saul to hurl a javelin at David. And in 2 Samuel, he sends an "angel" to punish his own people through pestilence. But as the angel is about to destroy Jerusalem itself, God repents of the evil that *He* has willed and stays the hand of the *mal'ak,* who, Russel points out, has almost gotten out of control—reflecting the conflict in the divine nature.

In the book of Job it is Satan who "tempts" God to try his faithful servant, and it is with God's permission that Satan, who has liberty to roam the world at will, torments Job. Eventually, Russel notes, the good aspect of God became "the Lord" and the evil aspect became "the Devil." During the Apocalyptic period of about 200 B.C. to 150 A.D., when the Jews suffered under Syrian and Roman rule, the Devil figured prominently, particularly in some of the writings that were eventually not included in the final form of the Hebrew canon. Some of the works of the period indicated that the world was under the power of the Devil but that the Messiah would usher in a new reign of justice (Russel, 1977, p. 176). In one of these books, it is the prince of evil spirits, Matsema, who slays the first-born of Egypt and who proposes to God that Abraham sacrifice Isaac as a burnt offering. In the Apocalyptic literature, as in Christianity, this dualism of good and evil is only temporary. Eventually, evil will be negated at the end of the world, through the will of God. Ultimate dualism is avoided—the good in God's nature triumphs.

In Greek legends of the classical period, the gods could be responsible both for human transgression *and* simultaneously demanding of its punishment. The legend of Oedipus, in fact, is a quintessential expression of this paradox. He was both fated to kill his father and to sleep with his mother and held accountable for these crimes.

I have felt it important to touch on these historical issues and trends because the Devil by whom Frank felt threatened, while it was the Devil of the Roman Catholic tradition in which Frank had been raised, was also a symbol that incorporates more than 2,000 years of history and a deeply felt concern with perplexing existential issues. Insofar as it was a symbol of intractable evil in the universe, the Devil was a personification of a conscious, malevolent will. As such it could symbolize the evil side of human nature.

The Devil and Projection

In its function as a projective screen, the evil that one unconsciously perceives within oneself is attributable to the influence of the Devil. The concept of the "projective screen" is a psychoanalytic interpretation which asserts that a person is repudiating responsibility for unacceptable impulses by making an external agency their author.

However, the doctrine of demonic influence prevalent in early and medieval Christianity presupposed precisely the reverse of projection. It signified *in*jection. In this sense, the fear of the Devil was not, *consciously,* a fear of the self, it is a fear of having something alien and beyond one's control inserted *into* oneself by a malevolent force.

Russel refers to this theme in the Apocalyptic literature, in which subjective psychological states are induced by the Devil: "As long as the dominion of Satan endures . . . the Angel of Darkness leads all the children of righteousness astray" (Russel, 1977, p. 213). In that view, the sins of Israel are the result of Satan's dominion, and Satan is made manifest in the evil inclination, the *yetser ha-ra* within men.

The Devil and Sexuality

There are also elements of an association between sexuality and the personified symbols of evil in the Hebrew literature. This is seen in the myth of the Watcher Angels, the *bene ha-elohim,* "sons of the Lord," who lusted after the daughters of men and who are also associated with the Devil's rebellious challenge to God. In another place, the serpent is accused of precipitating Adam and Eve's fall by poisoning the fruit with lust, the root and beginning of all sin. The Devil and his cohorts are tempters to sin of every kind, but "if fornication overcomes not your mind, neither can Beliar overcome you" (Russel, 1977, pp. 210–11). However, after the Apolcalyptic period, Russel (1981) observes, the Devil became, in Rabbinical tradition, more of an allegory of the human inclination toward evil—opposed by that toward good—rather than a near majestic adversary of God and humankind. The early Christian tradition, however, retained this concept, modifying it to become a struggle between Christ and the Devil.

As the early Christian church evolved, it did so in the direction of hierarchy and authority. St. Ignatius, bishop of Antioch and martyred in 107 A.D., had already enunciated the doctrine that anyone who propagated false doctrines and acted without the bishop's advice and consent adored the Devil. St. Polycarp, martyred in 156 A.D., understood those who disagreed with the emerging orthodoxy—heretics—to be of the Devil. Russel points out that views such as this laid the foundation for the demonization and persecution of heretics and non-Christians in later times.

This tendency to view opposing trains of thought as emanating from the Devil was also seen in the characterization of pagan deities as demons.

One also finds, as a major theme in the writings of the early church Fathers, an explicit association between subjectively felt sexuality and the agency of the Devil. The body itself was not regarded as evil—that was a doctrine that, while frequently proposed, was always rejected as heretical and ultimately inconsistent with the belief in the resurrection of the body. Erotic fantasies and the temptations of lustful thoughts were, however, directly attributed to the Devil. In a very real sense, the Devil injected himself into a man's very mind. Origen, born in Alexandria in 185 A.D., is characterized by Russel as the most inventive diabologist of his time. His devotion to poverty, asceticism, and chastity led *him* to self-castration.

As the monastic movement began, and isolation in the desert was seen as an ideal of Christian devotion, a dominant theme in monastic thought became the Devil as lord of matter, using the human body as the vehicle for his temptations. Having left the temptations of society, monks found that temptation followed in the form of the Devil (Russel, 1981). Demons especially used lust against younger monks and could also send dreams and hallucinations.

In our own cultural terms, some of these assertions seem paranoid in their extravagance. Yet, while extreme, the equation of matter and the body with baseness or even evil was seen in Greek philosophical—though not religious—thought of the pre-Christian era. And secular asceticism was a theme in the late Roman Empire. Early Christianity seemed divided on the subject. The *body* was not evil, but lust could be. And once one had committed oneself to the ascetic life in imitation of Christ, it most emphatically was. I do not think it is possible to know for sure why Christianity, especially in the West, took such a stance on sexuality that was so ambivalent as to be almost completely rejecting of it. However, there are some clues in P. Brown's very thorough study, which traces the theme of sexual renunciation from its beginnings in Christian thought until the fifth century (Brown, 1988).

Symbolic Meanings of Sexual Renunciation

The theme of sexual renunciation seemed to symbolize, as a continuing motif, the view that the *relationship* to God had precedence over any other relationship. The body—through its sexuality—was the medium through which powerful, competing relationships with others could threaten the primacy of the relationship to God. As part of this motif the surrender of sexuality came to symbolize the complete *submission* to God's will and the relinquishment of one's own. The hoped-for ideal was the elimination of all sexual desire, the fading out of sexual fantasy, and the cessation of sexual dreams. When this had been achieved, the monk could truly say to God, ". . . you have possessed my inward parts" (Brown, p. 232). The implied sexual metaphor is not, I believe, accidental, nor is the following utterance by Origen: ". . . oh, that I could be the one who might yet say: His left hand is beneath my head, and his right arm reaches around me" (Brown, p. 174). When, at the age of twenty, Origen had himself castrated, he ensured that no earthly sexual partner could compete with God.

The surrender of one's sexuality, then, symbolizes submission to God in a relationship that will brook no earthly competition. God's rightful claim to one's person was seen in the ideal of virginity epitomized in the doctrine that Mary remained a perpetual virgin. Ambrose, another of the early shapers of church doctrine, cites as justification, the lines of Ezekiel 44:2: "The gate shall be shut, it shall not be opened, and no man shall enter in by it . . . because the lord, the God of Israel hath entered in by it, and therefore it shall be shut" (Brown, pp. 354–55). Insofar as Mary is seen as an ideal for womankind, the claims of God over women's bodies would appear to take precedence over the claims of any mortal lover.

However, God also had claims on men that took precedence over the claims of women's love. Thus in the *Acts of John the Evangelist,* John says to Christ, "Thou who has kept me also till this present hour pure for Thyself and untouched by union with a woman; Who, when I wished to marry in my youth, didst appear to me and say: . . . 'John, if thou were not mine, I should have allowed thee to marry.' " The relationship to God—or Christ—envisaged in these vignettes is as passionate and intense as any sexual relationship and even uses imagery associated with sexual passion. But these are passions that are disembodied, as it were, befitting a relationship to a wholly spiritual deity.

The intensity of the passion for union with the divine is poignantly echoed in the words attributed to Saint Paul (Brown, p. 164): "I could desire to be dissolved and to be with Christ: for it is better." And it was Paul's agonized struggles with the "flesh" that Brown feels served as the template for the conflict-laden Christian view of sexuality. "In all later Christian writing, the notion of the 'flesh' suffused the body with disturbing associations; somehow, as 'flesh,' the body's weaknesses and temptations echoed a state of helplessness, even rebellion against God, that was larger than the body itself" (Brown, p. 48). Four hundred years later, Augustine was to propose the doctrine that the very fact that sexual desire is experienced as beyond one's own willful control symbolized man's first rebellion against God in Eden: ". . . the hiatus between will and sexual feeling had been inflicted on Adam [by God] and on all his descendants as a *poena reciproca,* a punishment to fit the crime. Hence its immense symbolic power" (Brown, p. 416). Sixteen centuries later, Frank was to recall having been sternly warned against "the world, the flesh and the Devil."

It is apparent that, having made sexual renunciation the ultimate symbol of devotion to God, even those who fervently chose this path of devotion suffered severe inner conflicts caused by resurgence of the competing needs for other, earthly partners, needs symbolized by the stirrings of the body's sexuality. Sexuality, then, came to symbolize the rejection of God's claims to precedence over any other possibility of love. In Hindu thought, too, there is the tradition of practicing austerity and sacrifice, including asceticism, to honor a deity or as a prelude to asking for a boon. However, in contrast to the Christian tradition, the temptation to deviate from self-imposed austerity is not attributed to any adversary of the deity. But in a development fateful for Christianity, the Devil—the cosmic adversary of God and Christ—came to be firmly and forever identified as a source of the sexually symbolized human needs that tempted the Christian to swerve from the difficult path of exclusive devotion to God.

With the passage of the centuries, the concept of living a chaste life by those able and willing to perform such a sacrifice, a concept seen in the writings attributed to Paul, seemed to have become increasingly transformed. In this transformation what was once experienced as a difficult path freely chosen became a coercive demand for the surrender of sexual freedom, enjoined and often enforced by external authority and internalized as the critical and prohibiting voice of conscience. It is true that the vast majority of believing Christians did not attempt to live lives of celibacy. But in the religion that nevertheless tempered their world view and that shaped the Christian conscience as it has been passed down from generation to generation, a decisive development had taken place. For Christianity, sexual symbols—with all their complex meaning, evocative power, and expressiveness in human consciousness—had become inextricably tangled with the symbol of ultimate, cosmic evil. As such, these elements formed a multifaceted, multilayered symbol—or symbol complex—such that the evocation of one aspect of this symbol complex was almost sure to evoke the other. I do not think that our civilization has succeeded in separating the two main aspects of this symbol—the sexual and the demonic—to this day. There is, however, another aspect to the symbol of the Devil that is associated with the thematic strand of evil. This is the aspect of the

Devil as a symbol of any kind of rebellion against God, sexual or otherwise—an association that was transformed by the emerging hierarchy of the early church into an opposition to constituted religious authority. This authority with the conversion of Constantine, (Fox, 1986) was to become a formidable establishment.

In consciousness, the Devil became a symbol of evil, lust, and rebellion. These represent some of the main subjectively experienced constituents of the symbol. But from a perspective outside the culture in which the symbol took shape, it is possible to make several additional observations. From a theological point of view the Devil unconsciously symbolized the dark, split-off side of divine nature. From a psychological point of view, repudiated parts of individuals' motivations, for example, sexual impulses, were projected onto the symbol of the Devil—who was perceived as injecting these impulses into consciousness. From a historical point of view, the repudiated aspects of the pre-Christian and non-Christian religions were also associated with the Devil symbol.

The Depiction of the Devil

No picture of the Devil survives from before the sixth century. However, the figure of the Devil is almost always male. In some early depictions, he is seen as a large, dark, muscular man with human hands but with clawed feet and tail. He is usually naked but sometimes wears a loincloth. He is usually black, but sometimes blue or violet. (It is interesting to recall that in one of Frank's dreams, the Devil appears as a blue figure.) The muscularity and nudity imply phallic sexuality. Russel (1981, p. 190) cites Jerome's comparison of the Devil with Behemoth, a huge being with "strength in his loins, force in his navel," and inordinate sexual powers.

The iconography of the Devil also drew on depictions of the repudiated pagan deities. Thus the Copts, Egyptian Christians, often saw demons in likenesses of the Egyptian deities, with human bodies but heads or faces of animals. In the West, the iconographic influence of the minor Greek deity, Pan, was enormous for the depiction of the Devil (Russel, 1977). Pan was the son of Hermes whose symbol was the phallus. In fact, Dover (1978) points out that a stylized "Herm" figure stood outside the entryway to most Athenian homes. It consisted of a stone pillar, surmounted by a head of Hermes and adorned, halfway down with genitals, with the penis erect. The phallic imagery here clearly had a benevolent,protective meaning. It seems ironic that Pan, phallic like his father, but also hairy and goatlike, became something of a model for the Christian representations of the Devil. Pan symbolized sexual passion, even frenzy, sometimes wild and uncontrolled. At the same time, he was a pastoral deity with a gentle side to his nature, associated with the arts and especially music, through his symbol, the flute.

There were other iconographic signs from the Greek and Roman pantheon. The wings often shown on the Devil's legs seem borrowed from Hermes himself. Also, Poseidon's trident was, of course, a frequent prop, for the Devil himself and for subsidiary demons. Vales and glades that were often sacred in classical times came under suspicion as places frequented by demons. It is as if Nature itself became tainted with the demonic, even as the Devil was referred to as "the lord of this world."

Russel (1977) points out that, in Greek myth, as in other traditions, there is an association among sexuality, fertility, the underworld, and even death. Hades presided over the underworld, populated by the souls of the dead; however, he was wed to Persephone, whose emergence thence in the spring coincided with the earth's rejuvenation. And Hermes himself led the dead to the underworld. Russel (1977, p. 128) notes, "Sexual passion, which suspends reason and easily leads to excess, was alien both to the rationalism of the Greeks and to the asceticism of the Christians; a god of sexuality could easily be assimilated to the prince of evil. The association of the chthonic with both sex and the underworld, and hence with death, sealed the union."

Greek culture, in spite of conflict, had been able to accommodate both sexuality and rationalism. The emergent Christian culture, however, did not succeed in finding the means to an analogous accommodation. The struggle against sexuality—which the classical world incorporated in its symbols and world view—found its way into the iconography of the Devil. In many respects, Christianity strove continually to suppress the remnants of the symbols and world view of classical civilization. The homosexual symbols that so troubled Frank are, of course, among the reminders of the classical world view upon which Christianity sought to superimpose itself. The repudiation of homosexuality was only part of the effort to suppress the sexual symbols of the earlier civilization. That effort, I believe, continues to this day as part of the tension between Christianity and the persistent classical elements in our civilization.

The Suppression of Clerical Marriage

Anne L. Barstow (1982) has provided a detailed examination of the debates on the issue of clerical marriage that flared up in the middle of the eleventh century, which eventuated in the destruction of that institution. I am going to argue that the manner in which this issue was resolved can plausibly be viewed as significant both for the meaning of the Devil symbol and for the issues that, centuries later, troubled Frank and continue to trouble others.

I think it may not be realized by many that the majority of priests in the early church are now generally thought to have been married. However, this institution came in for debate in the fourth century. Then, from the fifth century onward, priestly marriage was permitted, but with the proviso that priests not have sexual relations with their wives. That this was an ideal rather than a practical expectation is indicated by the fact that priests, deacons, and subdeacons not only married but regularly fathered children.

Surprisingly, the notion of marriage as a sacrament did not really develop until the late medieval period. Barstow observes that the working definition of marriage had always been the consent of both parties, ratified by sexual intercourse. In fact, even concubinage was not condemned by the medieval church. Early on, a schism between the Western (Latin) and Eastern churches began to become apparent on this issue. In 692, in a ruling reflecting the views of the Eastern majority (Barstow, p. 19), it was declared that there could be marriage before but not after ordination except for monks and bishops (who could never marry) and that priests could and should live with their wives, in contrast to the attempts at enforced separation between husband and wife being made in the Western church. This issue separating the two branches of the church was an important factor in disagreements between them that led to the excommunication in the eleventh century of the Greek patriarch by the emissary of the pope, who compared the Greek church to "the brothel of Jezebel" and declared all priestly marriage to be heresy (Barstow, p. 54).

It was in fact the papacy that spearheaded the renewed drive to destroy clerical marriage, and Barstow points out that Pope Gregory VII was singularly effective in his aggressive use of ecclesiastical legislation toward its destruction. In his first synod in 1074, Gregory decreed that no one would be admitted to orders without a vow of celibacy and actually forbade the laity to attend the services of an unchaste priest. In fact, the concept of cultic purity—purity of the altar—was one of the psychological motivations in the opposition to married priests, even though its theological justification was dubious. As Damian, one of the most aggressive spokesmen of the papal party, succinctly put it: "The hands that touch the body and blood of Christ must not have touched the genitals of a whore" (Barstow, p. 59). In fact, to the Gregorians, all clerical wives were regarded as concubines, not wives. While the rationale was put forward that a priest could not serve both God and a wife, the rhetoric reflected a deeply antisexual and misogynistic position. "A priest's wife is nothing but a snare of the devil, and he also must afterwards pass into the hands of friends and totally perish" (Barstow, p. 38). In all the decrees attempting to enforce clerical chastity, it has been observed none showed the slightest concern for the wives and children of these men.

Pope Gregory and the Gregorians were unrelenting, and Gregory used the hierarchical structure of the church by demanding that individual bishops comply with his decrees or be faced with escalating threats and punishments culminating in excommunication. Succeeding popes kept up the pressure—and the rhetoric. Calixtus II, in 1119, said at the Council of Rheims, "We forbid absolutely the cohabitation with concubines or wives by priests, deacons, or subdeacons. If any of that kind, however, should be found, they are to be deprived of their offices and benefits. . . . Indeed, if they will not have corrected their filthy ways, they should be deprived of Christian communion" (Barstow, p. 47). Leo's earlier anathematizing of married clergy and condemning them to perpetual damnation had not been enough to end the institution. The doctrine of papal infallibility was not officially enunciated until the nineteenth century and in the period under consideration, the papacy was very much a temporal power still. The pope was subject to open criticism and disagreement of a kind that seems unthinkable in our more secular modern times, both by secular authority and the clergy. Thus, when Gregory's celibacy decrees were announced, the German clergy said about him, ". . . the man was clearly a heretic and of unsound mind, who by violent interference would force men to live in the manner of angels, and while denying the ordinary course of nature, would release the restraints on fornication and filthy behavior; that if he should proceed to confirm the decision, they would choose rather to desert their priesthood than their marriages . . ." (Barstow, pp. 68–69).

Barstow notes that another theme in the counterattack against Gregory's moves was the charge that the real papal agenda was not moral reform, but rather the assertion of power; that by forcing men to give up their wives, the movement sought to gain greater control over men's lives. In fact, Barstow sees this as one of the important underlying motivations in that movement, noting that the popes most concerned with asserting papal primacy—Gregory VII, Calixtus II, Alexander III, and Innocent III—were most concerned with priestly celibacy. In this struggle for power, the laity, oddly enough, was more sympathetic to the papal party than to the married clergy because the latter were perceived to be more allied with the immediate secular authorities who ruled and sometimes oppressed them. In the end, the papal party won, as Pope Innocent's ruling at the second Lateran Council in 1139 declared, "[For priests, deacons, subdeacons, canons regular, monks, and lay brothers] we sanction that copulation of this kind, which was contracted against ecclesiastic rule, is not matrimony" (Barstow, p. 47). And now married clergy were effectively prevented from ministering at the altar. Pockets of resistance held out, in parts of Norman England for example, but by the end of the twelfth century, clerical marriage had effectively been wiped out.

The clergy, as Barstow notes, had become a race apart as the ascetic and monastic ideals of the early church were now *forcibly* made the norm for all clergy. Being closer to the angels, as it were, they were seen as superior by the laity, who gradually lost power as priests became more powerful. In the quest for papal primacy and ecclesiastical power, the clergy were forced, in Pope Nicholas's rendering of the phrase from the gospel of Matthew (19:10–12), to become "eunuchs for the kingdom of heaven" (Barstow, p. 109).

In the course of the intensely emotional debates on this issue, the group opposing clerical marriage was sometimes accused of turning a blind eye to the more serious vice of sodomy, or indeed of being sodomites themselves. There does not seem to be much evidence for this charge. Damian, one of the most vituperative critics of women as well as a dedicated opponent of priestly marriage, was vitriolic on the subject of homosexuality as well. Boswell (1980) points out that the period under discussion was a remarkably open one with regard to the expression of love between males, including even homosexual love. However, Boswell also notes that, after the end of the twelfth century, a gradual shutting down of openness and tolerance for these sentiments was seen. I think this development is understandable because the debates on clerical marriage were not about homosexuality versus heterosexuality but rather about sexuality versus chastity. They were also about power—the power to dispose of one's body and to allocate one's feelings as one wished versus a submission to a discipline that regulated both of these. As Barstow asserted, more now than before, "Life was seen as an endless struggle between flesh and spirit, a conflict which Christian thought has not entirely resolved to this day" (Barstow, p. 190).

Psychoanalytic theory might formulate forcing the priesthood to adopt the role of "eunuchs for the kingdom of heaven" as tantamount to castration. And since a succession of popes succeeded in imposing it, it could be understood as a castration at the hands of the father—the Holy Father, to be precise. There was anguish, rage, and open rebellion, but in the end resistance was overcome, and the clergy had to accept their role in the power structure of the church as it consolidated itself further or to be utterly cast out from its protection. These developments had, I think, consequences for the meaning of the already complex and multilayered symbol of the Devil. Subsequent sections will deal with those consequences.

The Devil, Homosexuality, and Politics

In his book on the trial of the Knights Templar, Malcolm Barber (1978) tells that Pope Gregory XII, in 1233, sent letters to several important German dignitaries in order to stimulate action against certain heretics in the Rhineland. These letters detailed description of certain rites associated with their heresy. When a novice entered the sect, he went forward to meet a pallid man with very black eyes and an emaciated figure, whom the novice kissed. After the kiss, "the memory of the Catholic faith totally disappears from his heart." After a meal, the novice, the master, and others of the order would kiss the statute of a cat on the hindquarters. The candles were then extinguished, and there followed "the most disgusting lechery." However, "if by chance those of the male sex exceed the number of women . . . men engage in depravity with men." Candles were lit again, and from the dark corner emerged a man "from the loins upward gleaming more brightly than the sun, so they say, whose lower part is shaggy like a cat and whose light illuminates the whole place." The master then picked something from the novice's clothing and said to the figure,"this which has been given to me I give to you." The figure replied, "You have served me well and will serve more and better" (Barber, p. 180).

The above scenario, Barber pointed out, could have served as the text (and possibly did) for the charges that were brought against the Knights Templar, by Philip IV (the Fair) of France in 1307. These charges had the following preamble: "A bitter thing, a lamentable thing, a thing which is horrible to contemplate, terrible to hear of, a detestable crime, an execrable evil, an abominable work, a detestable disgrace, a thing almost inhuman, indeed set apart from all humanity" (Barber, p. 45). The charges that followed were: First, when the new Templar was received, he denied Christ and was told that, since Christ was a false prophet who was crucified for his sins, there was no hope of salvation through him. The new member was made to spit on the crucifix or on the image of Christ, or to trample or urinate on it. Second, idols were presented. These were in the likeness of a cat, or a head that sometimes had three faces. The head was worshiped as a savior and venerated as a giver of plenty which could make trees flower and land germinate. They touched or encircled it with small cords worn around their waists. Third, they did not believe in the sacraments and Templar priests omitted the words of consecration during mass. Fourth, the Grand Master and other leaders took it upon themselves to hear confessions and absolve from sin. Fifth, new entrants were brought naked to the senior Templar who kissed them on the mouth, navel, stomach, buttocks, and spine. Homosexuality was encouraged or even required. Sixth, the Templars sought gain by any means, lawful or not. And seventh, if a Templar should reveal what happened at meetings to any outsider, he would be imprisoned or killed.

The motives of the king and his chief minister, Guillaume de Nogaret, seemed, in reality, to have been entirely political and venal. The Templars were an international order who had achieved fame in the Crusades in the Holy Land. They were also quite wealthy and, during much of the thirteenth century, acted virtually as royal treasurers to the French monarchy. However, by the end of the century, they had lost that position. They were a celibate order, embodying the ideal of chastity that had gained increased prestige among the laity with the suppression of clerical marriage.

According to Barber, Philip was in constant need of money and had perfected techniques of extortion, accompanied by the blackening of the reputations of his opponents. History seems to concur that the charges against the Templars were groundless. However, Philip had at his command the machinery of the Inquisition, put into place by Pope Gregory IX in the first quarter of the thirteenth century and empowered to use torture by Pope Innocent IV in 1252. The Templars were arrested in a dawn swoop throughout France on October 13, 1307.

Philip eventually achieved his aim of destroying the order and, most important, confiscating most of its properties and those of its members. That Philip customarily used trumped-up charges of heresy and sexual irregularity against political opponents is seen in his attempt to force the then pope, Clement V, to institute an inquiry against his predecessor, Boniface VIII, on the grounds of heresy, witchcraft, magic, and homosexuality. Boniface had been Philip's political opponent and since the late pope's sympathizers remained an influential political force, he wished to discredit his memory by any means possible. Accusations of sexual orgy, Russel (1984) points out, were frequently included in the charges against heretics, who were also assumed to be either consciously in league with the Devil or to be unconsciously serving his ends. Barber, working as a political historian, leaves little doubt that Philip's motives were essentially cynical. Nonetheless, it is very important that the successful manipulation of the Devil symbol and its associations were crucial to his success. In Pope Gregory's letter, the "pallid man," the kissing of whom causes complete forgetting of the Catholic faith, seems transparently demonic. In the scenario imagined for the Templars, the Receptor for the order bestows the kiss. The head is a significant element in this script, recalling its meanings as symbolic of fertility, discussed in Chapter 5.

As we have seen, the enforcement of priestly celibacy required that men had to relinquish a phallic role, both in the sense of sexual intercourse and in the sense of generation and fertility, since they were not permitted to have children. The rituals falsely ascribed to the Templars include the following forbidden elements: rebellion against the teachings and authority of the church; adoration of a symbol associated with phallism and fertility; indulgence in a form of sexuality associated with the suppressed cultures of the classical world. The Devil, while not physically in evidence, is present spiritually so to speak, through these elements with which he is associated.

I do not know if there is any significance to the charge of homosexuality cropping up in both the charges against the Templars and against Pope Boniface. But Barber reports a somewhat enigmatic quote attributed to Bernard Saisset, bishop of Pamiers, who compared Philip to the owl, purportedly chosen by the birds of antiquity because he was the most beautiful. However, the owl was worthless and good for nothing, the bishop observed, adding, "such was our king of France, who was more handsome than any man in the world, and who knew nothing at all except to stare at men" (Barber, p. 29). To presume that this meant that Philip's trumped–up accusations reflected a reaction formation against something in himself that he unconsciously feared would be to presume too much.

It is striking that Frank, who knew neither of the Pope's letter nor the charges against the Templars, dreamt, almost 700 years later, that the man who kissed him turned into—not the priest, the "Father" who actually kissed him behind the altar with such violent passion—but the Devil. Over the intervening centuries, the figure of the Devil seems to have continued to symbolize *something* which, though never enunciated in theological terms, was part of the dark shadow cast by this formidable figure—its unconscious meaning as a power to whom one submits sexually—and homosexually. It is remarkable that Frank intuitively grasped this meaning, suggesting that cultural symbols, even when their meanings are not in consciousness, can color and interpret an inner experience which is also not in consciousness.

Frank was suffering from an obsessional symptom, and the connection between the Devil obsession and the fear of homosexuality had to be painstakingly discovered through psychoanalytic means. Modell (1958) reported on a psychotic patient for whom the Devil was a conscious and dreaded sexual partner. This patient, whose father had been a violent man, believed himself to be possessed by the Devil, saw him in visions, and hallucinated performing fellatio on him.

The imagined initiation ceremony and the papal letter on which it was probably based imply a long historical continuity in the association between the Devil and homosexuality. While Philip may have been indifferent to the truth of these charges, the inquisitors who served him undoubtedly were not. As the church tightened its grip on the clergy through the destruction of clerical marriage in the twelfth century and introduced the systematic use of torture as an instrument of terror against the laity in the thirteenth, could the perception of the goodness of God—whom the church claimed to represent—remain unaffected?

I have proposed that the Devil was a complex symbol with both conscious and unconscious meanings. Some of these meanings could be understood as projections of forbidden impulses within the self, especially sexual feelings and inner feelings of protest and rebellion against church and God. But the meaning of the Devil as symbolizing the split-off dark side of God, that part that permits and even wills human suffering, is not a projection. It is a displacement from God himself to the figure of his chief adversary, his "doublet." The figure of the Devil as he appears in these fantasies—and they were fantasies made up by the clergy—is erotic. However, he is also a power to be reckoned with, one that demands and gets submission. The Devil symbol is then a composite, a condensation in fact of two main constituents—one constituent being made up of projections of forbidden impulses from within the self; the other representing the alien, intrusive, outside force that seizes hold of the self and uses it for its own purposes. These meanings conform exactly to what the Devil symbolized for Frank.

In the destruction of clerical marriage, men were not *invited* to surrender their sexuality, the better to open their hearts to God. Rather, the church forcibly took possession of their bodies and ruled their most cherished earthly relationships to be "filthy" and "not marriage." The perceived difference between this kind of authoritative control over body and soul and possession by the Devil must have been measurably diminished. The Inquisition, in turn, perpetrated tortures that could rightly be described as "devilish" against laity suspected of heresy.

The hierarchy of the church was essentially male; the inquisitors were male; the pope was male; the God they presumably served was male; and so was the Devil. Greenberg (1988) theorizes that the suppression of clerical marriage intensified the pressure to channel sexual need into homosexual outlets. The tightening up of the strictures against homosexuality was, he feels, an unforeseen but understandable outcome of this increased pressure. While I would not disagree with this,

I would propose an additional explanation, one at a different level of meaning. The figure of the male was becoming more powerful and more destructive, more of a threat to emotional fulfillment and even physical safety. The dangers to life and liberty from arrogant princes, invading armies, and marauding brigands had always to be reckoned with. As the church sought to extend its control over people's lives, wishing to penetrate into the most private places of their minds, it too could threaten life, and most certainly liberty.

I am proposing that the increasingly strict prohibitions against the taking of a male sexual object—against homosexuality—reflected the growing hatred of the male by people whose lives were oppressed by male authority and a male deity. Consciously, they owed obedience and perhaps even reverence to the men who ruled them, and most certainly to the God in whose name these men ruled. Their fear and hatred of these men and even of God himself was, I am proposing, moved onto—displaced onto—the figure of the Devil, whose phallic aspect symbolized the quintessential expression of the invasive power of both God and church.

But there was another class of beings that the Inquisitors were even more concerned with than they were with so-called "sodomites"—a class of beings who were, by their most essential nature, given to consorting with the powerful, hated male that the Devil symbolized. These beings were women.

The Devil During the Witch Craze

We are fortunate in having an excellent, even loving, translation of the major and definitive treatise on witchcraft of the Late Middle Ages. The treatise in question is *Malleus Maleficarum* ("The Hammer of the Witches"), written by two Dominican monks, Heinrich Kramer and Johann Sprenger. First printed in 1489, the work was commissioned by no less than Pope Innocent VIII. It was intended to be the definitive handbook on witchcraft, detailing how witches were recruited, how the Devil and his subsidiary demons worked their evil will with their assistance, and how suspected witches were to be interrogated and dealt with. The date of this work (1489) is noteworthy—by this time the Renaissance had been in full swing, and the contract between the two universes—that of the cool classicism and pagan voluptuousness of the one, and the demon-driven visions of hellish carnality of the other—is stunning. It was also a period on the brink of the Reformation.

The first English translation of this work, which went through ten printings before 1669, was not until 1928. The translation was by the Rev. Montague Summers, (Summers, 1928), whose admiration for the authors of the work—which he regarded to be as timely in 1928 as it had been in 1489—was only surpassed by his admiration for the pontiff, Innocent VIII, who had sponsored it. The Rev. Summers, who saw the worldwide conspiracy of witches operating in modern Bolshevism as well, agreed fully with the authors of the *Malleus,* in refuting those skeptics who did not give credence to the reality of witchcraft. Kramer and Sprenger had observed, "Therefore those err who say that there is no such thing as witchcraft, but that it is purely imaginary, even although they do not believe that devils exist except in the imagination of the ignorant and the vulgar, and the natural accidents which happen to a man he wrongly attributes to some supposed devil. For the imagination of some men is so vivid that they think that they see actual figures and appearances which are but the reflections of their thoughts, and then these are believed to be the apparitions of evil spirits or even the spectres of witches" (Kramer & Sprenger, 1489, p. 2).

The above passage, except for the phrase, "those err" would strike the modern student of psychology as an excellent explanation for delusions and hallucinations. However, the passage quoted above continues, "But this is contrary to true faith, which teaches us that certain angels fell from heaven and are now devils, and we are bound to acknowledge that by their very nature they can do many wonderful things which we cannot do. And those who try to induce others to perform such evil wonders are witches. And because infidelity in a person who has been baptized is technically called heresy, therefore such persons [who reject the reality of witchcraft] are plainly heretics" (pp. 2–3).

This last passage is truly chilling. It signals that the authors are in a world of faith that is impervious to the rules of empirical evidence, and the skeptic is reminded that to insist upon such rules of evidence is technically—in fact plainly—heretical. Such a reminder at a time when the Inquisition's branding of a person as a heretic could lead to the stake was surely meant to give dissenters pause. The authors were equally clear about the divinely decreed penalty for witchcraft—death.

In conformity to well-established doctrine, the authors state that the actions of both the Devil and of witches are only possible with the sanction of God. The witch, however, always willfully entered into a pact with the Devil who, in turn, did not actually need witches to do his evil deeds but ensnared them to effect the perdition of their souls. Witchcraft was differentiated from all other heresies by this conscious, willful pact. Four actions characterized this "abominable evil": First, to renounce the Catholic faith; second, to devote themselves body and soul to all evil; third, to offer up unbaptized souls to Satan; and fourth, "to indulge in every kind of carnal lust with Incubi and Succubi and all manner of filthy delights" (pp. 20–21).

In conformity to long philosophical tradition that bodily and material things were on a lower scale than pure and spiritual intelligence, which plane both angels and devils occupied, devils were deemed able to control what was beneath them. So, they cold collect and make use of human semen. As the treatise progresses, it becomes apparent that sexuality occupies a central position in transactions between humans and the Devil or his agents. They observe, "And although they have a thousand ways of doing harm, and have tried ever since their downfall to bring schisms in the Church, to disable charity, to infect with the gall of envy the sweetness of the acts of the Saints, and in every way to subvert and perturb the human race; yet their power remains confined to the privy parts and the navel. For through the wantonness of the flesh they have much power over men; and in men the source of wantonness lies in the privy parts since it is from them that semen falls, just as in women it falls from the navel" (pp. 23–24). They quote St. Augustine as testifying to the fact that satyrs and fauns ("which are commonly called Incubi") had appeared to wanton women and obtained visitations with them, another indication of the demonization of the figures of classical mythology.

The authors assert that it is upon the venereal act that the Devil is allowed to cast a spell rather than upon any other human act. They say, ". . . the foulest venereal acts are performed by such devils, not for the sake of delectation, but for the pollution of the souls and bodies of those to whom they act as Succubi or Incubi.

". . . although the Scripture speaks of Incubi and Succubi lusting after women, yet nowhere do we read that Incubi and Succubi fell into vices against nature. We do not speak only of sodomy but of any other sin whereby the act is wrongfully performed outside the rightful channel. And the very great enormity of such as sin in this way is shown by the fact that all devils equally, of whatever order, abominate and think shame to commit such actions.

"And it seems that the gloss on Ezekiel XIV means this, where it says, 'I will give thee into the hands of the dwellers in Palestine, that is devils, who shall blush at your iniquities, meaning vices against nature. And the student will see what should be authoritatively understood concerning devils. For no sin has God so often punished by the shameful death of multitudes" (pp. 29–30).

As to why there were so many more female witches than men, they explain that women are feebler than men in mind and body and are more carnal. There follow citations from many sources, including pre-Christian ones—the level of scholarship in the treatise is impressive—on the defects of women and how men's need for them leads to grave problems. They note, "If we inquire, we find that nearly all of the kingdoms of the world have been overthrown by women." And, "There is no man in the world who studies so hard to please the good God as even an ordinary woman studies by her vanities to please men." And still, ". . . without the wickedness of women, to say nothing of witchcraft, the world would still remain proof against innumerable dangers" (p. 46).

Their version of the Fall is unequivocal in fixing blame: "For though the devil tempted Eve to sin, yet Eve seduced Adam. And as the sin of Eve would not have brought death to our soul and body unless the sin had afterwards passed on to Adam, to which he was tempted by Eve, not by the devil, therefore she is more bitter than death (p. 47). And further, ". . . since the first corruption of sin by which man became a slave of the devil came to us through the act of generation, *therefore greater power is allowed by God to the devil in this act than in all the others*" (p. 48). ". . . God allows the devil more latitude in respect of *this act, through which sin was first spread abroad,* than of other human acts." (Italics added.)

In these passages, it appears that the concept of the original sin of disobedience has been overshadowed or confused with the sexual act. In this act, woman stands implicated: "To conclude, all witchcraft comes from carnal lust, which in women is insatiable" (p. 47). And even love is gravely suspect. St. Jerome is cited: "He who loves his wife to excess is an adulterer. And they who love in this way are more liable to be bewitched" (p. 170). ". . . infatuate love proceeds from the evil works of the devil" (p. 52).

In all these passages, two major themes stand out. The first is the Devil's motivation in the recruitment of witches. That is clear: to harm the Catholic faith. The second is the means vital to the achievement of this end. That also is clear: sexual seduction by the Devil or a surrogate, in male guise (Incubus) to seduce women; in female guise (Succubus) to seduce men, keeping in mind that even devils would shrink from committing vices "against nature" (homosexuality and acts other than vaginal intercourse).

Of the various meanings of the Devil symbol, these two are paramount, opposition to the church; and illicit sexuality, for all sex outside of marriage was a mortal sin. The Devil is the quintessentially evil, sexual—phallic—fallen divinity, who uses sexuality not for his pleasure but to degrade and corrupt humankind and to wean it away from the true faith. It is human weakness, especially unbridled female lust, that makes the body—specifically the genitals—the gateway to the soul.

The zeal with which the inquisitors pursued their mission is appalling. Russel (1984) estimates that between 1400 and 1700, 100,000 people were put to death, most by burning after having endured torture, and most were women. This was a movement whose motive forces seem to have been far more irrational than were Philip's in his destruction of the Templars. Greed is understandable and can be satisfied, if not satiated, when its goals have been fulfilled. Philip brought down a wealthy order of influential men in order to expropriate their property. The witchcraft craze hauled in victims primarily from the poor and powerless classes, and especially poor old women. Lacking any rational goal, the process of suspicion, torture, and conviction could go on indefinitely.

Russel points out that the witchcraft mania was primarily promoted by the educated elite—the scholastics and the inquisitors. Interestingly, the authors of the *Malleus* note that there are three classes of people that witches cannot harm: those who carry holy water, those blessed by the holy angels, and significantly, those (like themselves) who administer public justice against witches. And even more significantly, they add that witchcraft is not practiced by learned men (like themselves) but by the altogether uneducated. I do not think one needs to be a Marxist to get the point.

It also cannot escape one's notice that the educated elite who ferreted out and condemned witches came from the class that an earlier pope had extolled as "eunuchs for the kingdom of heaven." Even as Sprenger and Kraemer convicted women of lewd sexual connections with the Devil, they were aware of the battles that men of their own class had daily to fight. Fortunately, some were aided by the holy angels who purified them in their genital functions so that witches could not affect them in those functions. They also spoke of how the "gift of chastity" had been bestowed on several holy men, taking away all feeling from their sexual organs, or through the illusion of having their testicles removed; with the desirable result of eliminating all sexual desire, "that natural desire which is aroused even in babes and sucklings" (p. 95).

That the church would have fought deviation in matters of faith even with the cynical motive of maintaining its power would be understandable. That the church in the late fifteenth century might feel anxiety about the potential for great cultural changes that might weaken faith—the Renaissance and the early warning signs of the Reformation—is also understandable. But the witchcraft mania did not seem to be addressing any serious social or even theological issues. It was addressing, it seems, psychological issues, and psychological issues that were pertinent, not for the laity, but for the clerical body of the church itself, for its professional membership rather than for its congregation. I would propose that the toll exacted by the need to be "eunuchs for the kingdom of heaven" was too heavy to bear, both for the institution itself and for many individuals in it, just as the defenders of clerical marriage had predicted. However, in spite of the deep misogyny expressed in the witchcraft mania, the heart of the matter, the real enemy, was in the end, the Devil, or more precisely what he symbolized—not the women who were the chief victims of the inquisitors' mania.

The Devil Symbol: Conscious and Unconscious Meanings

Throughout this book, it has been consistently held that symbols have meanings at both conscious and unconscious levels. For Frank, it was the unconscious meaning of the Devil symbol that gave it its aura of uncanny feeling and its obsessive character. But Frank, though a Catholic, had never been devout and was living in a secular age when the Devil symbol had lost much of its power as a focus for the expression of religious fervor or moral concern. However, in the time when *Malleus Malificarum* made its appearance, the Devil remained a significant rallying point for religious feeling. Nevertheless, as its authors acknowledged, there was also skepticism—not about the reality of the Devil, but rather about the reality of witchcraft.

Johannes Weyer was born about a quarter of a century after the *Malleus* was published and in 1563, as a mature physician, Weyer published his *De Praestigiis Daemonum.* There is no English translation of this two-volume work, but G. Zilboorg (1969) has given an excellent summary of Weyer's views. These views were that so-called witches were utterly incapable of doing any harm by supernatural means. He bluntly referred to the propositions of Kramer and Sprenger as "silly and often godless absurdities . . ." (Zilboorg, p. 118). His own point of view, he asserted, was completely opposite to theirs. Weyer was the personal physician of the enlightened and liberal Duke Wilhelm of Jülich-Cleve-Berg upon whose protection he could count. (While the Inquisition could condemn a heretic, it had to depend on secular authority to be willing to carry out the sentence.)

Certainly Weyer felt that many accusations of witchcraft were entirely groundless. However, he was a careful investigator and felt that some women actually had the delusion of being able to perform harmful acts through supernatural means. These delusions he attributed in some cases, to natural causes, such as illness or toxic substances. As Zilboorg points out, however, Weyer was also a psychiatrist in the best sense of the word, combining medical knowledge and remarkable psychological acumen with a pragmatic and compassionate temperament. In one sense only could he be said to differ from his modern psychiatric counterparts. He was sufficiently of his time to view the Devil seriously as a force that could and did operate in the everyday world. His views are succinctly expressed in his assertion, ". . . that witches can harm no one through the most malicious will or the ugliest exorcism, that rather their imagination—inflamed by the demons in a way not understandable to us—and the torture of melancholy makes them only fancy that they have caused all sorts of evil." And addressing the duke, who is sympathetic to this point of view, he remarks, "You do not, like others, impose heavy penalties on perplexed, poor old women. You demand evidence, and only if they have actually given poison bringing about the death of men or animals, do you allow the law to take its course" (Zilboorg, p. 119). He was forthright in condemning cruelty when perpetrated by Christians and, especially, by the clerical demonologists, whom he contemptuously referred to as the "encowled." It was they who were truly the servants of the Devil in the sense of doing the kind of evil the Devil willed. Weyer's book enjoyed some success and went through several printings, the last, five years before his death. However, he was listed on the Index of 1596 as an author whose works were prohibited in their totality. As of the 1969 edition of Zilboorg's book, his name had not been removed.

I have felt it important to cite Weyer's views because they demonstrate that even a cultural symbol as powerful as the Devil was not experienced uniformly by everyone in the culture. For Weyer, its meaning seemed to be confined to its *consciously* acknowledged meanings as the chief opponent of Christ on the one hand and, on the other, the personification of willful evil and malice. It is undoubtedly relevant that Weyer, unlike the authors of the *Malleus,* had no stake in maintaining the power and prestige of the church hierarchy, nor was he bound by any vow of celibacy. Evil he conceptualized as the perpetration of injustice and unwarranted cruelty. That he was not concerned with that part of the symbol that referred to the Devil's inspiration of heresy is seen in his proposing that Christians could take lessons in compassion and mercy from barbarians such as Alexander the Great and Saladin.

For Kramer and Sprenger, too, the Devil was Christ's chief adversary. For them, too, he was the personification of evil. Evil, however, in this instance seemed to be mainly defined as opposition to the articles of the Catholic faith, of whose power structure they were a part, and as instigation to carnal lust. In their measured and deliberate exposition of the orderly steps in which torture should be used against suspects, in their chillingly casual reference to "those whom we have caused to be burned . . ." there is no evidence that evil was defined as the deliberate inflicting of pain and suffering upon sentient beings.

However, their obsessive and unrelenting persecution of the women (and men) whom they suspected of being the Devil's consorts and collaborators could be taken to be fairly indicative of the operation of unconscious motivations. These motivations, I am proposing, had to do with the *unconscious* meanings of the Devil symbol that were particularly relevant to the priesthood rather than to the laity.

I would like to begin by focusing on the indispensable element in the contract between Devil and witch, her lust-driven accession to sexual intercourse with Incubi, the male personifications of the Devil himself or of his demons. (With men, the Devil assumed a female shape.) These accusations, in their extravagance and inaccessibility to reason and the normal rules of evidence, seem like grotesque exaggerations of neurotic jealousy, precisely the kind of jealousy from which Frank suffered. In Frank, it was shown that his jealousy was motivated chiefly by his unconscious reactions to the male in the fancied triangle, not by the behavior of his wife or girlfriend.

The iconography of the Devil leaves no doubt that he is male and either human or humanoid in form, with the phallic figure of Pan serving as one of the most widely used models for how he was pictured. The Devil, then, was a male of inordinate sexual powers, as St. Jerome had long ago observed. And he and his cohorts had the power to torment Christians by injecting lustful thoughts into their minds and were even able to enter the body through its orifices. Again and again it seems apparent that destructive phallic power was an important component of the Devil symbol. That part was in fact conscious. What was unconscious was the relationship between the witch-hunters and this destructive phallic figure.

A further clue to this relationship may be provided by Russel's observation that the figure of the Incubus arose from scholastic theory and had not been important before the twelfth century, the century when clerical marriage was once and for all suppressed. That the cold-hearted and celibate inquisitors were yet capable of feeling lust is indicated in their envy of those holy men who, by grace, had been relieved of all genital sensation. Nevertheless, few had chosen to follow Origen's third-century example and literally make of themselves "eunuchs for the kingdom of heaven." In the imaginations of these men Incubi were constantly committing the "filthy" acts that they themselves had renounced. I think it would be reasonable to conclude that part of the relation between these persecutors of women and the Devil was an unconscious identification with his phallism, forbidden to them by church authority and therefore experienced as evil.

However, that element does not, I think, exhaust the components in the unconscious meanings of the Devil symbol for the Inquisitors. The protests, bitterness, and rebellion against the papal attacks on clerical sexuality are well documented. The history of psychoanalysis attests to the enormous difficulties and problems attendant upon the attempt to repress the exercise of the sexual function. The spiritual and material motivations that drew men to holy orders obviously did not imply an ability to give up eroticism without a struggle in any but a few. This must have been especially true in the medieval period when clerical vocations were so important as avenues to security, mobility, and power.

Consciously, the Devil was seen as seducing people to renounce the Catholic faith. Yet, it was this faith itself that imposed the rigors of celibacy. The Devil was also the chief rebel against God. This aspect of the symbol lent itself to the other major projective element in the Devil symbol—rebellion against the rigors of the faith and against the papal authority which had been decisive in the suppression of priestly sexuality. The spiritual authoritarianism of the medieval church and its brutality in dealing with heresy must have had a chilling effect even in the privacy of an individual's thoughts. Hence, the Devil could symbolize the unconscious suppressed and heretical dissent within the self.

We come again to a third and one of the most significant unconscious meanings of the Devil symbol: its meaning as a displacement of the perception of the evil in God.

In Freud's hypothesis of the primeval father, only he was permitted to be phallic. He kept the women to himself and threatened the sons with castration if they attempted to approach them. Eventually the rebellion came in which the sons rose up and killed their father, and traces of this guilt, Freud felt, linger in the memory of the human race. Anthropological research and theory have not dealt kindly with this hypothesis. Nevertheless, even if it is regarded as a myth, I think it is a myth which demonstrably carries some psychological truth. That elements of the myth—or primeval history, depending on one's preferences—were present in the medieval church seems self-evident.

In the history of the medieval church prior to the witchcraft mania, the Holy Father had wielded *his* power to take away the "sons' " sexual right to women. In the lore of diabology, submission of a sexual sort was always part of yielding oneself up to the Devil. This submission could be in direct sexual intercourse, as women were charged with, or, in men, it could be in the "obscene kiss," the *osculam infame,* where the Devil or his surrogate was kissed on the genitals or buttocks. The church required the "sexual submission" of its sons, just as the Devil did. But whereas the Devil forced initiates to engage in sex, the Holy Father demanded that his sons refrain from it. The end result was the same—subservience to a more powerful male.

It may seem paradoxical to suggest that the phallic figure of the Devil could symbolize even the dark side of the supreme head of the church, who presumably reigned under the banner of chastity. But the anthropological and historical data demonstrate that the phallus can symbolize destructive power as one of its meanings. The phallic power of the Devil, in that sense, would have connoted ruthless papal power, not papal sexuality. However, in a supremely ironic historical coincidence, Innocent VIII, whose papal bull ordering unquestioned compliance with his inquisitors Kramer and Sprenger made little effort to hide its tone of brutal menace, married his son Franceschetto to the daughter of Lorenzo de' Medici in great splendor at the Vatican in 1488—one year before the publication of the *Malleus Maleficarum* (Summers, 1928).

Strikingly, this equation of papal authority and the Devil was sometimes openly implied in a satirical genre of the thirteenth and fourteenth centuries, the so-called Devil's letter. Among its purposes, Russel says, was to satirize the corrupt morality of ecclesiastics, especially the Roman curia. From the fourteenth century on, the satire became more political, attacking the governance of the church by papal authority. Russel (1984, p. 88) cites the following satirical salutation, modeled on the preamble of a papal or other legal charter: "Satan, emperor of the realms of hell, king of shadows, and duke of the deepest district of the damned, to his most faithful servant John Dominici, archbishop of Ragusa and abettor of all our works, sends good health and eternal pride." The most famous letter was the "Epistola Luciferi," composed in 1351 and widely circulated. It began, "To all members of our kingdom, the sons of pride, particularly the princes of the modern church . . ." and concludes, dated "at the center of the earth in our shadowy kingdom, in the presence of hordes of demons specially summoned for this purpose to our treacherous consistory" (p. 89).

In fact, the proposal that the Devil symbolized the hated and resented side of papal authority in some *literal* sense is an unprovable hypothesis. However, the image of the powerful and potentially destructive male constitutes an enduring theme in male psychology, with the phallus capable of symbolizing that power. This image existed before the Christian era and exists in regions where monotheism has been unknown. In the Devil symbol the image of the destructive male, with the phallus the premier symbol of that destructiveness, seems to have attained something of an apotheosis. Why?

I have tried to show that the escalating demands for sexual renunciation by the hierarchy of the Western church can plausibly be understood to have been experienced by the clergy as an inexorable encroachment by the powerful male representatives of a male deity. These powerful male figures demanded the subordination of the individual's will in an all-consuming relationship whose only rewards were forcibly desexualized. I have argued that the Devil symbolized not only the sexual impulses forbidden by these male authorities and the suppressed rebellion against them, but also the hated and feared aspect of these powerful males—an aspect that was split off and displaced onto the Devil, who could be overtly hated and resisted. Because the Devil obsession sprang from an inner conflict impossible to resolve, the energy that fed it was inexhaustible—as long as it could be replenished by a continuous supply of victims. The Enlightenment and the increasing secularization of society eventually put a stop to the witch-hunts and the burnings. But the Devil is far from dead. Rather, he seems to live on in secularized if less majestic forms. One of these forms, as the case of Frank demonstrated, is encountered in the revulsion against homosexuality.

8
Symbolism, Culture, and Sexuality

In the previous chapter I tried to show how the symbol of the Devil—itself a powerful metaphor for transcendent evil in the universe and simultaneously a symbol of the part of God that tolerated or even instigated human suffering—historically came to symbolize a rather different set of concerns. In its function as a symbol for that aspect of deity that permitted or even willed evil the Devil was eminently suited to symbolize the unconscious side of other important and ambivalently regarded relationships. I tried to show how the figure of the Devil could have come to symbolize not only the forbidden and therefore repressed feelings within the men of the church, but simultaneously, the powerful male figures who were the prohibitors—and whose very prohibitions led to the repression of those feelings. These powerful male figures included both the church hierarchy and the male deity whom they served.

The manner in which Christianity evolved seems to me to have fostered and perpetuated a sense of oppression by powerful males and thus reinforced the image of the powerful, destructive male that is both a concrete reality in human history and a menacing shadow on the fringes of human consciousness. In ways that I discussed in the last chapter, sexuality became the focus and the phallus the prime instrument of the Devil's destructive power.

In our contemporary society, the Devil is no longer a frequently used symbol of baleful evil, except in more evangelical interpretations of Christianity. But the revulsion against homosexuality is widespread. In my chapter on bisexuality, I argued that the rejection of Freud's views on bisexuality was based on this revulsion against the hypothesized homosexual capacity that Freud felt was universal. I would now state that this purely secular revulsion against homosexuality can also be understood as symbolic and that it symbolizes precisely the same thing that the Devil obsession symbolized for Frank—and the men of the church—*fear of the destructive, phallic male.* For Frank, the bartender figure eventually replaced the Devil in symbolizing that man. He saw that type of man as cruel, selfish, exploitive—and sexually charismatic to women. In consciousness, he felt only jealousy with regard to this figure, not fear. However, the fear emerged in his dream where he was afraid of the handsome criminal to whom Jenny, in the dream, was attracted, as he accused her of being in waking life.

That the fear of the destructive, phallic man is a central meaning symbolized by the revulsion against homosexuality is more clearly evident in the less highly educated strata of our society who do not have access to the better rationalized defenses of the psychologically more sophisticated classes. Thus, in prison, the "wolf," as he used to be called (Sykes, 1958), embodied this figure—calculating and predatory, he manipulated or bullied weaker men into surrendering to his desires. The "wolf" was understood to play the phallic, penetrating role, and not thought any less manly because of his homosexual predilections. In fact, Sykes pointed out, he was not himself considered to "be" homosexual. Rather he forced or persuaded *others* to be—if only temporarily.

P. H. Gebhard et al. (1965) of the Institute for Sex Research founded by Kinsey reflected on the meaning of contact with the phallus of another man in our culture at a time when homosexuality was still illegal in most states in this country. They observed, in considering who might or might not be arrested for homosexual acts, "Apparently the crux of the matter is this: the man bringing the other man to orgasm is the 'real' homosexual; the man being brought to orgasm is not. To put it another way, the policeman may feel that seeking an orgasm is not really blameworthy even in a homosexual situation, but that being interested in bringing another male to orgasm is an unmitigated perversion" (pp. 324–25.) The masculinity of the person who comes into contact with the phallic "other" and brings him to orgasm is seen as compromised or damaged by this destructive contact.

When we compare this attitude to the rites of Sosom among the Marind-anim, where the first step along the prolonged ritual initiation into manhood begins with the boys undergoing promiscuous anal intercourse all night long, it seems impossible to ignore the profound importance of culture for understanding the meaning of sexual imagery and action; it also emphasizes the futility of discussing sexual imagery and action without reference to meaning.

If we consider the sexual action of intercourse between a man and a young adolescent boy, it becomes clear how culture can assign radically different meanings to the same action. In our culture, a sexual action of this kind symbolizes the gross sexual abuse of a minor. Among the Marind, it symbolized the beginning of the boy's initiation into men's secret rites and of the passage into the world of the adult male head-hunter.

The anthropologist Clifford Geertz has regarded symbolism as central in his approach to cultural analysis (Geertz, 1973). Geertz views culture as "an historically transmitted pattern of meanings embodied in symbolic forms by which men communicate, perpetuate, and develop their knowledge about and attitudes towards life" (p. 89). Meanings, he points out, are stored in symbols, a view that is thoroughly consistent with the approach taken in this book and wholly applicable to the cultural component of sexual symbols. The Sosom ritual does indeed "store" meanings that are *directly* experienced no more than once a year during the *déma*'s annual visit. The term *sexual abuse* also "stores" a set of meanings that the culture strives to prevent the young from ever directly experiencing.

Geertz also considers the concrete symbols of religion. He says, "They both express the world's climate and shape it. They shape it by inducing in the worshipper a certain distinctive set of dispositions . . . which lend a chronic character to the flow of his activity and the quality of his experience" (p. 95). This statement seems most applicable to the symbol of the Devil in the early Christian era and medieval periods.

But what Geertz says of the concrete symbols of religious belief can also be applied, I think, to sexual symbols. Is it really possible to speak of, let us say, male psychosexual development without taking into account the shaping effect of cultural symbols? To consider this question further, I would like to turn to P. Blos's views of the resolution of the negative Oedipus complex. (Blos, 1985.) The issues he addresses are certainly directly relevant to the case of Frank. Blos identifies the early, preoedipal period as one in which the little boy's relationship has no element of competitiveness and exists alongside an analogous relationship with the mother. He terms these parallel, noncompetitive relationships, "dyadic," as opposed to the triangularity—with its competitiveness and ambivalence—of the "triadic" Oedipus complex.

Freud (1923b) also took note of the early, preoedipal relationship between the boy and his father, and described it as characterized by a direct and immediate identification. This direct identification is distinguished by Freud from the later identification that replaces the sexualized feeling toward the father as well as rivalry with him. In any case, Blos notes that the dyadic, or preoedipal, relationship fuses into the later negative Oedipus complex. Like Freud and most other analytic theorists, he feels that the "positive" Oedipus complex of the boy is resolved at the beginning of latency. However, in contrast, he feels the negative Oedipal feelings, fused with the earlier dyadic complex, await adolescence for their resolution. The strength of the revived early feelings for the father can be frightening to the boy. One of the reasons for this is that, with the onset of puberty, these feelings get drawn into the physical realm, generating homosexual trends. In the terms of this book, these feelings tend toward finding expression in sexual symbols. When the unconscious longing for the father is at its height, Blos says one is likely to see a sort of compulsive, emotionally shallow, heterosexual behavior that is essentially defensive and typified in the "one-night stand." In other words the culturally approved heterosexual symbols replace the homosexual ones that the longing for paternal love would generate. As Frank said, "You can't love a man. That's wrong. You love a woman."

Blos sees it as an essential developmental step that the boy surmount the longing for the father that would either keep him as a boy in search of a father forever—or, by displacement, lead toward a homosexual solution. (In this concern, he reflects our cultural stance.) The working through of this complex is marked by the consolidation of the adult ego ideal, which then has the function of blocking displacement onto the homosexual solution: "In the case of the male isogender [same sex] attachment emotions a homosexual potential is either fleetingly or more lastingly evoked. This disquieting emotion is diverted by the formation of the adult ego ideal, which by its consolidation affirms its roots in the narcissistic sector of the personality and carries it forward as a self-acknowledged system of guiding principles devoid of object libido. This task is accomplished by the male adolescent in his resolution of the isogender dyadic and triadic complex" (p. 152).

Not only is dealing with the father complex a very important issue in therapy with adolescents, but Blos notes that it also makes its appearance regularly in the analysis of adult men as well. I would certainly attest to this, not only through my work with Frank, but also with most other men I have worked with. In fact, I am prepared to believe that Blos has drawn attention to an issue for male psychology that is present in all cultures and has at least as much general significance as the positive Oedipus complex.

However, although the issue of the boy's confrontation with the multilayered father complex at adolescence undoubtedly has genuine universality, the way in which this confrontation is handled is culturally specific and variable. Blos's observation that the ego ideal diverts the "disquieting homosexual potential" of this complex might be true, but I think it must be acknowledged that our culture offers the adolescent little other choice. However that did not seem to be the case among the Greeks, where the boy was permitted to effect precisely this kind of displacement of the father complex onto a relationship where he took the role of *eromenos* to an older male's *erastes*. Among the Marind-anim, the boy had a special relationship with his *binahor*-father, who called him "son," and for whom the boy was, for a while, a sexual partner. The fact that the *binahor*-father was, where possible, the boy's maternal uncle indicates that the displacement from the father himself was not very distant.

It seems to me that the sexual symbols a culture provides—or forbids—to its young have the power to affect consciousness, identity, defense, and what inner emotional trends will be allowed to grow or be nipped in the bud. Would a Greek boy in Athens of 500 B.C. have to indulge in the frantic pursuit of some equivalent of heterosexual "one-night stands" in order to fight off the implications of his father complex? I think not because accepting the role of *eromenos* would not have represented taking on an identity that was either invidious in his society or that prevented him from looking forward to adult married life. However, since entering into a sexual relationship with an older male would have exactly those consequences in our culture, a sexual solution to the issues surrounding the father complex must be ruled out.

My own view has gradually become that the so-called Oedipal issues are, in reality, lifelong ones since they manifest themselves at different stages of male life in different areas—family; emotional and sexual relationships in adolescence and adulthood; work; and in social and political life. And I would agree with André Green (1979) when he asserts that the negative Oedipus complex necessarily refers back to the positive, and that it is the essential nature of the complex never to exist in the simple state but in the double.

While the core Oedipal issues remain constant, the different contexts in which they are experienced radically modify how they are expressed and handled. Here is an example of what I mean. A young man I worked with for a while had, when he was seventeen and still in high school, run away from home with a male teacher who had been giving him lessons in a specialized field. The boy had been having some difficulties with a domineering father, and there were other tensions in the home as well. He telephoned his parents and told them that he would be living with this teacher and that he (the boy) was gay. The teacher, in fact probably old enough to be his father, had promised to help him achieve proficiency in his field and to open up many doors of professional opportunity to the boy. The reality turned out to be much less rewarding. He was selfish, demanding, and alcoholic, and did not come through on his promises. In addition, the boy felt no physical attraction for him. However, he tried to convince himself and even the teacher that he was indeed gay, to the extent of submitting to an attempt at anal intercourse that was cut short when he found it painful. After a little time, he left the teacher and returned home. He began to date, became engaged while in college, and married around graduation.

The cultural context strongly affected how this young man consciously experienced what he was doing. There were major psychological issues that both Greek and Melanesian patterns took into account. The older man's attraction to the boy was emphatically erotic. His to the older man was not, which was accepted, in the fact almost a theoretical ideal, in the Greek pattern. Among the Greeks, it was also expected that the older man would be a mentor who would have the boy's welfare at heart. The boy whose case I have cited had hoped for such concern. The relationship of *binahor*-father among the Marind-anim had similar elements. However, in neither the Greek nor Melanesian examples did the relationship imply a change in sexual identity on the part of the youth, as it does in our own culture.

If we conceptualize the situation I have just described in psychodynamic terms, multiple elements are evident. Identification with an admired teacher, the desire to be appreciated and wanted by a father surrogate, and rebellion against the actual father's domineering attitude. He had not gone for the sex, he said, but the experience had really turned his sexual ideas upside down. That the announcement about being gay might have been a further rebellious act against his conservative father is plausible—but it would not have occurred without our intense cultural insistence upon the characterization of personality in terms of sexual identity and the further dichotemization of sexual identity into homosexual and heterosexual.

Another example of the effect of cultural context on how inner emotional themes are experienced and symbolized is sexual interaction among adolescent peers. Following Blos, one would expect that elements of the father complex would tend to be transferred to male peers and that sexual attraction for friends and contemporaries could occur. In our culture, fourteen-year-old boys are quick to use the epithet "faggot" or even "gay" against each other. Their sense of their own masculinity needs to be reconsolidated, and there seems to be an energetic defense against homosexuality.

One of my graduate students had done a case study for me on an adolescent boy of Puerto Rican background who had grown up in New York. He had spent a few days in the Rikers Island jail where he had seen some homosexual play that appalled him. Some time later, he and his friends were together at one of their homes and they saw, hanging about outside, another boy who they believed to be gay. They went out and beat him up. My graduate student also had some adult Pakistani friends. Once, in discussing their sexual experiences as adolescents, they freely acknowledged that they had all engaged in sexual play with friends in adolescence.

In the contrasting reactions of the Americans and the Pakistanis, one can see how culture permits or prohibits the symbolization of adolescent homosexual potential and how it assigns added meaning to it. For the Pakistanis, it was a stage that boys normally went through; for the Americans, it was a declaration of identity.

What is striking in the case of the Greeks, of the Sambia, and the Marind is that the homosexual experiences of their adolescence seemed to be an integrated part of their progress toward manhood. These experiences were obligatory for the New Guineans, but optional for the Greeks. History has not left much in the way of subjective reports by the *eromenoi*, but there is no reason to feel that they felt that role to be degrading or distasteful. Rather the reverse would seem to be the case.

Although Herdt's account leaves no doubt that the rites of fellatio are part of a complex systems of beliefs and attitudes that are not without their anxieties and contradictions, the subjective reports on experiences in both roles—of course every individual did play both roles—were on the whole positive.

Culture, Consciousness, and Inner Experience

Devereux (1970) makes the point that "The view that impulses, wishes, fantasies and other products of the human psyche which are completely repressed in one society may be fully conscious and even culturally implemented in another society is, today, almost a scientific commonplace. This means that, instead of being an axiom, it has become a dogma or even a platitude. In undergoing this metamorphosis, the insight in question has, in fact, lost its provocative and thought-provoking character and has consequently failed to stimulate attempts to explore all of this deeper implications" (p. 70). Devereux goes on to say that it was the simplicity and obviousness of this axiom that led to its sterilization. However, I would compare the effect of this axiom to an interpretation offered to a resistant patient. The patient may listen politely and even find the interpretation "interesting." However, as Freud observed, he will now only have in his awareness information we have given him, but will be no closer to an awareness of his own unconscious than he was before.

As I noted earlier, cross-cultural data have long been available. The response has seemingly been to find it all very interesting but hardly consequential for analytic theory which, after Freud, remained decidedly but unacknowledgedly culture-bound. Westerners have no monopoly in viewing their own civilization as the "normal" yardstick against which all others are measurable deviations. Geertz notes that in Java, where he had done much of his work, people would quite flatly say, "To be human is to be Javanese" (Geertz, 1973, p. 52).

An issue raised in the case of Frank and, I think, far-reaching for the understanding of sexuality, is then, the influence that cultural symbols have not only on the consciously ascribed meaning of experience, but also on the nature of *inner* experience. Symbols, through their power to evoke meanings and feelings, affect the quality of inner experience, whether we are speaking of a religious ritual, a work of art, or the sexual images and actions into which one is expected to channel sexual energy and emotional need. I think it would be fair to say that certain kinds of inner experiences can only be mediated through sexual symbols. I do not think that any analyst would deny that, in the heterosexual realm, sexual intercourse expresses and evokes emotions that are simply not available without the mediation of the symbols of sexual action. Similarly, it seems plausible that the sexual relationship between adolescent boy and older male can make possible the direct experience of meanings and feelings that cannot be experienced through other means. I do not deny that there can be large overlapping areas between such a sexual relationship and a nonsexual one between a boy and an encouraging and admired teacher. I am certain there can be, but I am not certain that it can be the same. In fact, in our society, there might be considerable discomfort in many people if one suggested that the meanings and feelings of the two relationships were the same.

I think it is clear by now that phallic contact can symbolize multiple and contradictory meanings. Our culture obviously stresses the destructive meaning of phallic contact when it occurs between males and most especially between adult man and adolescent boy. But what of the other meanings, including that of love stressed, in striking contrast, by the Greeks? Is this meaning simply not understood in our culture? Or, is it an unconsciously understood but nevertheless forbidden meaning? I again recall Frank's heartfelt outburst of "You can't love a man . . ." Was he expressing an intuitive understanding of a reason for the prohibition of homosexual symbols—the prevention of an inner experience that the symbol is capable of mediating, that of love between men? A culture may prohibit certain symbols and thereby discourage or make improbable certain inner experiences, for example, those expressed and felt in a sexual transaction between adult male and adolescent boy.

In the symbols that a person uses, as in all other aspects of his mental and emotional life, he is deeply influenced by the culture in which he develops. However, it is not correct to assert that a person is nothing except a cultural product, a clone off the social assembly line. If that were so, social change would be almost nonexistent and individuals would never feel at odds with their culture. The individual human being is a symbol-making animal, to which the nightly creations of symbols in dreams are eloquent testimony. The truth is that a person is both a product of his culture and, at the same time, in a dynamic and potentially confrontational relationship to it. In his creation and use of symbols, he can be responsive to imperatives of human nature that transcend cultural dictates as well as to the unique configuration of his own life experiences and needs.

Our culture has authoritatively tried to banish homosexual symbols not only from action but even from consciousness. The effort has been and must continue to be a failure because these symbols are, I think, too deeply expressive of powerful complexes of feelings within men. Under consideration has been one of these deeply embedded complexes—the intergenerational one between younger and older males. The symbolic expression of this complex is one of the most strenuously disapproved in our contemporary culture. The symbols nevertheless persist, but in a shadowy and often desperate underworld. In a contemporary newspaper (Bollinger, 1988) there is a journalistic account of the widespread prevalence of teenage prostitution, both of girls and boys.

"Young boys and girls hang out in front, selling their bodies or smoking crack . . . Some move over to 'the loop' at 53rd St. and Second Ave.—one of the biggest spots for young male hustles in the city. The age range for 'the loop' is as young as 13, but you start seeing the kids in large numbers at age 16 . . . The older guys in their 20s are washed up. Youth sells for boys on the street. The older you are the less well you'll sell" (p. 22). These last were the observations of the director of an outreach program. In a separate box, the following lines appear: "The kids' story is one of desperation—of turning a trick for $5 in the back seat of a Mercedes-Benz with a man old enough to be their father" (p. 23).

Many of these young people are rejected runaways who live on the streets and in squalid shelters. Blos has emphasized the feelings of the adolescent boy and the man for the father. However, a current that seems deeply rooted in male psychology is the attraction that the man feels for the youth including the youth young enough to be his son. Because or in spite of the fact that our culture holds this to be a perversion, there is relatively little theoretical concern with this pattern. The fact that many of the young people who offer themselves are runaways would make it likely that, in addition to the very real pecuniary motivation, an additional one is feeling desired and valued by men who, however fleetingly, are father surrogates. The sexual symbols through which this feeling is realized has become assimilated to the clandestine role of prostitute in the context of urban anomie and its accompanying culture of heartless commercialism.

In classical Greece, the desire of man for youth was obviously thought to be quite normally masculine. From another cultural tradition, we have the words of the Persian prince Ibn Iskandar in a book of statecraft written to advise his favorite son and heir. He opens his chapter entitled "On Taking One's Pleasure" with the advice, "Let it be clear to you, my son, that if you fall in love with a person, you should not indiscriminately and whether drunk or sober indulge in sexual congress. It is well know that the seed which issues from you is the germ of a soul and a person. . . ." He continues, "As between women and youths, do not confine your inclinations to either sex; thus you may find enjoyment from both kinds without either of the two becoming inimical to you. Furthermore, if, as I have said, excessive copulation is harmful, (complete) abstention also has its dangers." He closes the chapter by saying, "During the summer let your desires incline towards youths and during the winter towards women. But on this topic it is requisite that one's discourse should be brief, lest it engender appetite" (Levy, pp. 77–78).

This book, the *Qābūs Nāma* (*A Mirror for Princes*), was written in 1082 A.D., the Islamic year 475. The prince, in this excerpt, seems sensitive to concerns of the spirit as well as the flesh. However, the advice he offers his son about tempering his sexual enjoyment so as not to exclude either sex seems well beyond any imagined father/son discourse in our time. Throughout the book, when sexual attraction or passion is mentioned, it is not initially clear whether the object is male or female.

I think that a symbolic approach to sexuality facilitates an understanding of this attraction of man to youth. The core of the experience symbolized by this transaction seems to be father/son love whether the relationship is initiated by the older or the younger partner. And even if the boy is selected for his feminine grace, an indispensable component of his attractiveness remains his masculinity. It must almost strike the modern reader as an anachronism in this era of fatherless families, when Freud observes, "I cannot think of any need in childhood as strong as the need for a father's protection" (Freud, 1930, p. 19). The strength of that need was seen in Frank's life history, as it is, Blos points out, in the lives of many other men. That a man might want vicariously to recreate elements of that relationship symbolically through a sexual one with a youth seems altogether comprehensible. The fact of youthful androgyny might add to the appeal but is not itself decisive.

Love and "Pathology"

In Part I of this book, we examined two motivational components in Frank's feelings about men: the fear of the destructive, phallic man; and the search for components of the father/son relationship. In Frank's longing for his father and his search for father substitutes, there was as Freud understood, the desire for a protective, loving relationship. Why would analytic theory have regarded the expression of these needs through sexual symbols as pathological? In *Civilization and Its Discontents* Freud (1930) speaks of the search for happiness through love. He says, "*One of the forms in which love manifests itself—sexual love—* has given us our most intense experience of an overwhelming sensation of pleasure and has thus furnished us with a pattern for our search for happiness. What is more natural than that we should persist in looking for happiness along the path on which we first encountered it?" (p. 29, italics added). The need for love also seemed pivotal in Frank's feeling for his friend Nick. In the dream in which he had intercourse with Nick, the aura of love surrounded this scene.

As Freud's career and life lengthened, the insight he offered into the great themes and dilemmas of life seem to me to have attained great depth. Eros, tending toward life and love, quintessentially expressed in sexuality, was, he came to feel, opposed to the instinct of pure destructiveness and death. Itself not erotic, the latter could, Freud felt, combine with its opposite, the erotic instinct, to form an alloy of which concrete sexual actions could actually be composed. This fits in with Stoller's hypothesis of the "desire to harm" as a significant element in sexual excitement. However, my reading of Freud indicates that, with the exception of sadism and machochism, Freud saw the balance very much on the side of Eros—of love—when it came to the symbolic meanings of sexual actions.

But the point about Eros that is particularly relevant to Frank's dream about Nick, is the following: ". . . towards the outside . . . the ego seems to maintain clear and sharp lines of demarcation. There is only one state—admittedly an unusual state, *but not one that can be stigmatized as pathological*—in which it does not do this. At the height of being in love the boundary between ego and object threatens to melt away. Against all the evidence of his senses, a man who is in love declares that 'I' and 'you' are one" (Freud, 1930, p. 13, italics added). It strikes me that when a man seeks intercourse with another whom he loves, as Frank did in his dream, he is seeking precisely the sense of oneness and of unity that Freud has described. If the gender of the other is male, does that necessarily make the act of intercourse *less* symbolic of love?

I am afraid that this question would be answered by a resounding "yes" in our civilization.

C. W. Socarides is an eloquent spokesman for our cultural stance when he outlines how a "homosexual" must be reeducated: "His homosexuality has been a constant course of anxiety, requiring that he repress his hatred of male rivals and substitute 'love' of them in its place. *He has to become aware that his main competition is with men; love and comfort are to be found with women.* He no longer needs to forcibly repress his aggressiveness and self-assertive urges in competition with male figures" (Socarides, 1968, p. 228, italics added).

Frank himself said the same thing rather more simply, when he nervously asserted, "You can't love a man. That's wrong. You love a woman." Analytic opinion was, at that period, in agreement, evidently feeling more comfortable with conceptualizing male-to-male relationships in competitive terms. Socarides's use of quotation marks around "love" in the above citation could only constitute a sarcastic commentary on its authenticity. It is remarkable how infrequently reference to love—without the use of invalidating commentary—was made in the professional literature on homosexuality up until the time I had begun to see Frank. In my own experience, on some occasions when a heterosexual man has reported a homosexual fantasy or even experience, the denial of its emotional meaningfulness with respect to the need for love has been striking. A man I once saw related how he and his cousin, when they were teenagers, used to be involved in mutual masturbation. One day, his cousin tried to embrace him and he recoiled in horror. To embrace each other, he felt, would define what they were doing as "truly" homosexual instead of simply providing each other with a sexual outlet in the absence of women.

In the case of another man who had conscious homosexual fantasies, he imagined himself being essentially forced to submit to rape by a more powerful man. Another man, also heterosexual, imagined a situation in which another's powerful erect penis was the sole focus of his attention, with no question of an affectionate or even personal transaction. Both men, in different ways, had lost a much longed for father, one through death during the patient's boyhood, the other through progressive disillusionment. For both these heterosexual men, the conscious imagery, however, was more concerned with power than it was with love, consistent with the symbolic meaning of the phallus as an instrument of dominant power. However, whereas in the Melanesian cultures, that power was used on the boy's behalf to help him grow to manhood, in our own the same actions can constitute a symbolic demasculinization. The desire for phallic penetration as symbolic of love may find some acknowledgment where women are concerned, but this meaning tends to be denied consciousness in men in conformity with the cultural injunction, "You can't love a man." With the loving meaning of the symbolic action repressed, therefore, what remains is the opposite meaning that phallic penetration can also have—symbolized in our culture both by the Devil and by revulsion against homosexuality—that of an intrusive and overwhelming evil.

How anxiety about the acknowledgment of feelings of tenderness or love in a homosexual liaison might, in practice, lead to the imagery of force and domination was, I think, seen in the treatment of an actual episode that a young American, Billy Hayes (1977), describes in his autobiographical account of his experiences in Turkish prisons, where he was incarcerated on a drug charge. In those institutions, the qualities of human compassion and kindness tended to disappear in an environment of thoughtless cruelty and bleakness. Nonetheless, the capacity for friendship and warmth among the prisoners was not entirely lost and Hayes describes how a friendship between himself and another prisoner, a Scandinavian, deepened into a loving and sexual relationship. In the film made on the basis of his autobiographical account—called *Midnight Express*, as was the book—the friendship is depicted but there is a scene in the shower where the friend kisses Hayes and indicates his wish for a sexual relationship. In the film Hayes is made to shake his head regretfully as he declines the sexual invitation. Perhaps the makers of the film felt that the large audiences that the film was targeted for would have difficulty having the heterosexual hero accept a consensual homosexual relationship while in prison. However, in an unsparing scene, the young man is brutally beaten and then understood to be raped by a sadistic guard right after his arrest. The end of the film has Billy killing this same guard in self defense as he fends off another rape and then escaping from prison wearing the guard's clothes.

In fact, although he was savagely beaten after his arrest, in reality no rape took place and his escape from the island prison later was not occasioned by any rape attempt. It seems the filmmakers suppressed the consensual sexual relationship that was part of the consoling and loving relationship between two men who found themselves in a horrible life situation. They then replaced it with images of rape and finally distorted the circumstances of an already heroic escape by depicting it as a triumph over homosexual rape. In analogous fashion, the suppression of desire for a loving relationship may lead to its replacement by images of force and domination in the homosexual fantasies of men. In Frank, there were images of imminent rape, pursuit, and capture in his dreams and the fear of possession was itself the quintessential act of domination by another.

The filmmakers seem to be saying of the hero that "He didn't want it—it was done against his will." The loving component is denied. The distortion of the ending itself might be explained by an actual incident I learned of while working in a penal institution for young men. One boy of eighteen had recently been transferred from another institution where, the grapevine had it, he had been raped by several other inmates. In the group therapy session that I was observing one of the group members accused him of not defending himself vigorously enough, indicating that he had a homosexual desire. The young man so accused heatedly said that he had been powerless to resist his attackers and swore to kill them if he ever had the opportunity. That vow seemed to satisfy his accuser, since it was the naturally accepted method for redeeming his masculine honor. In the film, the killing of the guard, accidental though it was, seems part of the hero's redemption as well. The sequence seems significant. The acknowledgment of the willingness to make love with another man is replaced by an image of sadistic force which then leads to redemption through an act of defensive violence. In an individual, this sequence would be a classic formula for paranoia.

As in paranoia, however, when sexual imagery in the absence of love or tenderness breaks through into consciousness, it is, paradoxically, even more threatening because one is more likely to feel like a potentially helpless victim of the phallic power of another man, in a way that is destructive of one's own sense of masculinity.

Herdt (1987, p. 162) reports that, among the Sambia, boys and youths who began to become infatuated with each other feared being stigmatized as unmanly. Even in a culture that mandated homosexuality, there was uneasiness about its potentially loving dimension.

The Themes of Love and Power

In Frank, two overarching themes constantly intertwined in differing configurations—the theme of love and the theme of power. Anger was a powerful and complicating current that could accompany both of these main themes. Both love and power are powerful emotional complexes that seek symbolic expression. This posed a massive dilemma for Frank. The intensity and the nature of his need for love, both in terms of offering and receiving it, were such as to seek expression in the energy of sexual symbols. But as soon as this symbolic energy was subliminally perceived at the shadowed edges of consciousness, another emotion was summoned up that blocked the emergence of these symbols into the light. This emotion was evoked in the form of the substitute symbol of the Devil.

I think it is clear by now that I do not feel that it is always possible fully to explicate the meaning of symbols. But, in this instance, Frank himself consciously felt that possession by the Devil meant humiliation, degradation, and reduction to a contemptible slavery. However, Frank did not speak of the unconscious meaning that actually clinched the utilization of the Devil as the symbol for what he feared. That component was the Devil as a symbol of evil, phallic power, the aspect that figured so prominently in the early and medieval portrayals of the Devil. For Frank, possession by the Devil symbolized possession by the phallic power of another. A critically important consequence of such possession would be the destruction of Frank's own masculinity.

Freud (1926) points out that touching and physical contact are the aims of both love *and* aggression. Eros desires contact because it strives to make the ego and the loved object one, to abolish all spatial barriers between them. Frank's need for love did, in fact, impel him in the direction of contact with another male, including his penis. In the dream about Nick, Frank did the penetrating with *his* penis. However, a few weeks later he had forgotten who had taken what role, indicating that both kinds of contact were implied in his feelings. His dilemma was that the need for love inexorably moved in the direction of a contact with the phallic aspect of the other that he simultaneously experienced as destructive to his sense of masculinity.

But the Devil was not only a phallic power; he was also an evil one. In that sense the Devil could be construed as the dark side of his father, the side that had hurt him and his family by his abandonment. The bartender also represented that side—"the guy in the bar" who ignored his family's needs and abused his son's feelings of tenderness for him. At one point, late in the analysis, Frank had spoken of how he felt all sexual relationships were essentially exploitive, unequivocally expressing his expectation that he would be hurt and disappointed in the still repudiated sexual relationship with another man.

Freud, in speaking of love in the transference situation, notes that it is true that it consists of new editions of old traces and repeats infantile reactions, but adds, "But this is the essential character of every love. There is no love that does not repeat infantile prototypes" (Freud, 1915a, p. 387). The experience of most therapists would lend credence to this idea.

Frank's need for his mother's love was transferred to other females during and after adolescence. As we have seen, this need was complicated by strong feelings of frustration and anger as well. Nonetheless he could consciously say to himself that he wanted to be loved by and to love a woman and to expect that love to find physical and sexual expression.

In analogous fashion, components of Frank's love for his father were also transferred to other males. This was most evident where older men were concerned. However, just as elements of love for the mother are transferred not to older women, but to female peers, elements of love for his father were transferred to male peers, especially his friend Nick. Not only did Nick have the classical handsomeness he envied, but he was also a warm friend with an athleticism that Frank prized in himself and others, which could plausibly be understood as an aspect of male strength—a quality Frank much admired in his father before it was lost to alcohol. There were feelings of idealization toward Nick that quite resembled the kind Frank had experienced toward women.

Love, Death, and the Oedipus Complex

The issues that revolved around males in Frank's emotional life seem common to the emotional life of men in general. Of the two themes—love and power—love was the one that most urgently pressed forward toward sexual symbolization. However, as the anthropological material has made clear, phallic contact can also symbolize the transmission of masculine power. Was there such a desire on Frank's part? It is true that, by the beginning of adolescence, Frank had lost the strong father of his early years. He desired to refind this strong father, to contact and ultimately, perhaps, to incorporate that strength in a loving relationship. This desire might also have pressed for sexual symbolization. It is also true that Frank had serious worries about his masculinity ostensibly because of the trauma of the fight incident of early adolescence. However, midway through the analysis the anxiety about his masculine adequacy had ceased being an issue but the force of the Devil obsession was not thereby diminished. I now believe that it had been the subliminally felt potential for sexuality in his feelings about men that generated the feeling of weakness and masculine inadequacy.

The male as desired object of love and sexual feeling was continually at odds with the male as competitor and enemy in Frank, and it was striking that these two opposing feelings about men appeared frequently in pairs in his dreams, a dream incorporating the one theme following upon the other. This juxtaposition of the two kinds of feelings was evident with great clarity when he reported the dream in which he described what he frankly termed "a homosexual relationship between me and Nick." In the other dream of this pair, he saw Anne with another man and although he "beat the shit out of him," it did not matter because Anne still did not want him.

While these dreams of competition were unpleasant and even painful when the other man repeatedly won the woman he desired, competition with another man was something that Frank, in accordance with the approval given it in our culture, could readily experience in consciousness. What he could not permit himself to experience was desire for another man. And what was very striking was how the man who was *desired* could become transformed into the man with whom he had to *compete*. In a later dream, Nick turns up as "Halsey," an actor who is Anne's new boyfriend. Two other of his very good friends appeared in dreams, coupled with Anne.

It would be possible to translate these two opposite elements in Frank's feelings toward men as reflections of the two poles of the Oedipus complex—negative and positive. While this would not be incorrect, I think it is more important to understand the meaning of each of these elements in Frank's adult life and to consider their relation to male issues in general. Our culture emphasizes the uneasiness around the issue of male-to-male attraction. A group ego ideal has coalesced around the unrealistic assumption that males never experience sexual attraction toward each other. In the religious/moral framework such attraction was sinful or the possible prelude to sin; in the biological/medical framework it was regarded as pathological; at the level of conscious cultural attitudes, it has symbolized masculine inadequacy and femininity.

In contrast, the competitive defeat of another male has enjoyed approval and encouragement. As male-to-male attraction has symbolized weakness and femininity, successful male-to-male competition has symbolized strength and masculinity. For Frank, vanquishing the other man had, then, an element of this culturally approved method of reassuring himself of his masculine adequacy. However, at a deeper level, these "twinned" figures of desired male and competitor were analogous to the "doublet" symbol in myth. One of the pair had reference to that aspect of the man he could love and want love from; the other part referred to that aspect of the man that he hated and felt threatened by. The bartender figure symbolized both of these.

In Freud's later works, the theory of the primeval father, first elaborated in *Totem and Taboo* (1918) becomes more and more prominent as part of the theory of the Oedipus complex. In *Civilization and Its Discontents* (1930) the dual-instinct theory becomes the other important thematic strand. The actual Oedipus complex, as experienced by the individual, becomes the product of three elements: the reality of the interactions in the actual family situation; the influence of the phylogenetically acquired memory traces of the primeval father and his murder which amplify both the child's aggressiveness towards his father and the guilt he feels as a consequence; and the struggle between Eros and the destructive instinct. In *Civilization. . . .* he says:

> Now, I think, we can at last grasp two things perfectly clearly: the part played by love in the origin of conscience and the fatal inevitability of the sense of guilt. Whether one has killed one's father or has abstained from doing so is not really the decisive thing. One is bound to feel guilty in either case, for the sense of guilt is an expression of the conflict due to ambivalence, of the eternal struggle between Eros and the instinct of destruction or death. This conflict is set going as soon as men are faced with the task of living together. So long as the community assumes no other form than that of the family, the conflict is bound to express itself in the Oedipus complex, to establish the conscience and to create the first sense of guilt.
>
> What began in relation to the father is completed in relation to the group. If civilization is a necessary course of development from the family to humanity as a whole, then—as a result of the inborn conflict arising from ambivalence, of the eternal struggle between the trends of love and death—there is inextricably bound up with it an increase in the sense of guilt, which will perhaps reach heights that the individual finds hard to tolerate (pp. 79–80).

As I said earlier, the theory of the primeval father was perhaps more congenial to the intellectual conventions of Freud's day than of ours. Nor has the destructive or death instinct really found wide acceptance, perhaps because it seems hard to know what to do with it in the treatment of the individual patient. But as soon as one shifts one's focus from the individual to the group and to the sphere of social action, the death instinct commands attention as a theory that must be taken seriously. How, after World Wars I and II, to say nothing of the many localized examples of massacre and genocide, including perhaps the only example of genocidal suicide in history—the self-inflicted holocaust in Cambodia—is it possible to dismiss the theory of the instinct of "destruction and death"? If it is not an instinct, it might just as well be, to all intents and purposes. Pragmatically, it makes more sense to view the destructive urge as something beyond rationality that requires the utmost in monitoring and vigilance to prevent it from getting out of control.

Analogously, even if the theory of the primeval father is regarded as an explanatory myth, it remains quite relevant to some aspects of social reality. The main threat to human life on this planet, it must be granted, has been in the form of male aggression, especially from armed men submitting to the leadership of a powerful male. In the era of the Vietnam war, leadership began to undergo a transformation and to become pure coercion. The president/father ordered the young men/sons to expose themselves to mortal danger for a course in which the security of the nation was not involved—except, as is now becoming clear (Goodwin, 1988), in the delusional system of the president's mind. It seems to me quite important that, in the Oedipus legend, his father Laios ordered that he be exposed and allowed to die on a mountaintop. It hardly seems necessary to point out that the protest against the Vietnam War had as one of its themes an intergenerational confrontation.

We can go so far as to dismiss the theory of the primeval father as an unverifiable bit of anthropological romance and yet grant it the status of a powerful metaphor—a symbol, in fact—for a multilayered psychological and social reality, the figure of the powerful, dominant, and destructive male. In this connection, Jung's concept of the archetype (Jung, 1964) comes to mind. The archetype is a tendency to form symbolic representations of certain motifs, which are themselves unconscious elements from the earliest prehistory of the human race. The archetype itself can be seen as a metaphor for certain universals of human experience, even if one does not agree with Jung's concept of a collective unconscious of which archetypes are a part.

I would like to return to the immediate issues of this book now by the route of the Oedipus legend. The early part of the legend, it will be recalled, recounts the abduction of Khrysippos by Laios, father of Oedipus. Either way this was an aggressive act; if it was a seduction, it was a violation of the rules of hospitality, for Laios was a guest in the house of the boy's father. If it was a rape, it was an aggressive act against the boy.

In the complete Oedipus legend, then, there is homosexuality as well as heterosexuality, with both of these themes in an ambivalent, intergenerational context. If we take the legend as symbolic of powerful complexes of conscious and unconscious feeling, then we can see both the positive and negative sides of the complex to which the legend gave its name. There is love between mother and son, polluted by incest. There is ambivalence between father and son. The figure of the father is both erotic and murderous. I would regard Khrysippos and Oedipus as succeeding images of the same son. The relationship between Laios and Khrysippos/Oedipus incorporates, then, representations of both the "Heavenly Powers" (Freud, 1930, p. 92) of the dual-instinct theory, Eros and death. As the love between mother and son is shadowed by incest, that between father and son is darkened by violence. Frank's resistance to homosexuality reflected the fundamental potential for ambivalence in the father/son and male-to-male relationships, in his expectation that opening himself up to sex with another man would also be laying himself open to emotional mayhem. Women have long been aware of this potential for male ambivalence. Men are aware of it in the prison setting where they become the openly acknowledged sexual objects of other men. And in the paradoxically violent landscape of modern America, the serial murderer John Gacy (Cahill & Ewing, 1986) seemingly identified with the image of destructive, phallic power and raped and murdered thirty young men.

The Revulsion Against Homosexuality

The Melanesian treatment of the relationship between father and son demonstrates that the erotic component implicit in it need not be attended by anxiety and defensiveness, nor must the sexual passivity of the boy be experienced as shameful and destructive to male identity. On the contrary, the exact opposite construction can be put on this aspect of the relationship. As I rather broadly hinted at the end of the last chapter, the revulsion against homosexuality is a secular successor to the witchcraft mania. The woman who gives herself to the Devil and the man who gives himself to the destructive, phallic man are equally guilty of going over to the enemy. This, as much as the fear of feminization, must account for the hatred of the male who takes a passive role, a hatred internalized by some gay men, as R. A. Isay (1987) has disclosed. There is ample evidence that Romans, though quite tolerant of the active form of homosexuality, always had some anxiety about the passive role (Richlin, 1983) as did the Greeks. However, Brown (1988) reveals that it was in the Christian era, the year 390, that Rome first witnessed the public burning of male prostitutes. The emperor, Theodosius, was shocked that " . . . a soul allotted in perpetuity to the 'sacrosanct dwelling-place' of a recognizably male body should have tried to force that body into female poses" (p. 383). This was a sinister foreshadowing of the terror that, centuries later, would claim the lives of so many women on similar pyres all across Europe.

From Isay's (1987) report, it seems that even for many gay man, contact with the phallic "other" in a cultural setting which has in the highest degree emphasized its destructiveness for the masculinity of the male at the receiving end of this contact can be deeply troubling. Isay says that ". . . self-hatred associated with what is perceived as passive and feminine in their sexuality was articulated by most gay men during their therapy" (p. 286). Isay goes on to say that these passive erotic longings originate in the feelings toward the father who, for the homosexually inclined child, is his son's most important erotic object, not the mother. Both the memories of these erotic feelings for the father and the adult passive wishes that originate from those feelings are the subject of varying degrees of repression and anxiety. Therapeutic progress is marked by recovery of the repressed erotic feelings for the father and the integration of the passive wishes into adult sexual relationships.

Isay says that the frequent report by gay men that their fathers were distant in childhood and that they lacked a sense of real closeness to them is a defensive distortion because of the anxiety about their erotic attachment to them, comparable to the ways in which heterosexual men deal with their anxiety about their early erotic attachment to their mothers. While I would accept Isay's analysis, I do feel there is a cultural dimension that must affect the way in which men—whether heterosexual or gay—experience the memory of their feelings for their fathers, as well as the way they react in adulthood, to their passive homosexual wishes.

The revisionist position, as I pointed out in Chapter 4, was to dismiss the notion of a normal erotic attachment to the father. If shown to be present, it was regarded as a response to anxiety or pathogenic family dynamics. However, the data on those societies of the Melanesian culture area (Herdt, 1984b) in which homosexuality was, together with heterosexuality, a regular part of the life experience of most males, are strikingly supportive of Freud's contention that an erotic attachment to the father—the "negative" Oedipus complex—is an important part of male development. In his introduction to this collection of essays, Herdt (1984a) ventures the opinion that an ancient [homosexual] ritual complex had become disseminated throughout this region. Although it underwent various transformations, ". . . the deep structure of ritual roles and symbols remained" (p. 54). In this ritual complex, erotic symbols linking father and son seem unmistakable.

In no society does sexual intercourse between father and son *actually* take place. But a special sexual relationship between a boy and an older male is a widely prevalent institution. These relationships—in some instances actual and in other classificatory—cluster around the father-son relationship and symbolically point to it. I have already mentioned that among the Marind-anim, this relationship was between boy and mother's brother. Among the Big Nambas (Allen, 1984, p. 89) boys are sent to their *grandfathers* with whom they remain in a sexual relationship until they marry. Among the Jaquai a man can send his son to sleep with an older man; the two have a relationship designated "anus-father" and "anus-son." (Herdt, 1984a, p. 29). Among the Sambia themselves, a male initiate's ritual sponsor (who is not, in this case, a sexual partner) is designated with the title of "mother's brother" (Herdt, 1984c, pp. 187–88). Among the Etoro, the ideal homosexual relationship is between a boy and his sister's husband or betrothed. In this society, the period of insemination is especially long, from age ten to the mid-twenties (Herdt, 1984a, pp. 35–36). Among the Kimam the mentor who is supposed to have regular anal intercourse with the boy in order to make him strong is designated with the title of "adoptive father" (Serpenti, 1984, p. 304). Among the Bedamini, insemination starts when the boy is eight to ten years old and is performed by a young man selected by the boy's father (Sorum, 1984). In all these cases, the purpose of insemination, as among the societies discussed in Chapter 5, is to make the boy grow to strong manhood.

I have already cited, in Chapter 5, the Keraki myth (Williams, 1936) which describes how the mythic ancestor had anal intercourse with his son to make him grow. Schwimmer says that a widespread mythic theme of the culture area we have been considering is " . . . that of a triangle involving a high god, his wife, and his male lover (a novice initiated by the high god). In these tales the novice and the wife have intercourse and are caught in the act. In spite of his strong love for the novice, the high god kills him because he cannot accept the triangle" (Schwimmer, 1984, p. 282). The Marind myth of Arememb, cited in Chapter 5, is a variant of this pattern.

In the Melanesian mythic tradition, we find elements of triangularity similar to those found in the Greed legend, arranged somewhat differently. However, the rituals and customs of the Melanesian culture area took as an important focus the *positive* symbolism of the erotic relationship between father and son. And in their rituals, rather than emphasizing the destructive potential in the competitive possibilities between the older and younger male, they fashioned a unique solution to the problems inherent in a sexual triangle. While among many of these societies, intercourse with women is forbidden boys during adolescence, another bond is offered instead: an erotic one between the adolescent boy and a father surrogate. This relationship is not only erotic but also nurturing and the boy understands that he is being strengthened so that he can become a man and enjoy manhood's privileges, including full rights to a relationship to a woman. Bonding among young males is generally promoted and in some, for example, the Keraki (Williams, 1936) it is understood that young bachelors will have sex with one another until they marry. Among the Marind-anim, a concern for the maintenance of bonds with other males was seen in the fact that the bridegroom will share his wedding night with other members of his clan.

It was in warfare that male-to-male aggression was given free rein. And it seems to be in the ritual of the headhunt that the destructive components in the father-son relationship were symbolically expressed, but so obscurely that it is only from the explanatory myths and a few clues in the ritual itself that this component can be inferred.

In the Greek legend, his father's decision to expose his baby son and his son's subsequent killing of his father had nothing to do with competition for the mother. One might be entitled to make the assumption that this element is implicit even if explicitly unstated. Nonetheless, the very element that is *unstated* in the myth became the *central* feature of the psychoanalytic interpretation of the myth, even where Freud was concerned and, after his death, the only feature that the revisionists accepted. Why did this process of selective interpretation of the Greek legend occur? I would hazard the suggestion that it occurred because the legend was regarded through the prism of Christianity.

The God of the Old Testament, who became the God of Christianity, demanded perfect devotion to himself to the exclusion of all other gods. A single act of disobedience led to the expulsion from paradise and repeated acts of disobedience led to the near destruction of mankind. In the Christian extension of this mythic tradition, the immortality lost by the first act of disobedience is regained through the death of Christ who is the first human to be born and live without sin. The relation between God the Father and the Son is both profoundly moving and paradoxical. He is loved by God, killed by God, and a part of God. Nowhere in all this is there any question of a triangular relationship that includes a competitive element for a female, either divine or human. Obedience, not sexuality, is the issue.

It is true that observance of laws regulating sexuality were represented in Jewish tradition as further obedience to God. In the evolution of Christianity, however, the regulation of sexuality became a central rather than an ancillary issue in the relationship to God. As Freud (1930) pointed out, our civilization has been fundamentally hostile to sexuality and as Brown (1988) permits us to see, this hostility had its origins in the renunciation of sexuality—above all heterosexuality—by both men and women in favor of the relationship to the father god. The so-called "positive" Oedipus complex, in which the son fears castration for his sexual wishes for the mother and feels rivalry for the father, seems to me to be a composite that results from passing the Greek legend through the filter of the Christian ideal of renunciation of heterosexuality as an essential component of the relationship to God.

As early Christianity emphasized, praised, and eventually demanded sexual renunciation, the incarnation of the primeval father was truly completed as, once again, he prohibited, through his church, sexual access to women by his sons. In *Moses and Monotheism*, Freud (1939) makes an observation applicable both to Judaism and Christianity when he says of the former that a religion that began by prohibiting the representation of God in an image developed more and more into a religion of instinctual renunciation. In the end God has become completely withdrawn from sexuality. When Christianity asserted that God fathered a son, it was a proposition that would not have surprised the Greeks. The simultaneous doctrine of this same son as an incarnation of God himself is fundamental to Hindu conceptions of divine nature. But both of those religious traditions conceptualize deity in *physically* sexual terms. Christianity did not do this. The conception was *spiritually*, not carnally, "sexual." The mother remained a virgin before *and* after his birth; the life of the son excluded sexuality.

In this myth, there can be no sexual competition between the high god and the son for the mother because there is no sexuality and the son is, in the end, identified as coequal with and part of the father. This is an idealized picture from which the potentially incendiary symbols of sexual passion and struggles for power have been excluded. However, if the Christian ideal of sexual renunciation and its deletion of physical sexuality from its sacred symbols aimed at reproducing in the life of the ordinary man or woman the idealized serenity that imbues the divine family, the attempt would have to be judged a failure. Sexuality was not so much transcended as not integrated. When it was denied symbolic expression altogether or only begrudgingly permitted, a false sense of serenity, at best, was purchased at the cost of repression. Much of this book is concerned with the way in which elements of sexuality that were denied symbolization in the conscious part of the self raged out of control in other forms.

Far from functioning as a model for a conflict-free father-son relationship the asexuality of the divine model seems to have contributed to the internalized representation of God becoming increasingly identified with oppressive, sexually prohibitive authority. As I have strongly implied in examining the consequences of this transformation of the image of God for the symbols of the Devil and the "homosexual," the prohibitions against heterosexuality directly contribute to the opposition to homosexuality.

It certainly is reasonable to suppose that there might have been a tightening of structures against homosexuality where the clergy were concerned, after the suppression of clerical marriage, as E. F. Greenberg (1988) suggests. However, Boswell (1980) points out that the third Lateran Council of 1179 was the first of the ecumenical councils to rule on homosexual acts—and for the *laity,* not just for the clergy. The prescribed punishment for a lay person was excommunication. Although it was in the second Lateran Council, in 1139, that clerical marriage was crushed once and for all, marriage for the laity was in no way impugned or degraded.

Greenberg also points out what continues to be evident in the pages of daily newspapers—that religious groups have led the opposition to the expansion of gay rights. These groups are mostly from the religious right: the Orthodox rabbinate, elements of the Roman Catholic hierarchy, and the more conservative Protestants. All these are groups that uphold the exercise of male authority in many areas, not the least of which is in control over male heterosexuality. However, in a religious hierarchy, those who control others are themselves controlled—by the internalized representation of the deity.

In his thorough critical review of the psychoanalytic theory of male homosexuality, K. Lewes (1988) theorized that the revulsion against homosexuality has its roots in gynephobia—fear of the female. Once again, I would not feel that this is incorrect. Once again, I would propose an additional and necessary factor: the fear and hatred of the controlling male—a variant of the image of the destructive, phallic male epitomized by the Devil symbol.

The preoccupation with dichotemous classification of men into "heterosexual" and "homosexual" which has prevailed in our culture is best understood in terms of the psychoanalytic concept of "splitting" or the mythic mechanism of doubling. The "homosexual" is a complex cultural symbol, a condensation of meanings. The first of these is, as I have stressed, the destructive, phallic male. Like the "bartender" figure in Frank's jealous obsession, he claims the woman for himself or, like the powerful men of the church, he prohibits access to her. Like the Devil of Frank's anxieties, or the father with the muscular arm of a killer, like the dream images of brigands or rapists he is capable of making both women and men his victims. But a second meaning of the complex symbol of the "homosexual" is the man, who like the witch, enters into a pact with this destructive, phallic figure. The perception that he has thereby sacrificed his masculinity symbolizes the same surrender to this "evil" power symbolized by the witch's sacrifice of her soul.

As one meaning of the "homosexual" symbol is the split-off, feared, and hated image of the father, the other meaning is the split-off, dark side of the self, the "doublet" of the "heterosexual" self. In this sense, the "homosexual" is the repudiated part of the self that *could* relate to the phallic man in the triangle of *female "other"*, *male self*, and *phallic "other."* On the other hand, "heterosexual" symbolizes not only the side of male feelings drawn to the female "other," but also the safety and protection from the phallic other that is found in the arms of the female. It will be recalled how, when he awoke in the middle of the night almost panicked by the thought of the Devil, Frank asked his wife to hug him for reassurance. Another man related a dream in which he and another male were having sex with a third person, one who was male in the lower half of the body and female in the upper half. When he saw his ex-wife looking through a window, he signaled her, whether to join him or rescue him he was not sure.

Martin Luther was constantly battling the Devil who, in addition to other, more overt harassments, even lodged in Luther's bowels (Russel, 1986, p. 39). In fact, Luther himself said that he found that one of the best defenses against the Devil was to go to bed with his wife.

In Meyerbeer's nineteenth-century opera *Robert le Diable* the hero's father is the Devil himself, though initially masquerading in the guise of Robert's best friend. He plots to draw his son to his side, finally reveals to him that he is both father and Devil, and tries to persuade him to sign a pact. At the last minute, Robert is dissuaded and thus saved by the thought of the woman he loves and by being read to from the Testament of his long-dead mother.

And in 1974, the Tate Gallery in London showed more than 200 oils and watercolors of the nineteenth-century painter Richard Dadd who, on a trip to Egypt, came to believe that the god Osiris had directed him to eliminate the Devil's influence. Accordingly, in 1843, he killed his father by cutting his throat because he believed him to be the Devil in human form. (Lewis & Arsenian, 1977.) For Dadd, there was no salvation.

Identification

There is another defense against the danger of the phallic "other." That is the mechanism of identification. It is a concept often discussed by Freud but for purposes of this discussion, I will draw on the one in *The Ego and the Id* (Freud, 1923b). As I have already mentioned, Freud notes that, in the early years before the Oedipus complex, the little boy already begins to identify himself with his father. I think this early timing is consistent with subsequent research on the development of core gender identity. For Frank, there seems no question but that his earliest and deepest identifications were masculine and his memories suggest that his father played a significant role in those identifications.

For Freud, identification subsequent to its initial primary stage, seems to be influenced largely by object relations. As a mechanism it is activated by the complexities of the Oedipus complex. The polarities of the complex with respect to the father are, of course, tender love and hostile competitiveness. Identification is a mechanism for dealing with both of these difficult sentiments. With some incentive from the castration complex, competition and hostility are relinquished through identification which, however, enables the little boy to retain the mother vicariously as an object. However, identification is also a substitute for a sexual object tie, and identifications with both father and mother reflect that mechanism. Freud sums up, "The father-identification will preserve the object-relation to the mother which belonged to the positive complex and will at the same time replace the object-relation to the father which belonged to the inverted complex; and the same will be true, *mutatis mutandis*, of the mother-identification. The relative intensity of the two identifications in any individual will reflect the preponderance in him of one or other of the two sexual dispositions" (p. 24).

I am going to reproduce a further quotation from the same work, already cited in Chapter 4, because of its relevance to another issue I am about to discuss. "Closer study usually discloses the more complete Oedipus complex, which is twofold, positive and negative, and is due to the bisexuality originally present in children: that is to say, a boy has not merely an ambivalent attitude towards his father and an affectionate object-choice towards his mother, but at the same time he also behaves like a girl and displays an affectionate feminine attitude to his father and a corresponding jealousy and hostility towards his mother" (p. 23).

I imagine that exception would be taken, in the above quote to the phrase "behaves like a girl and displays an affectionate feminine attitude towards his father." It implies overtly feminine behaviors of the kind that are associated with the extremes of gender nonconformity in boys but not in the normative relationships to which Freud was obviously referring. And yet, in some of Frank's dreams, he was clearly identifying himself with a female figure; in one of the most frightening dreams he reported to me, he felt identified with a severely disturbed woman whom the doctors could not help. As I have earlier noted, Frank seemed to have made the kinds of identifications and followed the patterns of interests that are stereotypically "masculine" in our culture. In these dreams, the feminine figure seemed to symbolize the part of himself that was drawn to relate sexually to another man. In this sense, the sexual potential between himself and a masculine "other" determined the "feminine identification" rather than vice versa. These observations support Isay's (1987) assertion that same-sex object choice precedes identification with the mother or the adoption of opposite-sex characteristics in the histories of those gay men who reveal such identifications. This causal sequence follows Freud's formulation. In "Dostoevsky and Parricide," Freud (1928) observes, both hatred of the father and "being in love with the father" undergo repression for different reasons: hatred, because of the fear of castration, and love, because replacing the mother as the father's object is *also* tantamount to castration. Whether one accepts the literalness of castration fear in a child or not, I think that Freud is here describing a complex of feelings that is psychologically very real to adolescents and adult men. Even among the Greeks, who had institutionalized homosexual relations, castration anxiety—in a physiological sense—had to be guarded against.

I would like to return to the situation of the male in our culture as he is confronted by the complexity of his feelings toward the female "other" and toward the male "other." Identification of oneself with the male "other" can be a solution to the potential dilemmas posed by the tendency toward a sexual movement toward him. Freud (1923b) suggests, "It may be that . . . identification is the sole condition under which the id can give up its objects" (p. 19). And, "When the ego assumes the features of the object, it is forcing itself, so to speak, upon the id as a love-object and is trying to make good the id's loss by saying: 'Look, you can love me too—I am so like the object.' "

I think this utilization of identification was seen in Frank rather clearly in two respects. The first was in the area of attractiveness. In the latter part of the analysis, when he was aware of a reaction to another man's handsomeness, he would say to himself that it did not mean that he was inferior or sexually drawn to the other man because he was also good-looking enough to attract women. And during sex, he tried very heard to be the best lover a woman ever had. In both instances, of course, part of his motivation *was* to ensure that he would be wanted by a woman. But the other motivation was to protect himself from the male "other." The mechanism of identification with the man for whom he could feel desire shifted the ground against which the picture of the man was experienced. This figure, the picture of a handsome or sexually powerful man, imposed itself, against Frank's will, upon his consciousness. But if the picture could be shifted and come to rest upon himself, if he could experience this man in himself, the consciousness of desire for another would be eliminated, and his self-esteem would be enhanced. This was exactly the reverse of what would happen if he felt desire for an object outside himself.

Looking at this process from the symbolic perspective, it is possible to see how all the facets of the Oedipal situation, as Freud envisaged it, are summed up in the heterosexual situation. As the strong and handsome lover, Frank could be like the idealized father of his boyhood even as his female partner symbolized the memory of his mother. But as he looked at himself through the eyes of the woman he was making love to, he was identifying with the same mother and retaining the sexual object tie to the father whose role he was also symbolizing. Thus, sexual intercourse symbolized, in the feelings and unconscious memories it expressed and evoked, *both* identifications and *both* object ties. However, although our culture permits transference from the object tie with the mother to other females, such a transfer is not permitted with respect to the object tie with the father; therefore the heterosexual man must rely on looking for the male object through the eyes of his female lover which can be accomplished if he can identify himself with that male object through projection of the latter's image onto himself. It seems to me possible then that, for men, the act of heterosexual intercourse can symbolically recapitulate—and perhaps very frequently does—the full Oedipus complex, and its transferences to other sexual objects, in a manner consistent with our cultural definitions of male identity.

Freud (1922) draws the following contrast with respect to the father: "It is easy to state in a formula the distinction between an identification with the father and the choice of the father as an object. In the first case one's father is what one would like to *be*, and in the second he is what one would like to *have*" (p. 46). I think it is clear that our culture approves only the first of these two alternatives. The second is prohibited, with the symbol of this prohibition being "homosexuality." This symbol evokes a complex of feelings both conscious and unconscious. One meaning is far more commonly discussed and researched and is more consistent with what is consciously feared—identification as female. If I am correct in surmising that such identification can normally be symbolized during heterosexual intercourse, it must depend for its exciting potential on remaining an unconscious meaning. I will now propose that a significant portion of the dread of a *conscious* identification as female stems from the fact that it symbolizes being in an impotent and helpless relationship to the dark side of the father image—the destructive, phallic male. The dread and even hatred of this dark side has, I think, been responsible for the stern prohibitions against homosexuality and the punishments—some of them lethal—that have been directed at men for homosexuality since the Emperor Justinian and his Empress Theodora prescribed castration and/or death for it in the Byzantium of the sixth century. Dover (1978) identifies that century as the terminus of the ancient Greek world, when the last vestiges of explicitly pagan thought and feeling were extinguished. The hysterical savagery of these punishments directed against passions that the ancient world believed to be divinely inspired by Eros seem grossly disproportionate to fear of femininity alone. Castration seems like an attempt to strike at a phallic power far greater than that possessed by the poor young man this imperial pair ordered tortured and mutilated (Boswell, 1980, p. 173).

Identification and Splitting

As in the witchcraft mania, there have never been any serious social issues to warrant the legal penalties and the hatred directed at those who practiced homosexuality. The issues are psychological, as they were in the witchcraft persecutions. An important shared element in these two varieties of persecution also has to do with the mechanism of identification. The persecuting authority identifies with the positive, idealized part of the powerful figure whose internal representation has undergone an unconscious splitting, or "doubling." The feared and hated aspect of this powerful, controlling figure is displaced onto another figure such as the Devil or the "homosexual" in ways that I have tried to describe. A frequent target of the authoritarian's attack is a group of people allied with the symbol of this unconsciously hated figure. I think this formulation has some claim to serious consideration with respect to religious authoritarianism in our civilization, for reasons that I have tried to demonstrate.

I would, however, permit myself to extend this hypothesis to the general situation in which a son identified with a father who demanded obedience but gave little love in return. Such a son *could* have rebelled as an alternative to identification, of course. However, an alternative that combined both identification *and* rebellion would be an authoritarian revolution, such as Hitler, who had such a father, succeeded in leading. He trampled contemptuously upon tradition while identifying with the image of the phallic, destructive man. In that role, he tortured and killed men who took as their sexual object the phallic male he both identified with and hated just as the inquisitors tortured and burned women who they imagined had sexual knowledge of the Devil, the dark side of male authorities they served.

The Primeval Father—Again

Freud was an iconoclast, even a revolutionary. A measure of his iconoclasm was the declaration of his belief that Moses was an Egyptian and that Jewish monotheism derived from the religion of the Pharaoh Akhenaton (Freud, 1939). In *Moses and Monotheism*, Freud returns to the theme of the murder of the primeval father, and makes the assertion that "Ambivalency belongs to the essence of the father-son relationship" (p. 172). Spinning out a highly speculative but not altogether unpersuasive line of reasoning, Freud proposes that the Jewish people were led out of Egypt by an important personage who had been close to the deceased Pharoah. This man, whom history knows as Moses, would have used this relatively unsophisticated people—who themselves were scarcely likely to have originated a religion of universal significance—as the instrument for the perpetuation of the monotheism that the established priesthood would not, in Egypt itself, have permitted to survive Akenaton's death. However, Freud continues, the people revolted against the rigors that the new faith imposed upon them and, rising up, murdered this Egyptian Moses. Freud compares the hypothesized murder of Moses by the Jews to the neurotic's acting rather than remembering. In this case, the Jewish people reenacted the murder of the primeval father. Freud goes on to say, "The poor Jewish people, who with its usual stiff-necked obduracy continued to deny the murder of their 'father,' had dearly expiated this in the course of centuries. Over and over again they heard the [Christian] reproach: 'You killed our God.' And this reproach is true, if rightly interpreted. It says, in reference to the history of religion: 'You won't admit that you murdered God' (the archetype of God, the primeval father, and his reincarnations). Something should be added—namely: 'It is true, we did the same thing, but we admitted it, and since then we have been purified' " (pp. 114–15).

Among other reasons for Christian hatred of the Jews, Freud suggests one that is thought provoking with regard to the issues raised in this book. He notes that many people were Christianized by force and have continued to harbor resentment for being forced to accept the new religion. The anger at this new religion can then be projected onto its source. Thus, the hatred for Judaism is at bottom the hatred for Christianity, seen in the Nazi hostility to both. It strikes me as not implausible that the continuing strain that the authoritarian and ascetic trends in Christianity generate might contribute to the kind of displaced resentment Freud suggests.

Freud makes another point that is relevant to issues in this book. "The origin . . . of . . . ethics in feelings of guilt, due to repressed hostility to God, cannot be gainsaid. It bears the characteristic of being never concluded and never able to be concluded with which we are familiar in the reaction-formations of obsessional neurosis" (p. 173). I would compare the seemingly endless preoccupation with "explaining" homosexuality as obsessive in just this way. However, this preoccupation is explicable if we assume that obsessions symbolically denote inner conflicts. Repressed hostility toward the father—in whatever guise—can explain the paradoxical fact that the most vigorous enforcers of the prohibitions against homosexuality have been male authority figures who, I think, have used identification as a defense against their own resentment of repressive authority.

One final element relevant to the father/son theme in Christianity must be mentioned. "Its main doctrine, to be sure, was the reconciliation with God the Father, the expiation of the crime committed against him; but the other side of the relationship manifested itself in the son, who has taken the guilt on his shoulders, becoming God himself beside the Father and in truth in place of the Father. Originally a Father religion, Christianity became a Son religion. The fate of having to displace the Father it could not escape" (p. 175).

It seems paradoxical that a religion that glorifies a male deity (Judaism) and one that glorifies this deity and his son (Christianity) have been so opposed to taking the male as a sexual object. For Christianity, a way out of the sensed paradox may be through identification, seen in the fourth-century Nicene Creed still widely used in Christian churches. It begins:

> We believe in one God, the Father, the
> Almighty, maker of heaven and earth, of
> all that is seen and unseen. We believe
> in one Lord, Jesus Christ, the only Son
> of God. Eternally begotten of the
> Father, God from God, Light from Light
> true God from true God,
> begotten, not made, Of one Being with
> the Father.

In the Christian doctrine as enunciated in the Nicene Creed, Father and Son are reconciled, but through identification. However, a sexual union on the part of the deity or with the deity is never imagined. This stands in stark contrast to some Hindu traditions in which the male worshiper adopts a feminine attitude in order to imagine himself in an erotic relationship with a male deity (O'Flaherty, 1980). But Hinduism has retained phallism as a symbol of the creative rather than the destructive power of the male deity. In one of his aspects, Shiva is depicted as lord of the beasts, horned, ithyphallic, and surrounded by animals. In early and medieval Christianity, he would, in this guise, have been instantly recognized as the Devil. And yet, without in the least denigrating the need to understand our place in the cosmos, or the need to create symbols through which to conceptualize forces greater than ourselves, individual religious symbols and the systems of belief they encapsulate *are* mental creations. Of the two important symbolic meanings evoked by the phallus, one religious system deified the phallus and another demonized it.

The peculiarly negative reaction that Christianity has shown toward phallism was compared with the more generally affirmative response to this symbol in other, especially older, religions in two papers read before the Anthropological Society of London in 1870 (Westropp & Wake, 1875/1970). The date of these lectures is interesting because it shows that well before Freud, indeed at the height of the "Victorian" era, the paradoxical omission of the symbol of the phallus from Christianity was noted. In his lecture, C. S. Wake says, "There can be no question, however, that, whatever may be thought of its symbols, the fundamental basis of Christianity is more purely 'phallic' than that of any other religion now existing. I have referred to the presence in Hebraic theology of an idea of God—that of a Father—antagonistic to the Phoenician notion of the 'Lord of Heaven.' We have the same idea repeated in Christ's teaching, its distinctive characteristic being the recognition of God as the Universal Father, the Great Parent of Mankind, who had sent His Son into the world that he might reconcile it unto Himself. It is in the character of a forgiving parent that Christians are taught to view God, when he is not lost sight of in the presence of Christ. The emotional nature of Christian faith, indeed, shows how intimately it was related to the older faiths which had a phallic basis. In Christianity, we see the final expression of the primitive worship of the father, as the head of the family, the generator, as the result of an instinctive reasoning process leading up from the particular to the universal; with which, however, the dogma of the 'fall' and its consequences—deduced so strangely from a phallic legend—have been incorporated. The 'phallic' is, indeed, the only foundation on which an emotional religion can be based. As a system of rational faith, however, it is far different; and the tendency of the present age is just the reverse of what took place among the Hebrews—the substitution of a Heavenly King for a Divine Father. . . . This cannot be, however, the real religion of the future. If God is to be worshiped at all, the Heavenly King and the Divine Father must be combined in a single term; and he must be viewed, not as the unknowable cause of being, but as the Great Source of all being, who may be known in nature—the expression of life and energy" (pp. 77–78).

Wake rightly pinpoints the paradox in Christianity, a religion of the Father and of the Son, in which the original sin that led to humankind's estrangement from its creator is intertwined with symbols of phallism. Wake points out that before the Hebrew legend of the fall, the serpent was a symbol of wisdom and healing. The sacred serpent was kept in Egyptian temples and the asp appeared in the crown of Isis, the goddess of life and healing. In the annals of the Mexicans, the first woman was always represented as accompanied by a great male serpent, which represents the Sun-god, Tonacatl-coatl, the principal deity of the Mexican pantheon. The goddess-mother of primitive man is called Cihua-Cohuatl, signifying "woman of the serpent." Of course, the story of the fall in Genesis does not literally state that original sin was a sexual act; however, it seems to be symbolically implied, both in the element of the serpent and of the forbidden tree, itself a symbol of the male principle. In any case, the authors of *Malleus Maleficarum* quite explicitly linked the sexual act with the transmission of original sin, which estranges God from his children, and which was why the Devil had been given free rein over this particular function. Phallism, instead of being symbolic of God's act of creation, becomes symbolic of the power of destruction.

Psychoanalysis is, in a sense, the science of the interpretation of symbols. However, the anthropologist Geertz (1973, p. 128) points out that symbols themselves have the power to order experience. Undergoing analysis is meant to ensure that analysts' interpretations will not be unduly biased by their own unconscious needs, anxieties, and defenses. However, when the analyst's cultural experience—and that of *his* analyst—has been ordered by symbols that store unexamined complexes of needs, anxieties, and defenses, these symbols will, without acknowledgment, enter into and even guide the analytic process itself. I think it is clear by now that the revulsion against homosexuality (and for that matter, "homosexuality" itself) is just such a symbol. In his comprehensive review of the treatment of homosexuality in most of the societies for which data on this subject are available, Greenberg (1988) supports my contention from the perspective of the sociologist deeply concerned with many of the issues of this book. He says, "It is axiomatic in psychoanalysis that people are not always aware of the psychological processes that limit and direct their thought and actions. The same is true of social factors" (pp. 495–96).

I have tried to show that Freud's concept of the Oedipus complex grew well beyond the confines of the nuclear family to take in sweeping issues of love versus death and the innate sense of guilt. More and more Freud sought to establish connections between individual and group psychology and to integrate these with the cultural evolution of humankind. The Oedipus complex was named after an ancient legend, which though recounted at a pinpoint in time, represents a symbol of deep meaning and sweeping evocative power. While individuals who have been in analysis might feel that they have successfully come to grips with the elements of the complex as it took shape in their families, I think it is fair to say that the issues symbolized by the legend continue to confront men on an ongoing basis throughout their lives. Furthermore, they are also stored in and experienced through our cultural symbols.

Men's preoccupation with competitive success and advancement in hierarchy is just one element of the complex that daily confronts men, psychoanalysts not excepted. The issues with which this book has been concerned are, in fact, Oedipal issues, in this broad sense. The sexual desire for another male has, as I once said to Frank, its prototype in love for the father, conceptualized by Freud as the "negative" Oedipus complex. The revulsion against it has its prototype in hatred and anger at the same father or his surrogates. In individual cases the "resolution" of the elements of the Oedipus complex in the nuclear family may be, or seem to be, successful. But what is to prevent the complex from living on at other levels of experience—the cultural, for example? Not much, if one fails to see that the cultural symbols that order experience can store and express the significant elements of that complex.

Identification and Sexual Object Love

Freud contrasts identification with a "sexual object-tie" in his portrayal of the dualism of a childs feelings in the throes of the Oedipus complex. The ego takes on the characteristics of the loved object instead of seeking sexual union with it. But are these two processes mutually exclusive?

Even in his concept of narcissism (Freud, 1914) "narcissistic" and "object" libido are in a constant state of reciprocal flux, rather like an electric charge flowing back and forth between two poles of a battery. As Lewes (1988) has observed in his critical examination of the concept of narcissism in analytic theories of homosexuality, the term came to be pejoratively associated with a more primitive mode of relatedness in which self-love is all-important and the capacity for genuine object-love is stunted. However, this kind of oversimplification is thrown into perspective by Freud's observation that "Parental love, which is so touching and at bottom so childish, is nothing but parental narcissism born again and, transformed though it may be into object-love, it reveals its former character infallibly" (Freud, 1914, p. 49). There is almost a tongue-in-cheek quality to this offhand comment that warns the reader against oversimplifying the complexities of loving. I need hardly state that parental love is probably the supreme example of altruistic affection in normal human experience. The unconditional nature of this love was long ago chronicled in King David's lament for his slain rebellious son: "O my son Absalom, my son, my son Absalom! Would I had died instead of you, O Absalom, my son, my son! (2 Samuel, 18:33).

Identification, which denotes an analogous kind of identity between self and object, does not have the pejorative ring of "narcissism" with its vernacular connotations of egocentricity and its analytic ones of primitivism. In contrast to the concept of narcissism identification *necessarily* assumes a relation to an object. I believe that in discussions of the homosexual component in men, the term "narcissism" has been confusingly applied to aspects of male-to-male relationships that would be more accurately described by the concept of identification.

Freud, it will be recalled, stresses the relation of the son to his father from the earliest years as one of "primary identification." Blos (1985) extends this concept to that of the "dyadic isogender [same sex] complex," independent of the complex of feelings about the mother, which reemerges anew to confront the boy at adolescence.

However, identification of a son with his father is a lifelong process. It is facilitated by a favorable relationship with a normally loving father at all developmental stages and is generally beneficial to a man's self-concept. I think it is also undeniably important in male peer relationship and friendships from early childhood to old age. And while identification also occurs in a boy's relationship to his mother and between a man and his wife, there is a sense in which identification felt between or among males cannot be duplicated in a relationship to a female. And the reverse is undoubtedly true.

A sense of identification was something Frank sought and enjoyed in his male relationships. When he said about Robert, "We're alike, just alike," it was with evident pleasure. I do not think this sense of identification with Robert was only a substitute for the repressed sexual "object-tie." His desire to feel the pleasure of identification with Robert was part of the *motivation* for the sexual object-tie. The desire for identification was also present in his feelings for older men. The beauty of his friends Sam and Nick, as well as their qualities as friends, stirred his admiration and gave impetus to a desire to feel a sense of identification with them in the context of a loving relationship, as in the dream of having intercourse with Nick. And with respect to gay men, one of the attractions that he felt about their interest was that, as men, they would understand one another better.

However, as these feelings about men moved toward sexual symbolization, another male image rose up to block this movement—the image of the destructive, phallic male. I have said that this image was reinforced in Frank by the hurtful experiences he had had with his father and with the aggressive peers of his adolescence. However, even if his previous male relationships had been entirely unclouded by such painful experiences, the image of the phallic, destructive male would have still stood in the way because it is a powerful cultural symbol whose meanings are internalized by males growing up in our civilization.

It is because of the prominence of this symbol in our culture that the sense of identification must be thought of in entirely desexualized terms. Among the Melanesians, identification among males seems to have been facilitated through sexual interchanges. In fact, identification and sexual love are not inherently contradictory. A spiritual sense of oneness and sense of oneness achieved through sexual union can be two facets of the coinage of love. Thus, the Renaissance paintings of Ganymede depicted Zeus, in the form of the eagle, carrying off the beautiful youth. A modern painting by the Yugoslavian Ferdinand Kulmer entitled *Ganymede's Flight,* shows the tall figure of a slender, naked youth, seen from behind. One foot is just lifted from the ground; instead of human arms and shoulders, however, he has the wide-spread wings of an eagle; and instead of the head and the neck of a youth, the wings are surmounted by an eagle's head and neck. In this apotheosis, Zeus and Ganymede have become one.

In a male-female vein, Shiva becomes one with his beloved Parvati when she doubts his love. He says, "Why do you torment yourself like this, when you could obtain whatever you want merely by asking me? You are the oblation and I am the fire; I am the sun and you are the moon. Therefore you should not make a separation between us, as if we were distinct people" (O. Flaherty, 1980, p. 315). Shiva then causes her to enter his own body, and their paired bodes became one because of their love.

The revulsion again the homosexual component reflects the continuation of unresolved elements of the "Oedipal" struggle at the cultural level—the conflict between love and hate between father and son, and men towards each other.

Let me cite one more piece of clinical evidence for this hypothesis: a dream of an adolescent boy as reported by Blos (1985, pp. 21–22). ". . . I am wrestling with my father—not fighting, just wrestling. Suddenly I feel that I am coming—I cannot control it. I get panicky and I yell, '*No, no— I don't want to make up with you.*' I repeat these words again and again, getting more and more panicky. I can't stop the orgasm. I have it." (Italics added.)

My interpretation, not necessarily Blos's, is that the orgasm symbolizes, involuntarily, the wished-for love in relation to the father—a wish that the boy strenuously does not want to give in to because he feels too angry with his father for the reconciliation that the orgasm also represents.

9
Bisexuality Reconsidered

Psychoanalytic theory has, since the time that I first began working with Frank, begun to reject the definition of homosexuality as pathological. Leavy (1985), Stoller (1985), Isay (1986), Liebert (1986), and Friedman (1988) all exemplify a growing rejection of the reactionary trend that dominated the thinking about this issue after Freud's death. Robert Friedman (1986) and K. Lewes (1988) have contributed comprehensive critiques of analytic theories of homosexual pathology. In contrast to the thinking of the earlier period, which virtually denied that bisexuality could exist except in the realm of the pathological, the newer school of theorists seems to accept that genuine bisexuality is possible. Bisexuality does not, however, seem to have drawn as much theoretical or research interest as homosexuality. I would like to reconsider Freud's bisexuality theory, taking into account the historical/cultural and artistic/symbolic frameworks for the understanding of sexuality.

Let me very briefly recapitulate the main points of his theory. First, there are two related assertions: that every male is *capable* of making a homosexual object choice; and that, in fact, he *has already made* such a choice, either in consciousness or in the unconscious. In the latter instance, it is likely to be the object of "vigorous counter-attitudes." Second, although the homosexual object choice resulted from a convergence of a number of factors, one of these was the constitutional factor. In the male, a "female" component in the constitution implied a corresponding inclination toward a male sexual object while the "male" component tended toward a female object. Third, the libido is distributed between male and female objects, in manifest or latent form. Fourth, exclusivity of sexual object choice—whether it was female or male—was not a "natural" state of affairs that required no accounting. Fifth, another major factor to be reckoned with was the Oedipus complex, composed of two major components. In its negative aspect, *every male* took the father as the object of his jealous love, just as he did the mother in the positive aspect of the complex. The dynamics of this complex were bound to be involved in the determination of sexual outcomes.

Finally, Freud felt that both sets of needs—toward males and toward females—had to be channeled in some way that permitted their satisfaction lest they wind up interfering with each other.

The revisionist theorists attempted to dismantle the various components of the theory. The attack began with the biological grounds for constitutional bisexuality. This was accompanied by the dismissal of the negative aspect of the Oedipus complex. The mutual interpenetration of love and sexuality reflected in the libido theory next became irrelevant as the sexual drive became conceptualized as virtually independent of love and then tied to a biologically determined heterosexual imperative. The universality of unconscious homosexual object choice was dismissed where heterosexual men were concerned while the universality of unconscious heterosexual object choice for homosexual men was affirmed. Sublimation of homosexual love became irrelevant as any homosexual inclination—unconscious or conscious—was regarded as a neurotic symptom to be dissolved. The universal *capability* of making a homosexual object choice was essentially ignored while supporting data—whether supplied by such modern research as Kinsey's work or by literary and historical sources—were refuted, rationalized, or ignored.

The Constitutional Component

The presence in men of a "female" constitutional component that inclines them toward other males is, in my view, the weakest part of the theory. The concept of "constitution" was a kind of anachronistic intrusion of the biological/medical framework into a theoretical approach—psychoanalysis—that avowedly rested on data derived from mental events, communicated or inferred. The attempt to find reliable correlations between homosexual choice and any independently identifiable "female" constitutional component has met with very little success. The argument that homosexual interests—whether exclusive or in tandem with heterosexual ones—reflect such a component is either circular or, at best, rests on the hope that the missing "constitutional" link will someday be discovered.

One the other hand, there is ample evidence to support Freud's view that a capacity for responsiveness to males as well as to females is completely consistent with normal male physical makeup in the fact that in some societies—the Melanesian ones discussed in this book—virtually every male goes through a homosexual phase.

Object Choice

I think Freud's use of the term "object choice" merits further consideration. The concept seems to imply an emotional zeroing-in on an individual object of love or desire. The concept is entirely appropriate to Frank's feelings where Nick was concerned, as well as a number of other men in his life. It would apply with equal logic to Anne and the other women with whom he was in love. However, while the term "object choice" seems to fit very well into *our* cultural tradition of lifelong—or serial—monogamy, it seems less appropriate when sexual behavior towards a whole class of individuals is expected or even prescribed by the culture. In these situations, the element of choice of a single "object" while not entirely absent, would not appear to be the primary motivator of the behavior. In the required rites of fellatio among the Sambia the *action* and not the object was what was important. A boy had to drink semen supplied by an adolescent who was similarly required to supply it. And while boys and adolescents often did have certain preferred partners, these preferences were incidental to the main purpose of these rites. Similarly, when Marind youths were subjected to promiscuous anal intercourse during the first night of their initiation into the rites of Sosom, questions of individual choice seemed far in the background.

These rituals obviously required the erotic arousal of at least one of the partners involved in the sexual transaction. Herdt (1987) makes it clear, however, that the exchange was usually an erotic one for both individuals. Whatever these sexual transactions actually meant for the individuals involved, however, they were undeniably *homosexual* actions, involving as they did two males in sexual contact. Perhaps it is because, with the ascendence of Christianity, overt sexuality has long been abolished from ritual in our culture that even Freud's theory does not account for these forms of ritualized sexuality. But I think the recognition of the symbolic function of sexual imagery and behavior as I have proposed it in this book fits both the phenomenon of "object choice" as seen in our culture (and in Freud's theory) and the phenomenon of ritualized sexual behavior as it was widely practiced in Melanesia. Sexual imagery and action can symbolize deep feelings of love for another individual male person: an "object-choice." They can *also* symbolize transactions of male power. In practice, I think it is impossible for a man to have sex with another person—whether female or male—without the involvement of the power dimension. I believe I could depend on agreement from the majority of men if I said that the issue of power in sex was quite important to them. Frank was far from unusual in being excited by the feeling of being sexually powerful when he was making love to a woman. In the dream with Nick, Nick was submitting to Frank's power, even as Frank was making love—and here that description exactly fit Frank's feelings—to Nick. Among the Sambia and Marind-anim boys were submitting to the power of older males, but it was clear that such submission was in their interest. Phallic penetration was part of the process whereby they acquired male power for themselves, not a psychological form of castration, which is our culturally assigned meaning for the same act.

Cultural Models of Bisexuality

Although the terms *heterosexuality* and *homosexuality* are concepts particular to our culture, their meanings undoubtedly overlap with categories that other cultures use to think about and describe sexual behavior. I think the addition of *bisexuality* rounds out the way *we* think about sexuality. *Bisexuality,* in our usage, implies the concurrence of two continuously energized currents of feeling in a single individual—one flowing toward males and the other toward females—the coexistence of two ongoing motivational systems that surge forward toward sexual expression. This internal state of affairs characterized Frank's feelings at the start of the second phase of the analysis. Isay (1986b), in referring to men who "are" bisexual in this sense, suggests that "The comfort of their lives as functioning heterosexuals will, I feel, depend on the degree to which they are made conscious and accepting of their anxiety provoking homosexual fantasies and impulses, which can then be used in the service of their heterosexuality and productivity" (p. 294).

This observation, while sympathetic and undoubtedly not inaccurate—although the idea of using homosexual fantasies and impulses in the service of heterosexuality deserves further explanation—describes an outcome that reflects an adjustment to the particular cultural realities in which the men referred to find themselves. These cultural realities are the same that existed in Freud's era. When Freud observed that the two sets of needs—toward males and females—had to be channeled in a way that permitted their satisfaction lest they interfere with each other, it was understood that the only *culturally* acceptable channel for the homosexual component was sublimation: a process of finding symbols other than sexual ones for the expression of the complex of needs and feelings about men.

While Freud was, I think, right, in his warnings about the two sets of needs interfering with each other, he was right with respect to our culture where they *must* interfere with each other. In the end, our concept of "bisexuality" is a conflict model. In cultures such as those of Prince Ibn Iskandar (Levy, 1951), where a much more conflict-free model of concurrent bisexuality prevailed, it was not assumed that the two sets of needs would interfere with each other and no sublimation was required. Hence, the prince could advise his son not to restrict himself to either males or females, but rather to cultivate the enjoyment of both.

A quite different model of bisexuality was operating in the case of the Sambia in whom homosexuality and heterosexuality were not concurrent but rather rigidly segregated into two different phases of life, with a very brief period when there was some overlapping. Among the Marind-anim, the model becomes even more complex with the institution of the *binahor*-father, a still more precisely structured homosexual relationship in the context of the broader chronologically regulated homosexual institution.

I think to refer to all these different ways of thinking about and regulating sexual intercourse between males and females and males and other males simply as "bisexuality" in the sense assigned to it in our culture is to obscure important psychological issues rather than to clarify them. The point of view I have advanced in this book is that the understanding of human sexuality—whether in the homosexual or heterosexual mode—is furthered by recognizing that sexual imagery and behavior are always symbolic of emotions and meanings deeply important to human beings. In any culture, its variants of "homosexuality" and "heterosexuality" consist of complex systems of symbols saturated with meaning and emotion. Cultures differ with respect to whether the same individuals can utilize both symbolic systems, when they can, and under what conditions.

Libido Theory

But even in the framework of our culture's bisexuality model, how is Freud's phrase of "homosexual object choice" to be understood? Certainly, it can and undoubtedly does refer to the erotic feelings for the father that Freud felt were universal. But there is nevertheless implied a genuine—albeit more usually unconscious—reexperiencing of these erotic components of the feelings for the father with another male object. As we have seen, these assumptions fit the case of Frank very well. Earlier, I mentioned Isay's (1986a, 1987) assertion that for the homosexually inclined child the father is the more important erotic object, rather than the mother. It seems to me that if Isay is right about the father being the primary erotic object for the homosexually inclined boy—and it makes perfect sense to me—it must be because the father has become the primary *love* object for the boy—or the model for it.

The intensity of the need for love seems to be a factor that makes its symbolization in sexual terms more likely and more necessary. I think the data in Frank's case give convincing evidence that his need for love was the most important factor that drew him to men as erotic objects. On the other hand, his feelings about women strongly reflected important transferences from his mother, so that in him, his needs for love were deeply entangled with both parents. The concept of "libido" now has an old-fashioned nineteenth-century creakiness about it, rooted as it is in a kind of psychological Newtonian physics. But I do not think the move to discard it has produced anything better to replace it. When Freud uses the phrase "homosexual libido" he is linking loving a man and having sex with a man together in an essentially seamless continuum of emotional and sexual "energy." In a very real sense, having sex is "making love." I think this is really much closer to the classical world view, analogous to the Greek concept of *eros*, denoting a love that was emphatically sexual but that, particularly in the hands of Plato and Platonists, could find expression in more ethereal and transcendent forms.

The libido concept also implies a continuity between genital sexuality and the diffuse sensuality of the body as interrelated strands of a broadly erotic continuum. While Freud himself viewed the inhibition of genital sexuality between men as the result of "vigorous counter-attitudes," he would hardly have felt that the kinds of physical intimacies I have mentioned among Nepali and Indian young men were anything but thoroughly comprehensible expressions of a normative "homosexual libido" in men who had their share of the heterosexual kind as well. The libido concept had the virtue of granting sexuality between men legitimacy as expressive of the normal "libidinal" ties—ties of affection, identification, and love—that bind them to one another. I have proposed that the prohibitions against homosexuality have their source in quite opposite sentiments of hatred for and mistrust of the destructive male, epitomized in the symbol of the Devil.

Regardless of any individual man's historical experience with the males in his life, this symbol and one of its secularized incarnations—the "homosexual"—stand as culturally imposed and at least partially internalized roadblocks to the sexual, that is to say physical, expression of libidinal ties between himself and other men. Our cultural prohibition takes the form "Don't even think about it." In my psychology classes, the subject of homosexuality provokes a great deal of animated discussion among students. In one class, after spending the greater part of the class in discussions provoked by questions and comments, most of it expressive of tolerance rather than condemnation, I asked them why, in their opinion there was so much hostility directed at homosexual people. One young man, a physical-education major and from the same sort of background as Frank, said, "I think it's because everybody, in the back of their minds, has felt something like that."

The intensity of Frank's needs eventually overwhelmed the—for him—thoroughly internalized prohibition against thinking or feeling anything "like that." But it is obvious from my student's comment that the prohibition is generally not completely successful in controlling consciousness. The point of view advanced in this book is that symbolic images and actions are uniquely expressive of feeling. Freud's view of the interconnectedness of love and sexuality fits very well with the proposition that the sexual—in the sense of the physical—symbolizes through the imagery and actions of the body, existing or hoped for bonds of affection, identification, or love—libidinal ties, as it were, between oneself and others. Freud's model of the interpenetrating qualities of love and sexuality—the libido theory—would predict the emergence of homosexual as well as heterosexual symbols in men's minds.

However, an acquaintance with our culture's "conflict model" of bisexuality would lead to the expectation that where these symbols had succeeded in getting past that threshold where repression attempts to halt the process of symbolization altogether, their emergence would be attended by evidence of conflict. And, in fact, one sees such evidence in the affective accompaniment of the homosexual symbolic image or action. Freud (1915b) compares an "unconscious affect" to an unconscious idea. The latter continues after repression, as an actual formation in the unconscious. However, to unconscious affect there corresponds only a potential disposition that is prevented from developing further. Thus, almost all the men I have seen who have identified themselves as heterosexual have at least entertained an idea or an image involving other males that could be called sexual. But the conscious affects accompanying these images betrayed more conflict—directly in anxiety or indirectly by the attenuation or absence of affect—than analogous images involving women. Let me give a few examples that will not be able to do justice to the complexity of these men's feeling or the varying life histories of which these are fragments.

One man, married and recently reconciled with his wife, would sometimes imagine himself and another man sitting, naked together—in a sauna, say—with a kind of "what if" feeling hovering in the background. This was the merest wisp of a revery. Another, whose sexual encounters with women were frequent and intense, found himself looking at a certain kind of delicate young man with what he anxiously recognized as sexual attraction. A third, who had not yet had intercourse with a women but did not feel he was gay, found himself appraising his friend's body on the other side of the tennis net, noting its outlines and contours.

He said, matter-of-factly, that the idea of having his mouth around a penis did not bother him, although he felt he had no particular desire in that direction. A fourth, very oriented toward women, yet despairing of finding a woman who could love him as he needed to be loved, found himself thinking when he was in the company of a gay acquaintance who seemed to like him—perhaps he could go home with him. When I asked him what role he would have imagined himself taking in this situation, he said, angrily and with a deliberately brutal directness, "I'd have been fucked up the ass." He experienced my question as an accusation and answered defiantly in kind. (At the time, without stating it, I was still influenced by the pathological model of homosexuality. He must have sensed that and my questions, in that context, offended him.)

Would these men have found a measure of emotional gratification if they had gone on from symbolic images to symbolic action and had a sexual encounter with another man? Is it possible for "heterosexual" men in our culture to do this? Perhaps, but it may be difficult to do it with sufficient comfort to make the experience emotionally worthwhile for many of them. When contact with the phallic "other" is experienced as inherently destructive to one's own masculinity, it is hard enough to allow homosexual symbols to be formed in consciousness, never mind going on to action. In my own sample of predominantly heterosexual men in our culture, about a fourth have had one or more homosexual experiences. Their feelings about these experiences included varying degrees of anxiety. In no instance, would the experience have been publicly acknowledged. I think that, for a man to feel comfortable in a sexual relationship with another man, the potential for being damaged by contact with the phallic other must somehow be defused. Cultures that require or permit utilization of homosexual as well as heterosexual symbols provide such safeguards while emphasizing the positive meanings of phallic contact.

I would like to mention one such cultural model for bisexuality because, on the surface, it also has elements that could more easily be adapted to our own cultural patterns. A. P. Sorensen (1984) describes it. It prevails among some of the river Indians of the northwest Amazon. In this culture, men often sit in close physical contact with much casual touching or hugging. Some youths develop "best friends" relationships. Intimacy between such friends and within the youth group—ranging from age fifteen to thirty-five—leads to a range of homosexual actions, and occasional sexual exchanges are expected among friends. When these occur in a group situation one might be considered unfriendly for not joining in, at least with a token gesture. Homosexual activity is limited neither to one's own age-mates nor to unmarried men. When groups of youths go visiting neighboring villages—with the prime intent of meeting girls—the young married men of the host community might accompany them when they go to bathe in the river and induce them into homosexual activity. Youths are often given "penis names" by older peers and these names are used in friendly banter. Homosexual activity is not regarded as unusual or a "problem," nor is it ritualized. All the males who engage in it expect to have a sexual life with women that is normative in their culture, which includes both sex in marriage and, occasionally, outside of it.

In this society, Sorensen points out, the "macho complex" familiar in the Latin culture with which these Indians have contact, is regarded as impolite and undesirable. It seems that the phallus as an instrument of destructive power is, in contrast to Latin culture, markedly deemphasized. That meaning may not be absent, but phallic contact seems largely to symbolize elements of friendship, truce—and identification—between males rather than competition or aggression. Had Frank and Nick formed their friendship in a culture that offered this kind of model for sexuality between males it seems certain that they would have expressed the emotional bonds between them in sexual terms.

Universality

I believe that Freud's assertion that everyone has, in fact, made a homosexual object choice, unconsciously if not in consciousness, requires some qualification. Frank had made some "object choices" and was, in fact, fighting the choices he had made. For the other men, however, sex with another man seemed to be more in the realm of the possible than having the quality of a "choice" already made.

I would prefer to recast Freud's proposal about the universality of homosexual object choice in these less restrictive terms: *A sensed sexual potential in their relations to other males is an integral component of male psychology.* One factor in determining the outcome of this generally sensed sexual potential is individual need. Frank's need for male love was more intense and focused than it was for the four other men I have mentioned. Interacting with need, however, will be the negative emotions of anger and fear, elements that seem to be virtually inevitable in the matrix of feelings directed toward the male "other." The third critical factor in determining the outcome of this universal potential is culture.

Culture affects not only the extent to which homosexual symbols may be utilized but, in addition, the particular meanings which these symbols express and evoke. Homosexual imagery and action can, it seems to me, symbolize libidinal ties along a gradient of intensity and passion, from ties of affection and friendship, as would seem to be the case in the society described by Sorensen, to the passion of some of the Greek *erastes-eromenos* relationships. One of the meanings our culture has attached to homosexual symbols is that of exclusive choice—*for* men and *against* women. As a result, men who are drawn to women must experience any homosexual potential within themselves with a sense of paradox. Nevertheless, my analytic experience seems to square with my student's appraisal of the awareness of homosexual potential even in a culture as decisively opposed to homosexual symbols as ours. Spoken with unaffected candor, his words took in both sides of the male-to-male equation: the acknowledgment of the accompanying fear together with the observation that everyone—at least "in the back of their minds"—had felt "something like that."

However, our dominant culture permits the sexual symbolization of emotional needs, regardless of intensity, toward the opposite sex only. But even though individuals tend to be exponents of their culture, they are not, as I have already said, clones off of a social assembly line. They also stand in a dynamic and even confrontational relationship to it. But to oppose one's culture can engender severe inner conflict and, of course, invite severe social sanctions. Were it possible for our culture to be equally permissive for sexual expressiveness toward both sexes, we would, I think, see significantly more sexual dualism in behavior. I doubt we would see some sort of golden age of human integration and joyful sexual expression. Rather, a more permissive culture would probably be analogous to democracy, as Churchill described it—the worst form of government except in comparison with all others.

Therapeutic Problems

However, since our culture has not evolved a more permissive attitude for sexual expressiveness toward another of one's own sex, what kind of stance can the therapist take toward the patient's conflicts about homosexual symbols? From my own experience, I would say that it can only be helpful for the therapist to examine his own inner feelings on this issue, just as it is in other areas of important human conflict that touch on therapists' as well as patient's lives. Many practicing therapists are likely to have last had their own analysis during the period when the goal of analysis was to help a person relinquish the need for love from another of the same sex and to be free from the desire for its symbolic expression through sexuality. And this same attitude is likely to be encountered in the patient who is self-identified as heterosexual. Even if the therapist has achieved a broader perspective on this issue, the patient is likely to think in terms of the dichotomizing categories of homosexual/heterosexual or gay/"straight."

When I was seeing Frank I used the phrase "homosexual feelings" in talking with him, and the phrase appears in Part I of this book. But from the perspective of the theory of symbolism developed in Part II, I would retrospectively regard that term as a condensation of two things: the homosexual symbols themselves and the meanings and affects expressed by those symbols. From the point of view of subjective experience, it is usually the symbol—an image or an action—not the motivation, that is "sexual." The motivations expressed in sexual symbols are uniformly multilayered, complex, and often contradictory.

For some time, after the successful outcome with Frank, I felt it was important to make the interpretation of "homosexual feelings" to some heterosexual men because it seemed evident that there was deep conflict about feelings toward the father and, by transference, to men. While my formulation of the dynamic issues was not much off the mark, therapeutically, the results were sometimes more negative than positive. In some instances, the generally good relationship between the patient and myself overrode the feeling that I was saying, as one man put it, "You really are homosexual, aren't you?" In the worst-case scenario, the therapy was prematurely terminated. The transference in those instances became excessively negative as I became identified with the feared image of the destructive, phallic male. The therapist is in a powerful position. The patient bares his secrets to him, while the therapist remains clothed in the protective garb of nondisclosure. Deep transferences to the father are stimulated. Under these conditions, the invocation of the culturally symbolic code word of *homosexuality* is likely to be interpreted at the conscious level as a castrating assault and at the unconscious level as a homosexual rape. In fact, avoiding the use of the culturally loaded term of *homosexual* in these instances allows therapist and patient to concentrate their attention on the more vital issue—the feelings about men. It is the feelings that are more important anyway, even when the sexual symbols do occur in consciousness.

And when they do emerge into consciousness, whether stripped of affect or accompanied by anxiety, the denial of their sexual status with such terms as *pseudosexual* is equally harmful. This kind of denial of their sexual status implies that some discovery has been made that should now alter all of a person's previously held assumptions about himself. But beyond and beneath the symbols lies what is symbolized and that is the proper focus of analytic discourse. In the end, the person must be left free to choose his own symbols. I think I have been most effective with my patients when I have neither tried to impose sexual symbols upon them—whether homosexual or heterosexual—nor attempted to deny the sexual status of their sexual symbols. I have been least effective when I tried to do the reverse. In the case of Frank, the malignancy of the Devil obsession and the jealousy syndrome left me little choice except to insist that the blocking of the sexual symbols was a far greater threat to his happiness and stability than was permitting them to emerge into consciousness. I was fortunate in having, in Frank, an unusually dedicated and trusting collaborator. I am sure every therapist reading this book has had the frustrating experience of a patient preferring to hold on to even crippling symptoms rather than face the anxiety of dealing with the conflicts that generated them—such is the power of unconscious resistance. As Freud long ago pointed out, our alliance is with the conscious part of the person that *does* seek health, and the real relationship of mutual trust is what makes therapeutic success possible, against the odds.

In talking about the story of Frank with colleagues, the questions has arisen, "Did he become homosexual?" Understandably, the question tended to be phrased in terms of the dichotomizing symbols in which our culture frames thinking about sexuality. More and more, I have come to feel that the goal of therapeutic work is not only to uncover, but also to promote that creative capacity of the human personality and intellect to figure out what to do with what has been uncovered—or, to put it in the terms of the concepts of this book—to find those symbols that work, that bring together, express, and so allow one to really experience what is important in one's inner life.

In seems to me that Frank has done this about as well as anyone I know. Frank and I had little choice except to work in the cultural context that surrounded us. As I have said, had Frank and Nick lived in a different place or different time, they would probably have had a physical relationship that symbolically expressed its emotional components. But there are few signals available to men who "are" heterosexual to test the possibilities of physicality between them, even if the idea has reached consciousness.

However, in the protracted journey that Frank undertook, he not only learned how the denial of his need for love from men had cost him his peace of mind and made him fear for his sanity. He also came to understand how angry he had been with the women from whom he had sought love. In the course of the analysis—and in the continuing evolutionary process that has followed it—he was able to find the symbols that seem to work for him. His need for love from men seems to be able to find expression within the bounds set for it by the dominant culture without too much of a sense of deprivation, and his need for love from a woman has been channeled into marriage. Although it is not a marriage without problems, these problems come from the differences between two individuals' needs and goals rather than from an explosive ambivalence on the part of Frank alone. Becoming a father was always important to Frank, and the fulfillment of that wish has been an important symbolic realization of his need for a father-son relationship, with him now as the father. It may be a helpful coincidence that he has had a boy.

It seems plausible to me that there are both men and women who would find a greater measure of emotional fulfillment if they could symbolize their needs in homosexual as well as heterosexual terms. The historical and anthropological data show that such symbolization need not imply either a definitive decision with regard to identity or a lifelong commitment to dualism in one's sexual life. However, under the conditions of our cultural life, it is probably unrealistic to expect this to occur for most of these people. For them, as for Frank, what therapy can do is to enhance self-awareness and—this, I think, is a therapeutic responsibility as well—cultural awareness. Out of both kinds of awareness, it is to be hoped that people will be able to forge for themselves an identity and find the symbols that satisfy their individual as well as cultural needs. The end result may well be a compromise, but I think it is the quality of the compromise that counts.

10
Summary Thoughts

As Frank read over an earlier draft of this book, he recalled that the frightening dream that had preceded the emergence of the Devil obsession had, in fact, been one in which the Devil appeared. He also realized its cause. That summer, he had been forced to drop out of graduate school temporarily because money was short. He was working with his cousin whom he idolized. He learned about working on cars from him and did the things that he could not do with his father. It was true that he was something of a "bum" because he was cheating on his wife. But, he said, "I was in love with him."

I have told how I missed some of the references to myself in Frank's dreams and associations when these would have involved a sexual aspect to our relationship. It is obvious that I did not want to deal with that aspect of male-to-male relationships that our culture has so pronounced so dangerous. Perhaps the course of the analysis would have been speeded up by a more timely recognition of this factor on my part, or perhaps their interpretation would have proved counterproductive. The feelings that were expressed in these threatening sexual symbols had to do with the desire to be loved and, uninterpreted, they constituted part of the positive transference and corresponding countertransference—that help to motivate and sustain a therapeutic alliance.

I have tried to show that the complexes of needs and feelings expressed in homosexual symbols are integral and important themes in the lives of men in general. I would say that we have gone about as far as we can in looking for differences between "heterosexual" and "homosexual" men, conceptualized dichotomously. The area of shared similarities between them is, I feel, much larger. I also think we have gone as far as we usefully can with "heterosexual" researchers investigating "homosexuality." Certainly, there are professionals in all of the social sciences and clinical professions whose primary sexual modality is with their own sex. I think progress on understanding male psychology will benefit enormously from their open collaboration. It seems to me that, in the Oedipal conflict between love and hate, men whose primary modality is with men have come down on the side of love. But since male-to-male ambivalence is deeply rooted in masculine psychology, it would be important to see how this ambivalence is dealt with in these relationships. These and other questions would benefit from unprejudiced and collaborative research by people from both sexual modalities.

Geertz (1973) regards culture as consisting of historically transmitted patterns of meanings embodied in symbols (p. 89). The Devil is such a symbol. Freud (1923) retrospectively analyzed a neurosis of demonical possession in a seventeenth-century painter. While some of the conscious meanings of the Devil symbol have changed since, the continuity in its unconscious meanings is remarkable, and is reflected in the common desire for the father in the seventeenth-century painter and in Frank, the twentieth-century professional.

I have made it clear that I feel there is reason to regard the symbol of the Devil and the cultural symbol "homosexuality" as signifying an important set of shared meanings, the one in a theological and the other in a psychological context. Both the Devil and "homosexuality" symbolize an aspect of the Oedipal relation. Working on this book has given me a deeper appreciation of the twin themes of love and hate between men that are symbolized by the Oedipus legend. Thus, near the beginning of the analysis, Frank literally protested, "You can't love a man. That's wrong." More than a decade later, when his compassion for himself had grown, he could say simply about the feeling that he now understood had started the whole Devil obsession, *"I was in love with him."*

In the hothouse fantasy that was his rendering of the story of Salome and John the Baptist, Oscar Wilde put these words into the mouth of the teenage Judaean princess who was Wilde's dramatic alter-ego: ". . . the mystery of love is greater than the mystery of death." Almost a century later, it remains true for us, as it was for him, that though physical science can explain with great precision how and why organisms die, it cannot explain why they love.

And yet, the erotic in our civilization continues to reflect its treatment as a chief principle in opposition to God and of human well-being. Counter measures against such a principle have been correspondingly drastic, as in severe punishments for sexual acts at different times and, most notably, in the burnings during the witchcraft mania. However, since it is especially the impulse to love and the need to be loved that generate sexual symbols it is supremely ironic that the loving element in sexual imagery and action is often no longer even grasped in consciousness. The loving self is experienced as evil because the sexual symbols that express it are regarded as such.

From the vantage point of one who, like Frank, was raised in the Christian tradition and who still finds value in its most positive symbols and ethical principles, I would put a question to Christian theology: Is it possible to find a way to undo the fusion between the erotic and destructive as it is exemplified in the symbol of the Devil? This century has decisively demonstrated the tenuousness of the checks on the forces that seem to strain toward the destruction of the species. Russel (1984, p. 207) contrasts the trivialized view of the Devil as personified in "snickering demons who humiliate sleeping persons as incubi and succubi" with the power that is capable of destroying the earth with nuclear weapons. That power, he describes as " . . . the presence of something dark, cruel, idiotic, and destructive in the pits of our minds and the secret places of the stars, raging for ruin."

Freud recognized the "dark, cruel, and destructive" aspect of human nature in the dual instinct theory. I think it is time to recognize that uncontrolled and escalating aggression is the prime mental health problem at both the individual and social level.

I think it is also time for psychoanalysis to repudiate, once and for all, the preoccupation with sexual conformity. The chief result of this preoccupation has been suppression of the life-affirming energy of Eros, whose liberation in the personality is necessary for individual happiness and whose mobilization in society is vital to survival.

References

Allen, M. R. (1984) "Homosexuality, Male Power and Political Organization in North Vanuatu: A Comparative Analysis," in G. Herdt, ed. *Ritualized Homosexuality in Melanesia*. Berkeley: University of California Press.

Barber, Malcolm. (1978) *The Trial of the Templars*. Cambridge: Cambridge University Press.

Barstow, Anne L. (1982) *Married Priests and the Reforming Papacy. The Eleventh Century Debates*. New York: Edwin Mullen Press.

Bergler, E. (1969) "The Myth of a New National Disease. Homosexuality and the Kinsey Report," in *Selected Papers of Edmund Bergler, M.D.* New York: Grune & Stratton.

Bieber, I. et al. (1962) *Homosexuality*. New York: Random House.

Blos, P. (1985) *Son and Father. Before and Beyond the Oedipus Complex*. New York: The Free Press.

Bollinger, Ann V. (1968) "Kids' Living Nightmare." *New York Post*, 6 September 1988, 4–5ff.

Boswell, J. (1980) *Christianity, Social Tolerance and Homosexuality*. Chicago: University of Chicago Press.

Brown, P. (1988) *The Body and Society. Men, Women and Sexual Renunciation in Early Christianity*. New York: Columbia University Press.

Cahill, T., and R. Ewing (1986) *Buried Dreams. Inside the Mind of a Serial Killer*. New York: Bantam Books.

Danielou, A. (1973) *La Sculpture Erotique Hindoue*. Paris: Editions Buchet/Chastel.

Desai, Devangana. (1975) *Erotic Sculpture of India. A Socio-cultural Study*. New Delhi: Tata McGraw-Hill.

Deva, Krishna. (1986) *Khajuraho*. New Delhi: Brijbasi.

Devereaux, George. (1969) *Reality and Dream. Psychotherapy of a Plains Indian*. Garden City, N.Y.: Doubleday.

———. (1970) *Ethnopsychoanalysis*. Berkeley: University of California Press.

———. (1979) "Fantasy and Symbol as Dimensions of Reality," in Hook, R.H., ed. *Fantasy and Symbol. Studies in Anthropological Interpretation*. New York: Academic Press.

Dover, K. J. (1978) *Greek Homosexuality*. Cambridge: Harvard University Press.

Edmunds, L. (1983) *Oedipus. The Ancient Legend and its Later Analogues*. Baltimore: Johns Hopkins Press.

Fouchet, M. P. (1959) *The Erotic Sculpture of India*. New York: Criterion Books.

Fox, R. L. (1986) *Pagans and Christians*. San Francisco: Harper & Row.

Freeman, D. (1979) "Severed Heads That Germinate," in R.H. Hook, ed. *Fantasy and Symbol. Studies in Anthropological Interpretation*. New York: Academic Press.

Freud, S. (1905) *Three Essays on the Theory of Sexuality*. New York: Basic Books.

———. (1910) *Leonardo da Vinci and a Memory of His Childhood*. New York: W.W. Norton, 1964.

———. (1911) "Formulations Regarding the Two Principles in Mental Functioning," in *Collected Papers*, vol. 4. New York: Basic Books, 1959.

———. (1912) "The Dynamics of the Transference," in *Collected Papers*, vol. 2. New York: Basic Books, 1959.

———. (1914) "On Narcissism: An Introduction," in *Collected Papers*, vol. 4. New York, Basic Books, 1959.

———. (1915a) "Further Recommendations on the Technique of Psycho-Analysis. Observations on Transference Love," in *Collected Papers*, vol. 2. New York: Basic Books, 1959.

———. (1915b) "The Unconscious," in *Collected Papers*, vol. 4. New York: Basic Books, 1959.

———. (1918) *Totem and Taboo*. New York: Vintage Books, 1946.

———. (1922) *Group Psychology and the Analysis of the Ego*. New York: Bantam Books, 1960.

———. (1923a) "A Neurosis of Demoniacal Possession in the Seventeenth Century," in *Collected Papers*, vol. 4. New York: Basic Books, 1959.

———. (1923b) *The Ego and the Id*. New York: W.W. Norton, 1960.

———. (1926) *Inhibitions, Symptoms, and Anxiety*. New York: W.W. Norton, 1959.

———. (1927) "Postscript to a Discussion on Lay Analysis," in *The History of the Psychoanalytic Movement and Other Papers*. New York: Collier Books, 1967.

———. (1928) "Dostoevsky and Parricide," in *Collected Papers*, vol. 5. New York: Basic Books, 1959.

———. (1930) *Civilization and its Discontents*. New York: W.W. Norton, 1961.

———. (1933) *New Introductory Lectures on Psychoanalysis*. New York: W.W. Norton, 1965.

———. (1937) "Analysis Terminable and Interminable," in *Collected Papers*, vol. 5. New York: Basic Books, 1959.

———. (1939) *Moses and Monotheism*. New York: Vintage Books.

Friedman, Robert (1986) "The Psychoanalytic Model of Male Homosexuality." *Psychoanalytic Rev., 13:483–519.*

Friedman, Richard C. (1988) Male Homosexuality. New Haven: Yale University Press.

Gebhard, P. H., J. H. Gagnon, W. B. Pomeroy, and Cornelia V. Christenson. (1965) *Sex Offenders*. New York: Harper and Row.

Geertz, C. (1973) *The Interpretation of Cultures*. New York: Basic Books.

Goldwater, R. (1979) *Symbolism*. London: Penguin Books.

Goodwin, Richard. (1988) "The War Within." *New York Times Magazine*, 21 August, 1988, 34–38ff.

Green, André. (1979) *The Tragic Effect*. New York: Cambridge University Press.

Greenberg, E. F. (1988) *The Construction of Homosexuality*. Chicago: The University of Chicago Press.

Harrison, Evelyn. (1978) "Sculpture in Stone," in *The Human Figure in Early Greek Art*. Greek Ministry of Culture, Athens/National Gallery of Art, Washington, D.C. (Catalogue)

Hayes, Billy (with William Hoffer). (1977) *Midnight Express*. New York: Dutton.

Herdt, G. (1981) *Guardians of the Flutes*. New York: McGraw-Hill.

———. (1984a) "Ritualized Homosexual Behavior in the Male Cults of Melanesia, 1862–1983: An Introduction," in G. Herdt, ed. *Ritualized Homosexuality in Melanesia*. Berkeley: University of California Press.

———, ed. (1984b) *Ritualized Homosexuality in Melanesia*. Berkeley: University of California Press.

———. (1984c) "Semen Transactions in Sambia Culture." in G. Herdt, ed. *Ritualized Homosexuality in Melanesia*. Berkeley: University of California Press.

———. (1987) *The Sambia. Ritual and Gender in New Guinea*. New York: Holt, Rhinehart & Winston.

Isay, R. A. (1986a) "The Development of Sexual Identity in Homosexual Men." *Psychoanalytic Study of the Child*, 41:467–89.

———. (1986b) "Homosexuality in Homosexual and Heterosexual Men: Some Distinctions and Implications for Treatment," in G.I. Fogel, F.M. Lane, and R.S. Liebert, eds., *The Psychology of Men. New Psychoanalytic Perspectives*. New York: Basic Books.

———. (1987) "Fathers and Their Homosexually Inclined Sons in Childhood." *Psychoanalytic Study of the Child,* 42:275–95.

Jung, C. G. (1964) "Approaching the Unconscious," in C.G. Jung, ed. *Man and His Symbols.* Garden City, N.Y.: Doubleday.

Kensinger, K. M., ed. (1983) *Marriage Practices in Lowland South America.* Chicago: University of Illinois Press.

Kinsey, A. C., W. B. Pomeroy, and C. E. Martin. (1949) *Sexual Behavior in the Human Male.* Philadelphia: W. B. Saunders & Co.

Kramer, H. and J. Sprenger. (1489) *Malleus Maleficarum* (trans. M. Summers). Great Britain: John Rodker, 1928

Kuhns, R. (1983) *Psychoanalytic Theory of Art. A Philosophy of Art on Developmental Principles.* New York: Columbia University Press.

———. "Tragedy: Its Contribution to a Theory of Objects and the Emotions." Unpublished manuscript.

La Barre, W. (1984) *Muelos. A Stone Age Superstition About Sexuality.* New York: Columbia University Press.

Leavy, S. A. (1985) "Male Homosexuality Reconsidered." *Int. J. Psychoanal. Psychother.* 11: 155–74.

Levy, Reuben. (1951, trans.) *A Mirror for Princes. The Qābūs Nāma of Ibn Iskandar.* New York: Dutton.

Lewes, K. (1988) *The Psychoanalytic Theory of Male Homosexuality.* New York: Simon & Schuster.

Lewis, D. N., and J. Arsenian. (1977) "Murder Will Out." *J. Nerv. Mental Disease* 164:273–79.

Liebert, R. S. (1986) "The History of Male Homosexuality from Ancient Greece through the Renaissance: Implications for Psychoanalytic Theory," in G.I. Fogel, F. M. Lane, and R. S. Liebert, eds. *The Psychology of Men. New Psychoanalytic Perspectives.* New York: Basic Books.

Linder, R. (1966) *Stone Walls and Men.* New York: Odyssey Press.

Modell, A. H. (1958) "The Theoretical implications of Hallucinatory Experiences in Schizophrenia." *Journal of the American Psychoanalytic Association,* 6: 442-480.

O'Flaherty, Wendy D. (1973) *Asceticism and Eroticism in the Mythology of Siva.* London: Oxford University Press.

———. (1980) *Women, Androgynes, and Other Mythical Beasts.* Chicago: University of Chicago Press.

Ovesey, L. (1969) *Homosexuality and Pseudo-homosexuality.* New York: Science House.

Rado, S. (1940) "A Critical Examination of the Concept of Bisexuality," in *Psychoanalysis of Behavior,* v. 1. *The Collected Papers of Sandor Rado* New York: Grune & Stratton, 1956.

———. (1949, revised 1955) "An Adaptational View of Sexual Behavior," in *Psychoanalysis of Behavior,* v. 1. *The Collected Papers of Sandor Rado.* New York: Grune & Stratton, 1956.

Richlin, Amy. (1983) *The Garden of Priapus. Sexuality and Aggression in Roman Humor.* New Haven: Yale University Press.

Russel, J. B. (1977) *The Devil. Perceptions of Evil from Antiquity to Primitive Christianity.* Ithaca: Cornell University Press.

———. (1981) *Satan. The Early Christian Tradition.* Ithaca: Cornell University Press.

———. (1984) *Lucifer. The Devil in the Middle Ages.* Ithaca: Cornell University Press.

———. (1986) *Mephistopheles. The Devil in the Modern World.* Ithaca: Cornell University Press.

Saslow, J. M. (1986) *Ganymede in the Renaissance. Homosexuality in Art and Society.* New Haven: Yale University Press.

Schwimmer, E. (1984) "Male Couples in New Guinea," in G. Herdt, ed. *Ritualized Homosexuality in Melanesia.* Berkeley: University of California Press.

Serpenti, L. (1984) "The Ritual Meaning of Homosexuality and Pedophilia among the Kimam-Papuans of South Irian Jaya," in G. Herdt, ed. *Ritualized Homosexuality in Melanesia.* Berkeley: University of California Press.

Socarides, C. W. (1968) *The Overt Homosexual.* New York: Grune & Stratton.

Sorensen, A. P., Jr. (1983) "Linguistic Exogamy and Personal Choice in the Northwest Amazon," in K.M. Kensinger, ed. *Marriage Practices in Lowland South America.* Chicago: University of Illinois Press.

Sorum, A. (1984) "Growth and Decay: Bedamini Notions of Sexuality," in G. Herdt, ed. (1984) *Ritualized Homosexuality in Melanesia.* Berkeley: University of California Press.

Stoller, R. J. (1979) *Sexual Excitement. Dynamics of Erotic Life.* New Haven: Yale University Press.

———. (1985) *Observing the Erotic Imagination.* New Haven: Yale University Press.

———. and G. Herdt (1982) "The Development of Masculinity: A Cross-Cultural Contribution." *J. Amer. Psychoanal. Assn.* 30:25–59.

Summers, M. (1928) Introduction to Kramer and Sprenger (1489) *Malleus Maleficarum.*

Sykes, G. M. (1958) *The Society of Captives; A Study of a Maximum Security Prison.* Princeton, N.J.: Princeton University Press.

Turner, V. (1979) "Symbols in African Ritual," in J. Dolgin, D.S. Kemnitzer, and D. M. Schneider, eds. *Symbolic Anthropology.* New York: Columbia University Press.

Van Baal, J. (1966) *Dema. Description and Analysis of Marind-Anim Culture.* The Hague: Martinus Nijhoff.

Vanggard, T. (1972) *Phallos: A Symbol and Its History in the Male World*. New York: International Universities Press.

Watts, A. (1971) *Erotic Spirituality. The Vision of Konarak*. New York: Macmillan.

Westrop, H. M., and C. S. Wake. (1975) *Ancient Symbol Worship. Influence of the Phallic Idea in Religions of Antiquity*. Preface by A. Wilder, M.D. New Delhi: Kumar, 1970. (Reprint of 2nd edition, 1875.) Two papers read before the Anthropological Society of London, Apr. 5, 1870.

Williams, F. F. (1936) *Papuans of the Trans-Fly*. Oxford: Clarendon Press.

Zilboorg, G. (1969) *The Medical Man and the Witch During the Renaissance*. New York: Cooper Square Publishers.

Index